About the Author

Born and educated in England, Jeremy Poolman has published seven books. His first, *Interesting Facts About the State of Arizona* (winner of the Commonwealth Writers' Prize, Best First Book) was followed by *Audacity's Song, My Kind of America* and *Skin*. His non-fiction includes biographies of Elizabeth Bacon Custer (*A Wounded Thing Must Hide*) and his great-great grandfather, *Gypsy Jem Mace*, the last bare-knuckle heavyweight champion of the world.

D1101987

The Road of Bones

A Journey to the Dark Heart of Russia

JEREMY POOLMAN

**SIMON &
SCHUSTER**

London · New York · Sydney · Toronto · New Delhi

A CBS COMPANY

First published in Great Britain by Simon & Schuster UK Ltd, 2011
This edition published in Great Britain by Simon & Schuster UK Ltd, 2012
A CBS Company

1 3 5 7 9 10 8 6 4 2

Simon & Schuster UK Ltd
1st Floor
222 Gray's Inn Road
London
WC1X 8HB

www.simonandschuster.co.uk

Simon & Schuster Australia
Sydney
Simon & Schuster India
New Delhi

A CIP catalogue for this book is available
from the British Library.

ISBN: 978-1-84739-797-3

Typeset by Hewer Text UK Ltd, Edinburgh

Printed and bound in Great Britain by CPI Croydon

For Sonia and for Joel. Always. Of course.

To know Russia, you must first know this road.

Isaak Levitan

The notebook in which I'm writing these words is a black Moleskine notebook, measuring approximately four inches by six. It was made in Italy by Modo e Modo and has cream-coloured pages and lines of the palest blue. I bought it six years ago for five dollars at the Metropolitan Museum of Art in New York, imagining (I imagine) that it would soon be filled with ideas for books and stories. This, however, was not to be the case. Somehow it just disappeared and was, I thought, lost for ever. It was only some years later, during an expedition to the attic in search of a bunch of old toys for my son, that I found it again, this souvenir from a life now long gone, and it is that – *this* – which sits open before me now as I wait at the airport in Zurich for my connecting flight to Moscow.

The pen in my hand is a blue Bic Cristal Grip, medium.

But to return to my notebook.

I write that there are three airports in Moscow, the third of which – Domodedovo, the one to which I am heading – being the oldest and, according to my guidebook, the location of what became known as the Russian Aircraft Bombings of 2004, during which two passenger planes were blown to pieces by Chechen terrorists, a pair of explosions

1

which together cost the lives of ninety people (including the four suicide bombers themselves) and proved to be only the beginning of a series of attacks which culminated in the hostage crisis in Beslan, during which 335 people lost their lives, many of whom were children.

But I'm moving ahead too swiftly. I should begin, as ever, at the beginning.

It was warm that summer two summers ago, Trafalgar Square thick with tourists, the Russian Landscapes exhibition at the National Gallery on its next-to-last day. I was there to see a picture I'd only ever seen in reproduction. It was a picture and an image I would end up chasing halfway around the world, and one that really would change my life.

I lodged my bag in the cloakroom and climbed the grand old marble steps. The rooms were choked with uncomprehending tourists and crocodiles of bored and restless schoolchildren trailing along behind their teachers.

'Do you see, children, how the painter takes the eye and leads us on?' said one such stooping, weary-looking man.

Before him, the group in purple blazers strained to see.

'And can anyone perhaps tell me who might have built such a road?'

The children shrugged; some shook their heads.

'Stalin?' he said.

The children looked blank; their teacher sighed. 'Never mind,' he said, an edge of wistful acceptance in his voice. 'Come on, then,' he said. He moved off. One by one the children followed him. I waited until they had gone, then stepped forward.

The picture – *The Vladimirka Road*, a landscape painted in 1892 – was sitting cool and sullen on that day that seems so long ago now, as bleak and unpeopled as ever, its stark severe beauty a sly challenge to the casual eye. I studied it hard; I squinted at it, trying to imagine it was a view from my window. I stepped back, then again drew closer. *Look at me*, it seemed to say, *do you know where I lead? Can you see the poor souls, chained and weary, further with every step from their homes and their families and closer with every step to the frozen gates of hell? And can you hear perhaps the ghosts that whisper in this tiny copse of trees?* I moved closer still, my ear to the canvas, but, of course, could hear nothing but silence, for paint and canvas and a gilt frame are as mute as the land. All that came to me was the smell of the painter's oils.

I turned my head (people were looking on, I was certain) and peered again at the brushstrokes; a distant chapel, a forlorn milepost, the rutted endless track. All was absence, and this absence seemed to me nothing more than evidence of what had once been – of the wretches, millions of them, who'd been thrust into the darkness of the rich eastern night and on to the road along which they would be bullied and beaten and on which many – the weakest and the youngest, the children, the sick – would stumble and fall and be left where they fell, their limbs close to useless, their will all but spent, their last hours and minutes passed alone on that dirt road until death rose to claim them and in time returned them – bones, blood and spirit – to the dark Russian earth from which long ago they had come.

In a while I turned away, all seeing done but all questioning merely beginning. I made my way to the cafe, where I sat drinking tea beneath a great picture window, while considering a postcard bought for sixty pence in the gallery shop. I turned it over. *The Vladimirka Road by Isaak Levitan.* I turned it back. Who exactly, I wondered, *were* these absent people, these long-gone victims – these men and women, these children? And where *exactly* was this road? Did *it* still exist, though *they* were gone? Did it still twist and turn through the landscape like a river? And who, finally, was this Levitan?

Questions, questions.

'Is this yours, sir?'

I looked up. The man – a gallery official, tall and thin, smartly suited – was frowning. On the palm of his outstretched hand sat my brand-new mobile phone. It had been lying, he said, on the floor behind my chair. I thanked him and retrieved it.

'You're welcome,' he said – and as if cued, then, by his words, the phone rang.

'Hello?'

Breathless, sounding distant, my wife said she'd seen him. It was Max, she said, she was certain. She'd been standing at the counter in John Lewis when she'd seen him.

'You mean,' I said, 'someone *like* him.'

She paused.

'Are you all right?' I said.

Yes, she said, she was fine. She just missed him too. Sometimes she couldn't believe he was really gone.

We arranged to meet in half an hour outside Marble Arch tube station.

'Did you see the picture?' she said. She was calmer now.

I said yes, I'd seen it. 'But what about you?'

It was nothing, she said – just a mind playing tricks. She took my hand. 'So this picture of yours,' she said. 'Was it everything Max said it was?'

I said yes, it was. To see the real thing at last had been like seeing him again, as bright and alive as once he'd been.

4

I turned to find her studying me, concentrating hard as if she were trying to divine something that was there but unseeable.

'What is it?' I said.

She smiled, what she'd sought clearly found. 'You're going to go,' she said, 'aren't you?'

I hesitated.

'Aren't you?'

'Would you mind if I did?'

She shook her head. She touched my shoulder. 'Hey, maybe you'll meet him there. Maybe he'll be one of the ghosts.'

I took her head in my hands. She was as beautiful on that day as she had been on the day I'd met her – on that day long before our son Joel's unexpected arrival, long after our friend Max had told me about the family he'd lost to Stalin and the Gulags, long before the first time he and I had talked idly of taking that trip down the road together.

She frowned.

'What is it?'

She said maybe I should take something with me – something of his.

'To Russia?'

'A gift,' she said, 'for his ancestors. Something you could leave there. Something to reunite the generations.'

The idea of taking his robe came to me then as clear and unexpected as a pale blue winter sky.

Sonia nodded. 'Perfect.'

And so as easily as that was the whole thing decided, my own willing sentence passed. I would take Levitan's *Vladimirka Road* as Max and I had one day long ago said we would – and take something of him along with me. We turned and descended into the gloom of the tube. *Yes*, I thought as the train for home approached, *I shall do it*. With his spirit beside me and the comfort of his Buddhist's orange robe in my hands, I would finally close the circle, at last turn my ear to the ghosts by the roadside.

A Muscovite and a chain-smoker and a man with eyebrows quite as thick as Leonid Brezhnev's, Nikolai Ilyanovitch opened his wallet and showed me a picture of a small, smiling boy. The boy's name, he said, was Roman.

'Like Abramovich,' I said.

'Yes. Like Abramovich.'

I wondered what he thought of him.

He shrugged. Abramovich, he said, was a thief. Like Putin.

I asked him what he meant – what exactly had been stolen. He looked at me as if I was half-witted. 'Russia,' he said, and I could see he meant *of course*, his grey hooded eyes heavy in that moment with what looked like the weight of a centuries-old burden. I wanted to ask him more, but then – as if cued by that particular word – they called us to the gate and we gathered our bags.

For six weeks I'd been poring over maps, skimming books about Russia, intending to extract just the minimum required but then being drawn in by the terrible stories of suffering, always suffering, suffering – stories of the wild and unmerciful Ivan the Terrible, who slaughtered his own son in a moment of vanity and rage, stories of the misery and death that accompanied the journey to the Gulag along that distant, often broken, bloody ribbon of a road. They were stories of the vastness and harshness of the great sweeping steppe, of the thousands of men, women and children who set out on the hard road of exile, thousands, of whom only a handful returned. There were stories too – little more, in fact, than imaginings – about the road itself, the earth and the stones that were its first constituents, and the words of scientists and men of God, both of whom claimed its creation for their own. Not that all was in dispute. All agreed, for example, that first there'd been nothing, just a wild, unpeopled land, but then – with the appearance of man by God or design and his fateful curiosity – a path was made from here to the horizon that would one day, thanks to centuries of toil, become the feared and bloody Vladimirka Road.

With the crew assembling at the departure gate and Nikolai Ilyanovitch beside me turning the pages of the *Moscow Times*, I opened my notebook and read again what I'd written about Levitan. He was the conscience, I read, the spine, the heart of Russian landscape painting.

'Hey, look at this.'

Nikolai Ilyanovitch had folded back the paper, so presenting a page of black and white faces, three of them – two men and one woman – headshots like mugshots, all ragged and staring as if at something a thousand miles away.

I asked Nikolai Ilyanovitch who they were.

He snorted. They were, he said, survivors of the camps of more than twenty years looking for compensation. Apparently, he said, they'd been denied their human rights by having been imprisoned more than 300 kilometres from their next of kin. The European Court of Justice, he said, was to rule on their case tomorrow or the next day.

I asked Nikolai what he thought would happen if they won – if their case was upheld. He shrugged. Nothing would happen, he said. The European Court of Justice could say what it liked. It had no authority in Russia, and, besides, the men and women were criminals, having been tried and found guilty – so who cared?

I looked at the faces. They were young but would now, of course, be old. I studied their faces and tried to imagine what manner of people they'd been. But their eyes were dead – like the windows of houses no longer occupied. But, of course, they weren't dead. Something within them had survived; somehow hearts had kept beating and the flickering flame of spirit or soul kept from being extinguished. And now here they were – the dead having returned and seeking justice.

The gate opened; a crowd formed. Beyond them, beyond the lightly smoked glass, the captain and first officer were getting themselves ready for the flight.

'So this boy of yours,' said Nikolai Ilyanovitch as we waited our turn, passports in hand, 'how old is he?'

He was five, I said.

He nodded, said it was a nice age.

Ten minutes later, as we sat in our seats, I took out the page I'd retrieved from the *Moscow Times*. There were three faces, three names, three stories. *Exiles seek justice.* I looked out of the window and thought again of Max – of how, had he been there beside me, he would have reminded me of a duty that the living always have to the dead. He would have told me, his face lighted up with that smile of his, that we all carry with us all those who went before, and that only through us – through the conduit of our voices – can their stories, that are our stories, be told.

I nudged Nikolai Ilyanovitch awake from his dozing. He looked at me, bleary-eyed. I pulled down his tray-table and spread out the page from the paper. I pointed to the first face of three and to the strange Cyrillic prose beneath and asked him if he'd tell me what it said. He looked at me sidelong, scowling. With a long sigh he reached into his inside jacket pocket and pulled out a pair of heavy-framed reading glasses. He cleared his throat like a man about to deliver a speech, then, shuffling in his seat in a vain attempt to arrange himself so that his large frame might be comfortable, he drew a breath and began to read slowly the first of the article's three stories.

He didn't cry, he said, until he read Solzhenitsyn's *One Day in the Life of Ivan Denisovich*. A free man for ten years thanks to the mercy of Joseph Stalin's death and his – and so many others' – subsequent release, he had not, he said, shed a single tear of pain or regret or even anger until he'd turned the pages and had seen himself there. Then, suddenly, as if a dam had been broken, those tears, and those he'd not cried on any one of the 9,126 days of his exile and imprisonment, had burst forth in a torrent so violent that he'd feared he might drown. Nothing, he said, could console him, and he could stand no company but Solzhenitsyn's words. He wetted them, he said, with his tears and tried to climb inside the book's browning pages, like a newborn baby who's seen the wretched world in the moment of his birth with its sharp capricious terrors and wishes with all his new strength to return with no delay to the safety and warmth of the womb.

Nikolai Ilyanovitch paused, then sat back, as if the task he'd been set had been done.

'Is that it?' I said.

He shrugged.

I asked him whether there wasn't surely some more – something, in all those strange words so impenetrable to me, to say what he's supposed to have done – to explain the reasons for his imprisonment.

Nikolai Ilyanovitch said the man was a terrorist – and that was all that mattered.

I asked him what the newspaper said he'd done.

Another shrug. The man, he said, had collected stamps.

'Stamps?'

I wasn't sure I'd heard him right. I asked him if he meant postage stamps – the kind you lick and stick on to envelopes.

'Of course,' he said.

I asked him if he'd read what the article said. Clearly reluctant and with a great and weary sigh, he drew his gaze back to the newspaper.

According to the *Moscow Times'* correspondent, the man – whose name was Maxim Guryanov – had been an engineer in a factory that had, in the twenty years before 1941 and the beginning of the Great Patriotic War, made lawnmowers and tractors; following the outbreak of hostilities, however, the factory had been re-designated as a producer of tanks for what some had already begun to see as the utterly shambolic Red Army. Thanks to Stalin's purges of the officer class and the introduction into each battalion-sized unit of political commissars, all discipline had evaporated and, consequently, any realistic hope of victory against Hitler's mighty Wehrmacht.

All of which, for the young Maxim Guryanov, had been no more than he'd expected, as, for him, as for any true philatelist, no better indication of a nation's state of health could be found than in the quality of that nation's postage stamps. This being so, and the implications of the general decline in the physical quality and pictorial ambition of philately during the rule of Stalin,[1] Guryanov and his fellow collectors kept to themselves. Not even in private was such a topic addressed, so insidious and widespread was the NKVD's network of informers. Despite these precautions, collectors were regularly found to have disappeared, and their collections sold overseas, the money from which – though officially intended for the betterment of the war effort – finding its way into the pockets of Party officials.

In the spring of 1942, following his factory's relocation east (in order to escape the Nazis' blitzkrieg advance), Maxim Guryanov was arrested at his lathe on a charge of treason and, within an hour of his arrest, had been sentenced to exile and life imprisonment. What happened to his collection (which included the very rare 50 Kopek Consulate tax stamp) remains a mystery, as, of course, nothing remained of it on Guryanov's eventual release.

According to the *Moscow Times*, Guryanov has spoken calmly during the hearing of his years in the Gulag, and has conducted himself with great dignity. Although he is fully aware of the unlikelihood of the current Russian government recognizing any conclusions drawn by the court, his hope is that his experience will act as a reminder to all those who think that the past, when past, is really gone. 'It lives,' he says, 'as long as the land upon which we live endures,' and it will, he says, unless we are careful, bury us all as surely as the sea rising over the land will bury us, or the flames of our brutal weapons engulf us.

---

1 Stalin's principal fear was that the kinds of images traditionally used on postage stamps would breed dissatisfaction in the general populace, and therefore act as an agent of counter-revolution.

Finally, when asked for the name of his favourite Russian stamp, Maxim Guryanov named neither the most valuable nor the most famous. His choice, instead, was a series of stamps produced in 1947, each one of which contained a portrait of a famous Russian painter. Of these, his favourite, he said, was the stamp on which had been reproduced the famous self-portrait by Isaak Levitan. When asked why this one in particular was his choice, he replied that the reason could be found in the Tretyakov Gallery in Moscow, in the famous painting *The Vladimirka Road*, for, he said, it was here and here alone that he could see again the faces of all those who'd died when he had somehow survived and only here, in contemplation of this picture, that their voices could still be heard.

Without a word, Nikolai Ilyanovitch folded the paper and passed it over. I slipped it into my pocket. In a minute I glanced over to find him sitting with his head back and mouth open, his eyes closed in sleep. I took out my postcard of *The Vladimirka Road*. How strange, I thought, that the man beside me had been reading about the very thing I was going to Russia to investigate, and how strange that simple brush-strokes on canvas can mean so much to so many people, and what a powerful, circular thing is absence, drawing as it does all those that are gone so close to the sad and mourning heart.

He was, people said, the conscience, the spine, the heart of Russian landscape painting. A Lithuanian Jew, Isaak Ilych Levitan abandoned the servility of his impoverished homeland for the cities of the great master, Russia. An orphan at fifteen, and a child thereafter atuned to the whispers of ghosts, he would wander the city's streets during the night's freezing curfew, watching the convicts – dreaded enemies of the tsar – as they shuffled through the streets, hands and feet manacled, their eyes cast down and spirits so low that nothing but the promise of freedom could revive them. Many walked barefoot; many were already grey-blue from the cold and would soon be dead, their still-warm corpses cut free from the caravan and left to cool and stiffen by the side of the road or on a deserted street corner, awaiting then the attentions of the sharp-toothed wolves that crept into the cities and the towns at night to feast on what man in his satiety had carelessly discarded. *I watched them fall*, said Levitan in his fiftieth year, *and, kneeling beside them, gave them what succour I could. I watched, too, the caravan depart, moving east and north, towards a land few had heard of.*

That land was Siberia, and though such was its name, to most it was simply *out there* – a place well beyond the reach of civilization. It was, people knew (how they knew it, they couldn't have said, but they knew it), a land of wolves, and the road one must travel to reach it a road without hope – the road of death, the road of bones, the road to a place so distant that even God, it was said, was unsure of exactly where it began and where it ended.

Nikolai Ilyanovitch sat up with a jolt as the plane rose and fell on a pocket of air. He looked around him. He'd been dreaming, he said, thanks to me, about Roman Abramovich – and about ducks.

'Ducks?' I said, not sure I'd heard right.

He nodded. It was ducks, he said, that got Abramovich started: a truckload of plastic yellow ducks sitting unattended on the Tretyakovst Proyez. Did I not, he said, know the story? I said no. Again the plane lurched. He drew a chubby hand across his brow.

According to Nikolai Ilyanovitch, quite how Abramovich parlayed such an unexpected bounty (no one ever, it seems, claimed the ducks when their whereabouts became known or even reported them as having been stolen) into a permanent apartment in the Kremlin on Red Square, not to mention a fleet of yachts and a vast portfolio of investments and mansions and Chelsea Football Club and goodness knows what else, no one, of course, is really quite sure. And those who *are* – those who believe themselves to be – speak out only quietly and from what they hope is a safe enough distance. Of one thing, however, all onlookers can be certain. In the far, frozen east – the wild east, so it's called, and for good reason – the land where the gas is endless and as priceless as it is endless, a land where the rule of law is nothing more than a distant abstraction and the idea of a code of morals so alien a concept as to be laughable, the ruthless man, if ruthless enough, will prosper, while others will dig and dig, their hands growing calloused and their backs breaking – and all for that day's daily bread.

'Isn't he,' I said, 'what the new, post-Communist, feeling-good-about-ourselves Russia's all about?'

As the plane climbed high heading east above the snow-covered Alps, Nikolai Ilyanovitch shrugged. Abramovich, he said, was a foreigner, a grandson of Lithuanian Jews cast out from their homeland following Stalin's occupation – a man, therefore, he says, with both commerce and thievery in his blood.

'So not a Russian, then.'

Nikolai Ilyanovitch sighed. On the contrary, he said. Abramovich, like Putin, was what Russia was becoming – had become. 'Like America,' he said. 'Only more BMWs.'

'Is that bad?'

Another shrug. Moscow, he said, as if in answer to my question, was about to host the Eurovision Song Contest.

'Isn't that *good*?' I said. 'The promotion of harmony between nations and all that?'

No, he said, it was bad. A humiliation. The real Russia – the old Russia – wouldn't have stood for it.

Foolishly (facetiously, perhaps), I mentioned the tendency in recent years for block-voting. I suggested the chances of victory were good. He smiled, rueful. 'Of course,' he said. 'If they want our gas in Uzbekistan, they vote for us!'[1]

---

1   In the event, the Russian entrant Anastasia Prikhodko finished in eleventh place. Curiously, as a representative of Russia, Ms Prikhodko was in fact born in the Ukraine and, as such, should have been ineligible. Her favourite pastime is chess and, as a patriot, would like to see all black people and those of Chinese origin either sent into exile or expelled from the Russian Federation.

'And the Chechens?' I said. 'Who will *they* vote for?'

He shook his head. All Chechens, he said, his manner suddenly changing, were barbarians.

'Because of Beslan?'

'Beslan?' he said. 'Forget Beslan. Blame Allah.'

'It's an Islamic thing?'

'For sure. They hate Christians. Ask the Georgians! Ask the Cossacks!'

'Are you a Christian?'

He shrugged. 'I believe in God. I believe in good order. I believe in Maggie Thatcher.'

I suggested she might have made a good Russian – given Stalin a run for his money. He shook his head and glanced around him, suddenly agitated. 'No joking,' he said. The man's children, after all, he said, were everywhere.

'Whose children?'

'Stalin.' He whispered the word like some evil incantation.

'Even here?' I said.

He nodded, glancing over my shoulder as if to confirm this. 'You see *him*?' he said, his voice suddenly low, like a spy's.

I turned. Three rows back on the aisle a man in a dark business suit was eating a breakfast of scrambled eggs and sausage.

'What *about* him?'

Nikolai Ilyanovitch hissed *Look at his shoes*.

So I did. The man in the aisle's socks were red. Whether this was significant or not I didn't know and, of course, never will.

Later, as the plane began its long, slow descent into Moscow, Nikolai Ilyanovitch told me the following joke.

A visitor from Chechnya was driving with a Russian through the outskirts of Moscow. Coming to a red light, he put his foot down and sped through. 'Hey,' said the Russian, 'you just went through a red light!' 'Chechens don't stop for red lights,' the driver replied. This happens a second and a third time. Eventually, arriving at a green light, the Chechen stopped the car. 'What are you doing?' said the Russian. 'The light's green!' Looking worried, the driver said, 'But a Chechen might be coming the other way.'

Existing in a state of war since its secession from the Russian Federation in the early 1990s, Chechnya, a largely Islamic republic on the northern slopes of the Caucasus mountains, has had a history quite ludicrously bleak. Since being conquered by the Russians in 1259, the Chechen people have, like the Cossacks, been regularly invaded and enslaved, and have often seen their homes destroyed and their children scattered like seeds thrown into the wind. Most recently, but long before the current and seemingly endless war, in the late 1940s the entire Chechen nation was dispatched by Stalin along the Vladimirka Road to Siberia – every man, woman and child forced with only a few days' notice to pack what they could carry and make the long journey north and east by unheated cattle-truck.

No food.

No medical attention.

No wonder that they feel as little a sense of fraternity with the Russian Federation as they did with the old Soviet Union. Clearly, sitting on the second-largest reserves of oil in the region has been scarcely a blessing. Clearly, the good fortune that gave a similar blessing to the murderous West-friendly regimes of Saudi Arabia and Kuwait hasn't visited poor Chechnya. Nor will it, it seems, as long as Moscow maintains the choking, disabling grip of post-Soviet Empire.

I asked Nikolai Ilyanovitch what he thought would happen in Chechnya.

He shrugged. The same thing, he said, that always happened. Russian boys would fight and die and Russia would win. And then lose. In the end the burden of victory and its prize of constant vigilance would prove too much.

'You mean the Chechen army won't ever be properly defeated?'

'Of course. If they want to be free of us, then in the end they *will* be. Such people will never forgive.'

'So what can you do?'

'Do?'

'To keep safe before peace comes.'

'Prime Minister Putin says we must be vigilant.'

'Which means what?'

'He says we must patrol the streets and gardens. He says we must watch and we must wait. We must carry our weapons and be ready.'

'Do you have a gun?'

'Everyone in Russia has a gun.'

I turned away then, filled with the image of a nation of vigilantes – a place where every citizen will shoot you as readily as shake your hand.

While the cabin crew prepared for landing, I glanced at my guidebook, at a page of quotes about Russia. *A rude and barbarous kingdom*, I read, the line sitting there as if waiting for my gaze. A few moments later I looked out of the plane window and, as we left the West behind us and crossed into Moscow airspace, a grey-painted Mig-29 Fulcrum rose up like a phantom to greet us.

Who can forget Beslan and the scattered toys on the schoolroom floor? And what father or mother does not remember the photographs of the victims pinned up on the gymnasium's far wall? Go there and stand before them and they look down on you now with that clear-sighted innocence peculiar to children.

And yet.

Look closer and there is surely something more. Alongside that innocence lies the mournfulness of future martyrs – a combination quite chilling and, it seems to me now, so *Russian*. Like the importance of understanding *duende* for a student of Spain, understand *strada*, people say, and you understand what it is to be Russian. Taken literally, *strada* means suffering – but that isn't it, for such literalism disguises much. In this case it disguises the fact of suffering not as the consequence of a wound but as an attitude – the prism of *expectation* of suffering through which all of life is viewed. As the plane broke through the clouds and the land below drew suddenly into focus, I was reminded of that old Russian joke: 'The doctor said, "To the morgue." "But what's wrong with me?" asked the patient. "The autopsy will show," said the nurse.'

Strada.

Strength and weakness in huge and equal proportions, and, above all, the absolute immensity of the land. Napoleon knew it and was afraid of it. *The vastness of this land will defeat us*, he said as he rode his horse Marengo east towards the fiery snowbound furnace of Moscow, while the Führer lost the better part of his army – and consequently the war – to the sheer inhuman distances involved and the terrible severity of the winter.

Max told me one afternoon as we lay stretched out in the back of his brother's pickup truck of the journey his great-grandfather had taken to Tomsk in Siberia, and it struck me then how strange it was and how wonderfully unlikely that that journey – that march of generations – should end with him in the blue-skied, clear-watered heat of a New Zealand summer.

Looking back, I realize now that I hadn't known until that moment – *Listen*, he'd said, *there's news and it's not good* – that he wasn't going to recover, and that the thing inside him that had for so long been growing and scheming and doing everything it could to rob him of his life (and, in the process, of course, kill itself by killing the host) was really going to succeed, and that, from that moment on, his life would be a series of *lasts* – a kind of farewell tour of all the stations of his life played out in the glare of a slow-setting sun whose heat was gradually failing and whose shadows, every day, were creeping ever longer.

'Are you sure?' I said.

Yes, he said, he was sure.

High above us, the blue southern sky was criss-crossed with vapour trails: planes full of people, young and old, those revelling in the thrill of it all – of leaving and arriving – and those terrified of the awful fragility of flight, some eating, others drinking, some watching *The Man Who Wasn't There* on the tiny little screen on the back of the seat in front. Every one of them, though – whatever they were doing – was living. Not dying.

'It's all right,' said Max, as if reading my thoughts.

Later that day, back at his father's house on Mount Eden Road, he told me some more about Tomsk – about his great-grandfather's exile and the road he'd taken north-east from Moscow, the road heading out to Siberia, where the comets that arced across the night sky were more numerous than the people whose lives were scratched out on the frozen earth below, and where a man would greet death as deliverance from his misery, and thoughts of warmth, of love, of summer's slothful ease as cruel postcards from a life that had surely never been. He spoke of the names – of Orekhovo-Zuyevo, of Elektrostal, of Omsk and Ufa, of Vladimir and Tomsk – and of the horrors of the camps his great-grandfather had called *Gulags*. What he wanted more than anything, he said, his voice already weakening, was to go there, to listen to the voice of his great-grandfather on the wind and to commune as best he could with the spirits of the dead. Then he turned to me and smiled.

'What is it?' I said.

He said what did I think.

'About what?'

'Well?' he said, wrapping himself in his saffron robe. 'Will you come?'

'Of course,' I said. 'When do we go?'

Again he smiled. It was the kind of smile that had once, for a bet, gained him entry to the Prime Minister's office at the Beehive in Wellington, from the window of which he had briefly flown the red and white sun and moon flag of the kingdom of Nepal.

That night, after fish and chips from Remo's and a half-dozen Steinlager Blues, we spread out the map on the kitchen table. For a moment each of us was silent, each astounded again by the sheer *size* of Russia. Max pointed to Moscow, then Tomsk in the east. It was, he said, one hell of a way – maybe too much for a Buddhist with a tumour in his head the size of a golf ball.

I looked to his father, who'd come in tired and hot from his afternoon's bowling. His father – nut-brown, a former rural policeman – without missing a beat, said, *No, of course you must go.* He knew, of course, that the trip now would never happen – but he *also* knew that there are times when a dream to a dying man is more valuable than the truth, and that even the man under sentence of death needs something to divert his attention from grim contemplation of the end.

'You think you can make it?' said Max.

'Sure,' I said, and I nearly said *If you can.*

I glanced again at his father. Duncan Boxall was gazing at his son as if from a great distance.

'Dad?'

And for a moment the vastness of Russia seemed like nothing.

'Hey, Dad – are you OK?'

But then the old man blinked, and his old eyes refocused, and that distance was suddenly, for the moment at least, reduced to nothing, as father and son just stood there looking at each other in that old wooden house on Mount Eden Road with a bond of love so strong that it was clear to me that nothing – not even death, not even distance – could ever really break it, neither in this world nor the next.

Happiness exists retrospectively; *I was happy*, we say, and the memory makes us smile. To say *I am happy*, however, is to issue a challenge to the very happiness it acknowledges – for, of course, in the moment of perception it is – like the *now* in which it lives – gone.

As the plane descended, I closed my guidebook (*A Short History of the Gulags* had gripped me with a horror that did not want to let me go) and gazed out of the window. As the sprawling mess and tangle of Moscow drew ever closer, I couldn't help thinking of Max and remembering that afternoon spent lying on the back of his brother's ute, and as I peered down, searching with the foolishness of a child for the point – *the exact place* – where the great journey of the Vladimirka Road begins, it occurred to me that for me, guardian of a spirit and a Buddhist's saffron robe, the pilgrimage to the end of the world had really already begun.

To write about such a road without mentioning the architect of its final, bloodiest use would be to write about Christmas without mentioning Jesus or the Austrian Anschluss without giving due credit to Adolf Hitler. Context, after all, is everything – setting the stage vital to some kind of understanding.

So. Joseph Stalin.

Not in fact a Russian at all, but a Georgian, Iosif Vissarionovich Dzhugashvili was the son of an impoverished bootmaker – the only one of four children to survive. A failed priest (he was thrown out of theological college for preaching against God and in favour of Marx), he discovered a talent for rabble-rousing, which talent brought him to the attention both of Lenin and Tsar Nicholas's secret police, the Cheka. The former embraced him as a likely successor, while the latter arrested him for treasonable activities and exiled him for life to Siberia – from which imprisonment in 1904 he escaped and fled to Finland at the exiled Lenin's invitation. Returning to Russia in 1913, he was again arrested and again exiled to the most northerly reaches of Siberia, where he stayed until an amnesty was granted to all political prisoners following the collapse of the tsar's imperialist regime and the formation of the first Russian Communist government. Awarded the role of Commissar of Nationalities (placed within his care, as a consequence, were all non-Russians resident in the Soviet Union), Stalin rose through the Party's hierarchy with a lethal combination of guile and brutality. A man with no conscience, he would kill with impunity and do to others what had several times been done to him without reference to or acknowledgement of the presence of any moral ambiguity. In 1922 Joseph Stalin was appointed General Secretary of the Communist Party, and within five years, following the deaths both of Lenin and Leon Trotsky,[1] he emerged as the vast state's new leader. What followed was nothing less than a holocaust as whole peoples numbering millions were slaughtered or sent into exile along the Vladimirka Road – the road along which he himself had been sent. His whim was utterly capricious, his power absolute, his legacy one of suffering, and his nation's ruination and eventual complete disintegration, and when he died he left nothing but scars behind him – on the flesh, in the minds of the people whom he'd terrorized for so long, and on the very land itself, where what remains of the death camps by means of which his power had been sustained can still be seen today – a vast network of prisons that some say have not even now been entirely abandoned.

As we sat on the plane and ate our chicken Kiev and drank our Russian wine, I asked Nikolai Ilyanovitch if what many people in the West said was true – that Putin and now Medvedev had secretly recommissioned some of the

---

1   While Trotsky's famous death by ice-pick in Mexico City was beyond dispute the work of Stalin's agents, the death of Lenin was clearly the work of nature, for not even Stalin dared raise a hand against such an iconic figure.

furthest-flung camps, specifically to accommodate those campaigning for greater democracy.

As usual when faced with a question, Nikolai Ilyanovitch shrugged. Were there not, he said, prisons in the West?

'But the Gulags were death camps,' I said.

He shook his head. The camps, he said, were *work* camps. The Russians, after all, weren't Nazis.

'But people died from overwork. If they got there at all.'

Another shrug. Anyway, said Nikolai Ilyanovitch, the past was the past. All that mattered now was today.

'And the millions who died?' I said. 'What about them?'

Nikolai Ilyanovitch sighed, clearly annoyed by my questions. The dead, he said, were dead – so who could help them now?

I opened my mouth to speak – to say something about remembrance and the value of memory. But something caused the words to stall in my throat. It was the sudden chill thought that maybe he was right – that maybe the dead really are simply gone and that to raise up their memory is both useless to the living and no service to the dead, disturbing, as it's bound to, the corpse lying still in its quiet, distant grave.

Those present at the death of Joseph Stalin on 5 March 1953 took turns, apparently, to poke the body, to assure themselves that life had indeed really fled. Some – those still cowed by the man's fearsome features – touched their fingers to his shoulder or his forearm, while the more reckless among them poked his cheek or pulled his ear. One even tweaked his nose. The death thus finally established, they stood around for a while like guests at a wedding after the bride and groom have gone and wondered what on earth to do now. In the absence of fear, they were bereft. In the absence of commands, life seemed suddenly arbitrary and fearful. One by one they left the room, some still looking back as if doubting even then that God had the power to remove life from such a man. Which, in a sense, of course, He didn't. The man's legacy of hatred and fear was so strong – so bred in the bone – that even after death it couldn't help but appear like a cancer in the flesh of the scarred ones left behind.

'Why are you here?'

I was standing in line, awaiting my moment beneath the flat, sullen stare of an immigration officer. At the flick of a finger I stepped forward to the line.

I was, I said, writing a book.

The eyes narrowed, as if what I'd said was easy code for *I've planted a bomb.*

'A book?' he said. 'Why?'

Why?

Now there was a good question.

'Yes?'

The book, I said, was to be about Russia.

The officer's gaze lightened. 'Stalin?' he said.

'Could I write a book about Russia without him?' I said.

He shook his head. Then, feeding my passport through the X-ray machine with one hand, with the other he reached down behind him and from somewhere out of sight produced a card advertising a Moscow pole-dancing club. This he slipped with some stealth into my passport.

'You may go now,' he said.

'Thank you,' I said. I took a step, a second.

'Hey . . .'

I stopped.

'Welcome to Moscow,' he said, no trace of a smile.

It was a joke written down on a piece of paper that did for Max's great-grandfather – three dozen words that bought him three dozen years in the wintry hell that was the Gulag[1] at Tomsk. The offending joke – so dangerous then, so harmless now – goes as follows.

One day, the great leader Stalin received a delegation of workers from the White Sea Canal. When they left, he discovered his pipe was missing. He called for Beria, his secret service chief, and told him what had happened. Beria told *him* that the matter would be dealt with and then left the room. A few moments later, the great leader discovered his pipe in his pocket. He sat back, lit it and puffed away happily, before calling Beria and announcing his discovery. 'What a pity,' said Beria. 'Why's that?' said the great leader. Beria paused. All the workers, he said, had already confessed and all had already been executed. 'A pity indeed,' said Stalin, whereupon he relit his pipe and, with neither a smile nor a frown disturbing the stillness of his face – as if, indeed, he was a man without a care – he drew casually and with evident pleasure on the pipe, then blew through pursed lips a great pall of smoke.

1 The acronym GULAG stands for Glavnoe Upravlenie Lagere. The English translation is the ironically prosaic Main Camp Administration.

We were sitting in Max's father's home on Lake Taupo, December's heat already fading, the chill of autumn coming on. I leaned forward, squinting hard without my glasses at the small piece of ragged lined paper set in a chipped wooden frame. It was the joke written out from memory by Max's father during his wartime service in the RAF protecting Russian convoys in the bitter Arctic Ocean.

'And for this he was sent to the Gulag?'

Max nodded. It was possession of just such a scrap of paper that had, all those years ago and so many thousands of miles away, seen him carted away in the dead of night and held for three days at Moscow's Lubyanka prison before his sentence of exile was ratified by the Punishment Committee of the local soviet.

He hung the frame back up on the wall. 'For that,' he said, 'and for being known to be a reader of books.'

'Like what?'

'Dickens, mostly. *Hard Times* was his favourite. But all sorts of things. It didn't matter. If a man could read, then a man could write, and a man who could write was dangerous. And so they took him, ripping him away from his family, and sent him down the Vladimirka Road to the Gulag. And when he got there, they beat him and worked him to death.'

'And his wife,' I said, 'your great-grandmother. Did she get to see him before his exile began?'

'Yes,' said Max. 'Once. They let her have five minutes with him in his cell before they sent him away. Not alone, of course. They were watched, every minute. She said she hardly recognized him. His face was swollen from the beatings, and when he stood he stooped like an old man.'

'How old was he?'

'He was twenty-nine years old. She said he could have been fifty. He reached out his hand when it was time for her to go, but the guard pushed it down. No contact allowed. And then she was gone, back out in the street with the rest of what was left of her life ahead of her.'

'What did she do?'

Max shrugged. 'Survived somehow. Somehow she stayed alive for her children. She made blankets out of scraps of material and sold them on the street. And when the war came she found work in a factory making shells. Did I tell you she met Stalin? Well, she did. He came to visit the factory when the Germans were only fifty miles from Moscow. She shook his hand. He asked her if there was anything she needed. When she said "My husband", he smiled and asked for his name. He said he would see that something was done. Two weeks later, my great-grandfather's rations were cut and the blanket removed from his bed. The blanket was burned before him, and he was forced to eat the ashes.'

'And your great-grandmother? What happened to her?'

'She was given a promotion and a Workers' Ribbon. With the extra money she fed her children. So you could say Stalin saved their lives. You could say he saved *my* life. What do you think of that?'

I said I didn't know. I said did that mean – could that *possibly* mean? – that he wasn't all bad? Did it mean that his was an evil that was learned and not simply a part of his DNA?

'How many times,' he said, 'has the prisoner become the guard? How many times has the victim of wickedness become its most enthusiastic practitioner?'

'Are you saying Stalin was a victim?'

Max nodded. 'Four times,' he said. 'Four times he was a prisoner of the tsar and four times he was beaten and starved and humiliated. And what he learned from his masters in the Okhranka[1] he remembered and later, at its height, when the system he built on the fear of his fellow citizens had become the very skeleton of the Soviet state, he used what he'd learned.'

'So are you saying he wasn't born a monster?'

'I'm saying that everyone is born a child, pure and untainted. Even Stalin. Even he, as a child, felt the sun on his face and the cool water of a stream in the heat of summer. I'm *saying* we all live by example. You strike your child, your child strikes *his* child and so on. On and on it goes until somebody says *no*. Until somebody takes that will to strike and smothers it like a boxer smothers his opponent's blows by wrapping him in his arms and holding him close. Haven't you ever wondered why the Jews didn't rise and fight when Hitler began his extermination? Why the six million didn't stand together shoulder to shoulder, raise their fists and say to the Nazis, who were fewer, that for every one of us you kill we will kill three of you?'

I said yes, I'd wondered, but had never got further than that.

'Well, think about it,' said Max.

I promised I would.

Later, back in London on the eve of my journey, I met a man – a Gulag survivor – quite by chance at a wedding in Highgate. He was small and sinewy with leather-brown skin. I told him what Max had said – how no man is born evil, just made so.

---

1   Okhranka – literally 'the guard' – was formed following several failed attempts on the life of Tsar Alexander II. It was the direct predecessor of Lenin's Cheka, which itself was forerunner to the notorious KGB.

'Max?' he said. 'Who's this Max?'

A friend, I told him, a former actor, a Buddhist.

'An actor?' said the old man, scoffing, dismissive, as if I'd said he was a hairdresser. He shook his head. 'Don't you know it's a wedding?' he said, his eyes on me – dark brown, almost black. 'Why are you telling me this?'

His words stung like a slap. He turned, and I watched him walk away, just as from inside the church the grand organ started up and the summer ceremony began.

A half-hour later, with the happy couple married and the guests dispersing to a rose-themed reception, the old man approached me. I braced myself, ready for anything but what came.

I said I was sorry for any offence caused, but he waved my words aside. Instead, he led me to a seat in the sun (a seat from which, incidentally, I later discovered, a taller man than I could see the very top of the gravestone of Karl Marx) and laid bare for me the bones of his story.

Now an old man of eighty-two, he had once, long ago, been a letter writer in the city of St Petersburg. Taken one day with no explanation from his home and his family (he had had a wife and three sons, none of whom he has seen since, and of whom he has no mementos, so swift was his expulsion from his home), he had been sent north in an open coal-truck, one of forty, all of whom had been forced to work on the infamous White Sea Canal. Of the forty, only one returned.

'And the others?'

They lay, he said, where they'd fallen and were buried in the concrete and stone of the canal – the great murderous white elephant that had consumed so many lives and proved useless – too shallow for commercial traffic – from the terrible day of its final completion.

How, I asked him, had *he* survived? He frowned, and I wondered what he'd say. Would it, I wondered, be God that had saved him, or luck, or the strength provided by the wish to bear witness?

But it was none of these things. What had saved him, he said, had been the cold. The cold – so bitter some days that men would die standing up, their spades still in their hands and their eyes open as if a great thought had struck them and not simply death – had, in time, frozen all hope, all love and all fear, and left him the husk of a man. He had, he said, neither wished to live nor to die; all that had come to matter were the strikes of his pickaxe – the numbers, the counting: a thousand, a million, and on and on – until one day he'd found himself quite alone in the vast white expanse, the crack of his pickaxe on stone the only sound. How long he'd gone on striking the solid ground he didn't know – or how he'd come to be alone, or even where on earth he was when he stopped. All he knew – all he remembered still – was the absolute, terrifying silence and the unbroken whiteness of the land.

I asked him what then? Where did he go?

He walked, he said, and he kept on walking. He must, he said, have walked south because in a while – after days and weeks, maybe longer; how long he doesn't know – the land began to thaw. It grew softer beneath his feet, and the sun grew warmer on his face. Then finally, after months of walking – of eating berries and leaves and anything growing in the ground he could find – he saw the golden domes of what he thought was St Petersburg but was in fact Moscow. He walked on. In a while he passed a milepost and a man in labouring clothes leaning against it. He paused and asked the man what year it was. The man told him it was 1953.

Nineteen fifty-three.

Stalin, the man said as if answering an unspoken question, was dead.

'At first I couldn't believe it,' he said. 'Men like Stalin don't die.'

'But he did. And you survived. And now you're here.'

He looked around him, then turned his face towards the sun. High above, a plane, then a second, then a third was drawing vapour trails slowly across the sky. He frowned; I asked him what was wrong, but he just shook his head, unable for the moment to speak. For the moment he was far too busy to speak – too busy counting the tiny distant aeroplanes and their graceful, drifting arcs so white against the blue.

The boys dropped their trousers and bared their pale skinny arses as the express trundled by. They watched the progress of the train that connects Domodedovo airport to the outskirts of Moscow without comment, their heads looking back from between their legs, their gaze consequently upside down. When the train had passed, they returned without enthusiasm to their broken-down basketball court and their lives lived for ever in the bleak concrete shadow of the grim 1950s.

'Excuse me. You are English?'

The girl on the train had been glancing at my copy of *Doctor Zhivago*.[1]

I said yes, I was English.

'That's good,' she said, and then said I was lucky. She was smiling and maybe fifteen or sixteen years old.

'Isn't it good to be Russian?' I said.

She nodded. Yes, she said, she was proud to be Russian, although she missed Primrose Hill.

1 *Doctor Zhivago*, completed in 1956, was immediately banned by the Soviet authorities. Though considered 'anti-Marxist', what really upset the censors was Pasternak's references to prison camps – camps which, they claimed, didn't exist.

'You've been to London?'

Aleksandra Rodianova had spent a summer in London as an exchange student in the house of the novelist Sebastian Faulks, the Faulkses' daughter having spent the previous summer in Moscow. There, in genteel Primrose Hill, she had practised her English until it had lost its strict grammatical rigour and gained in its place a colloquial fluency.

'Have you met him?' she asked.

No, I said. The man, after all, was a best-selling writer.

'But aren't you a writer too?'

'Did you read *Birdsong*?' I asked.

She shook her head. She looked clean and neat against the grime of the carriage.

'Overrated,' I said peevishly.

'Maybe you are jealous,' she said.

'Jealous?'

But then she smiled and so did I and from that moment on we were friends.

She was, she said, nineteen and studying to be a teacher. As the train rattled on, we talked about all kinds of things – books (she said she loved Gogol but couldn't stand Tolstoy, while I was the reverse), films (she disagreed with me about David Lean's *Zhivago*, thinking Julie Christie's beauty not a hindrance to the story but an advantage) and politics. When I asked her about Putin – whether or not his stepping down from the role of President to that of Prime Minister, leaving the former to his close friend Dimitry Medvedev, was really just a way to subvert the constitution – she just shrugged. Politics, she said, was coming to matter less and less. Medvedev or Putin, it didn't make any difference. They'd both become rich through GAZPROM, the largest extractor of natural gas in the world (a resource, she said, that belonged to the Russian people), and now Putin had said that it must be reformed, seeing, apparently, no conflict of interest in the fact of his having a 15 billion dollar personal stake in the company. No, she said, Medvedev or Putin or anyone else, there would still be people living in poverty and on drugs everywhere. 'Look,' she said, pointing out of the window at the twisted rusting fences and discoloured concrete and at the broken-down tower blocks beyond.

'Who,' she said, shaking her head, 'would like to live in a place like that?'

The buildings looked bleak and hopeless, clearly shoddily built. 'I don't suppose anyone *wants* to,' I said.

The glass was missing or broken in many of the windows, the poor-quality concrete crumbling at the edges and streaked with water stains beneath buckled and broken gutters.

She looked away. A woman with a supermarket trolley had appeared at the end of the carriage. The trolley was full of bottles of Coke Zero and Fanta and packets of sweets and magazines – Russian editions of *Hello!* and *OK!*.

'My father and my mother lived in such a place after their marriage,' she said. 'They were lucky. Sometimes it took ten years before the house commissioners said yes.'

'You paid rent?'

'Me?'

'Your mother and father.'

The woman with the trolley paused beside us. Aleksandra Rodianova shook her head. The woman moved on. 'No. It was free. A reward for being a good citizen. So you moved in – sooner if you were married. And then you paid back the money. So much every week. So many roubles.'

'Who were your parents paying?'

'They had to pay the man who had given the money to give to the house commissioners.'

'So it was a bribe?'

'Excuse me?'

'You had to pay to get something for nothing.'

'Pay? I think, yes. If you don't pay you have to leave. But at least in those days the windows weren't broken.'

I asked her how long her parents had lived there.

'Six years,' she said.

'And then?'

'And then my father becomes a professor at the university. He makes more money. He is given a new house. Not in a place like this.'

'Was that free too?'

She nodded.

'So was it expensive?'

'Excuse me?'

'Did it cost a lot, this free house? Many roubles?'

'Yes, many roubles,' she said, nodding, as the train slowed noticeably.

'Where are we?' I said.

The vast ring of tower blocks and scrubland was behind us now, replaced by the low-rise congestion always present at the outskirts of any Russian city.

'We have arrived,' said Aleksandra Rodianova as the train hissed and groaned into Paveletsky station. She looked at me quizzically. 'You have just this one very small bag?' she said.

Yes, I said, as the train slid to a grinding, reluctant stop, just the one.

The station was crowded – city workers at the end of the day waiting for the trains that would take them back out to their two- and three-room apartments on the fifth or twelfth or seventeenth floor. One woman in a headscarf was carrying a microwave oven. It reminded me of a headline I'd seen once on a Russian-language newspaper outside a newsagent's in Notting Hill. Translated by a friend from the Russian, it read: SOVIET UNION SENDS FIRST PEASANT INTO SPACE.

'But what will you do?'

'Do?'

'You'll need more things, won't you?'

'I'll get some new things – if I do.'

She looked at me then with a strange sideways look. She was certain, she said, that her father would like me. He was apparently quite reckless too. He'd often, she said, in the time of Brezhnev addressed classes at the university wearing a shirt with an antisocial slogan beneath his work clothes.

'What did it say?'

'The Five-Year Plan Is Not Working.'

'What was he teaching?'

She smiled. 'The victory of the Soviet planned economy.'

I asked her if he was still a professor.

'Yes,' she said. 'Only now he's the dean.'

'And the shirt?'

'Hidden,' she said. Then she asked if I would like to meet him.

'Your father?'

'You have somewhere else to go?'

'I have a hotel,' I said.

'Then tomorrow?'

Yes, I said, tomorrow would be good.

She stood up and fetched her bag down from the rack. For no reason I can recall now, something in her movement made me think of the boys looking glumly at the train from their broken-down basketball court. The army, sooner or later, I'd been told, would take them for their year's national service, their presence (often, these days, the result of 'enhanced recruiting' – that being a new name for the old exercise of 'press-ganging') an effort to shore up the slowly collapsing edifice that is the Russian army. Then, if they survived the brutality of the barracks (which some do not, returning home to their parents in cheap, sealed coffins), they'd be sent to Chechnya or Georgia or the border with Afghanistan. Here, under-trained and under-resourced, a third of them will take a bullet or shrapnel from a shell, and those who survive will return to their tower blocks and their basketball courts with their rusted chain-link fences, there just to stand and watch glumly, this time a lifetime older but scarcely any wiser, as the express train to Moscow rattles by.

Anyone who thinks it likely that they'll be served eggs at the breakfast buffet by a notorious mass murderer should really have made other hotel plans.

'Omelette?'

'Thank you,' I said, quite unable to keep my gaze from the man's extraordinary moustache. Though I was aware that beneath it his lips were working, they seemed to me to be producing no sound. 'I'm sorry?' I said, when all I wanted to say was, *Does anyone else see what I see?* I glanced at the little man beside me. He was Japanese and seemed to be taking the whole thing in his stride. I looked again at the omelette man. The moustache looked genuine, as did the swept-back bouffant hair.

The Japanese man leaned in close. 'Stalin!' he hissed. I nodded. Then, meekly accepting my breakfast, I turned and made my way back to my table.

'Is everything all right, sir?'

Katarina from reception was concerned. She had a booklet about the Tretyakov Gallery in one hand and some other papers in the other.

'I'm fine,' I said. As discreetly as I could manage, I pointed at the omelette man and asked her why he was dressed like Stalin.

'You mean Pavel?' she said.

'Is that his name?'

'Yes. Would you like to speak to him?'

'What?'

'For your book. He knows everything.'

'Everything?'

She nodded. He had, after all, she said, been Stalin longer than Stalin ever was.

The best story about Iosif Vissarionovich Stalin precedes by an hour or so the nose tweaking and hair pulling that followed the great teacher's final and incontrovertible death. Like that one, it too involves Lavrenti Beria, the chief of his secret police and perhaps the earliest and most trusted (which wasn't saying much) of his confidants. Again, it was the spring of 1953 and the generalissimo was known to be dying. One morning, those in his inner circle were summoned to his dacha at Kuntsevo, fifteen kilometres west of Moscow, to hear exactly who would be anointed as the great man's successor. On arrival, they gathered at his bedside – all the lackeys and sycophants – and were waiting for the word when, thanks to the actions of the young Nikita Khrushchev who dared to touch the great man's hand, they discovered that Stalin wasn't sleeping at all (he'd not said a word in two hours) but was, in fact, dead. Suddenly released from the chains of fearful subservience, Beria – always the most loyal, the most slavish in his attentions – leaped up and started cursing his erstwhile leader, telling everyone (including the man himself) how he'd never trusted him and what an ignorant peasant he was, etc., etc. In fact, he was just getting into his stride (Stalin, in his view – then most violently expressed – had been the child of the devil and a crippled Georgian cow) when suddenly the corpse coughed. All looked accusingly at Beria, who, without a moment's hesitation, dropped to his knees at his bedside, kissed Stalin's palm and declared again his undying, enduring loyalty and love. Such undying love, etc., wasn't, of course, to last, for ten minutes later – when death came for real – up he leaped again, and again started haranguing his once-revered leader (even spitting in his face this time), and in so doing set in train the events that would see him elevated to the post of leader himself. But not for long. Accused (and found guilty) of sexual perversion – including the systematic rape of young girls and children – he was arrested by his successor Khrushchev and shot in the head as a British spy.

An hour later, we were sitting in the hotel bar – Stalin and I – drinking strong sweet coffee from tiny china cups. I asked him where he'd been born. He was, he said, from Poti in Georgia on the shores of the Black Sea.

'Like Beria,' I said.

He frowned. 'I cannot speak about Beria,' he said.

We sat for a moment in silence – awkward, as if the man about whom he could not speak were there with us, watching us, his beady, sadist's eyes studying us, his pale, murderer's hands noting down our every move, every word.

In a while I asked him how it was that he spoke such good English.

He looked up, drawing himself back as if from the distance of a dream or a nightmare. 'English?' he said.

'Did you learn it at school?'

He shook his head. He learned it, he said, from watching premiership football on his son's satellite TV. And *The Waltons*. He liked *The Waltons*. That they were poor but always happy seemed to him a wonder. One day, he said, he'd like to go to America.

'You could be Stalin in Times Square,' I said.

He nodded, as if seriously considering my suggestion. His son, he said, had been to New York. Now his father's manager, he managed in all four Stalins, all of whom could be seen (and photographed for a price) most days on Red Square.

Didn't it ever feel strange, I said, the four of them dressed up as a man so hated.

'Hated?' said Pavel, his bushy eyebrows brought together in a frown. 'I don't understand. Who hates Stalin now?'

I opened my mouth to say, *Doesn't everyone?*, but something stopped me. And then I thought about Beria. He could talk about one mass murderer but not another – why? Instead, I asked him how long he'd been in his line of work. He'd been doing it, he said, since 1989; before that he'd been an athlete.

'What did you do?' I said.

He said he jumped with a pole. He'd even gone to the Moscow Olympics.

'Wow – that's amazing,' I said.

He shrugged. 'But now I live at my son's house,' he said. 'Now I watch Chelsea on TV.'

'Do you watch them because of Abramovich?' I said.

He shook his head. 'That Abramovich, he's a crook. A swindler.' But then he brightened. 'No, I like the nigger Drogba. Always he scores. And dances. I like the way he dances.' He looked at his cheap, clunky watch. 'But now I must go.'

'To work?' I said.

He nodded. We shook hands.

'May I walk with you?'

He shrugged. 'You walk with Stalin,' he said, 'and people will fear you.'

'Really?'

He lifted his head, raised his great bushy eyebrows and smiled.

A few minutes later he was waiting in the lobby when I stepped out of the lift with what little I'd brought with me.

'Shall we go now?' he said.

'Great moustache,' I said.

He raised his thick fingers and smoothed it down, a glint I'd not noticed before in his eye.

Mostly people smiled when they saw him coming, as if it were a joke and they got it. Some, though, did not. Some – almost always the older ones – seemed apprehensive, some crossing the street to avoid us, all looking away, anxious not to catch the man's eye. Even when they did and he smiled at them, this seemed to do no good. The smile, after all, for so many years had been the sly smile of death.

'You see them?'

We'd been walking for forty minutes and were now at the edge of Red Square.

'You mean at the wall?'

He nodded. It was Saturday in Moscow. Saturday in Moscow is wedding day. On the day of their wedding, a Muscovite couple will tour the city in a long limousine decorated with hearts and ribbons, stopping perhaps a dozen times in order to be photographed in front of famous city landmarks. The most important of these is the Flame of the Unknown Soldier just outside the walls of the Kremlin. Here, the couple will ask for the blessing of all those who gave their lives for the motherland in order for such traditions to be maintained.

The couple – he in an ill-fitting, cheap-looking shiny grey suit, she in a vast amount of snow-white netting – were posing for photographs in the shadow of the Kremlin wall.

We walked along in the shadow of the wall. There were some people – some friends – he wanted me to meet. For me, he said, they would be most interesting.

Tsar Nicholas was standing with Lenin by some dark red railings, the two of them posing, smiling broadly, in the company of a couple from Ostend and their two glum-looking children.

In a moment Stalin joined them, and the triptych was complete.

I stood back and watched them – watching too the looks of the people passing by. Though the three great leaders were fake – of *course* they were, and of course everyone knew it – there was, now and then, in the faces of the older people a look, it seemed to me, of something more than amusement or mere simple acknowledgement. Whether it was ghosts they were seeing – reminders, perhaps, of their own past blighted lives, of the voices, perhaps, of children lost to the terror or their own midnight fears – I can't say for sure. All I *can* say is that they would stand, these old people, just so close but no closer, lest, it would seem, some virulent infection thought long ago vanquished had somehow returned and would, given half a chance, once again infect them and cripple them like the beggars in the metro for whom warmth was a fantasy and comfort a thing known only to others.

'Hey!' Stalin beckoned me over. 'My friend here,' he said, 'has the secret to great happiness.'

'He does?' I said.

He turned to Lenin, urging him on. Lenin gripped his lapels, stuck out his chest and declared something loudly, proudly in Russian. Beside him, Tsar Nicholas nodded wisely.

'So?' I said. 'What is it? What *is* the secret to great happiness?'

Stalin glanced at Lenin. Something like a smile passed between them. 'The secret,' he said, 'is to have a bad memory. The secret is that what you cannot remember cannot cause you any pain.'

I looked at Lenin, but Lenin, with his balding head, steel glasses and heavy woollen suit, was stabbing now at his iPhone with his thick stubby fingers. Beside him, within sight of St Basil's, the most holy of Orthodox cathedrals, Tsar Nicholas had removed one white glove and was diligently picking the long royal nose.

It would have meant little to him that he lies with Shostakovich and Mayakovsky, with Khrushchev and Gogol and Raisa Gorbachyova in the city of Moscow's Novodevichy Cemetery; all that would have troubled Isaak Levitan would have been the absence beside him in the cold damp Russian earth of the bones of Anton Pavlovich Chekhov, his greatest and most enduring friend.

Born in the same year – 1860 – of the two, Isaak Levitan was in the end the first to go, just as the century turned and the overture of Russia's great upheaval began. Drifting into consciousness and then again into delirium, he lay on the porch of Chekhov's Crimean estate, returning in his mind to the days of his youth and his wanderings with Anton's brother Nikolai, with whom he'd painted en plein air, their easels erected like temporary churches on the banks of the Neva or the Moscow River. Forty years later, near death and in moments of half-lucidity, he'd ask for Maria[1]

1   Maria Pavlovna Chekhovna was a teacher who lived with delighted devotion in the shadow of her famous brother. Following his death in 1904, she appointed herself her brother's archivist, gathering all papers and lodging them eventually in the newly created Chekhov Museum at Yalta. Awarded the Order of the Red Banner in 1944 by Stalin, she died nine years later.

– whether hers was the hand he'd felt draw across his brow, and whether Anton would mind if he married his sister, so in love was he and so devoted to the family that to join it would be nothing less than sublime.

But there was no time for this, for death was approaching – and, besides, he was mistaken if he'd ever believed in the possibility of marriage: Maria, though affectionate to the painter, could harbour no love greater than that which existed for her brother. *He is my soul*, she would say, and when he too died four years later, she was as distraught as only a disciple can be. She closed the curtains and wrapped herself in her brother's memory. She would search for him sometimes in the rooms' long shadows, sometimes greeting him with a smile. Sometimes too she would meet the ghost of another man during her turns around the house, a tall man with a beard and dark piercing eyes; now and then this man would be standing at an easel, a smock draped over his shoulders and a look of great distance in his eyes. But then he too would fade, and the pale Crimean sun would rise beyond the curtains and another day of darkness begin.

'You want a guide?'

Take the Moscow metro out to Sportivnaya station, skirt around to the south of the convent and there you'll find the cemetery.

I said no, for who needs a guide in a cemetery?

But then, he said, for the price of 200 roubles he'd take me to the grave of Russia's greatest clown – and the deal, in that moment, was done.

Second only in prestige to burial within the Kremlin walls, interment in the earth of Novodevichy Cemetery is a sign – despite death – of arrival. If they bury your bones here, in the lee of the convent, then you somehow managed to rise to a position of some influence in your field without having had that influence misconstrued as a threat. Generals (victorious ones only), writers, painters, politicians and, of course, that solitary clown – all are represented here, and for the price of a ticket (and perhaps, in addition, a guide) all can be mourned at their final resting places.

Yuri Vladimirovich Nikulin was the most famous clown in both Soviet and post-Soviet Russia. Mourned by millions on his death, during life he'd been popular enough with the hierarchy of the Party to be the only performer allowed to publicly poke fun at them. Now, in death, he sits on the edge of his grave, a cigarette in his right hand, as if – fed up with the boredom and silence of death – he'd decided in the moments before you arrived to get up and have a chat and a smoke.

'You see his boots?' said my guide, lighting a cigarette of his own.

I looked down.

'They are not . . .' He held his fists out before him, as if each were tugging on the end of a small rope.

'Tied up,' I said.

He nodded. 'Yes. Tied up. Very funny.'

'He tripped up.'

'Tripped up?'

'Fell over.'

He smiled, clearly remembering great laughter in the past.

I asked him when he'd seen the great clown perform.

He shook his head.

'You didn't see him?'

57

His father, he said, had been a regional organizer for the Party and had not approved of some of the things the clown had said.

'But they say Stalin laughed.'

'But Stalin was not my father. My father was a little man. Stalin was a big man. Stalin could decide. One day funny and everybody laugh. Next day not funny and everybody dead.'

'So your father didn't laugh and he survived.'

'Survived, yes.'

'Is he still alive?'

He nodded. His father, he said, was ninety years old. He had fought at the siege of Leningrad and was a hero of the Soviet Union.

'So he met Stalin? What did he say?'

'Stalin?'

'When he gave your father the medal.'

My guide looked at the great clown's untied laces. 'He asked my father one thing,' he said. He looked up. His face seemed suddenly pale and undernourished, dark rings beneath his eyes, teeth yellow from too much smoking. 'He reached out his hand and put it on my father's shoulder.'

'And?'

'And then he asked him why he'd never laughed at such a funny man as the great Yuri Nikulin.'

Stories about Chekhov's death are legion. It is said, for example, that, fearing himself about to die (he suffered terrible – and terminal – tuberculosis), he called for a bottle of champagne, from which he drained a single glass before succumbing to illness. Also, several days before his death he is said to have told a friend that he believed his work would endure for no more than seven years. This, when pressed, he increased to seven and a half. As he believed he had only six years to live, he is said to have pronounced this arrangement 'quite satisfactory'.

The grave of Anton Chekhov is marked with a heavy, upright stone shaped to a point at the top on which has been added what looks like a small slate roof. The image of Christ on the Cross has been shaped into a panel set into the front, below which is carved the dramatist's name and dates. Appropriately, the monument is many things that the man himself is said to have been – strong, unwavering, a breaker of convention. And – as befits a man whose death was caused by fluid on the lungs – when the rain falls on Moscow, his little slate roof keeps him dry.

Not so Levitan. When it rains on *him* there is nothing to protect him – his monument of grey granite is lashed and battered with the storm's full force, in a way that he would surely have celebrated.

People say Isaak Levitan was a painter of landscapes, but this is only partly true, for he knew that, just as human beings cannot live without water, neither can the land. Hardly ever is it absent in his pictures: hardly ever is the great Russian steppe not surrounded by it or buried beneath its frozen brother, snow. It moves and shimmers, bringing life and hope to those cast adrift in desolate villages; it pulses and flows like the blood of the earth; it rises and falls, an inexorable, unbending spirit.

There are, of course, exceptions – *The Vladimirka Road*, for example. This road that, long before Stalin had made of it such a terrible conduit of endless death – a track that had already had, even before Levitan had set up his easel, a regular traffic in exiled, desperate souls – had seen so much thirst and the slow, aching death that thirst brings that to walk it even now is to know that to find water here you must dig and dig and dig. To survive here you must pause in your chains (though they'll not let you do so) and scratch at the earth like some burrowing creature. But you will not find it (they will not let you – they'll kill you before *that* with the butts of their rifles and leave your corpse for the bears to whom night there belongs) and so you'll move on, burning in summer, freezing in winter, nothing before you but a distant copse of trees, nothing behind you but all that is gone and will never be reclaimed.

We shook hands at the gate and I thanked my guide (whose name I never knew) for his time. He nodded and turned away. I turned back to Levitan – to his monument and the powder of his bones which lay beneath.

They say Isaak Levitan is buried with a mixture of the earth he'd gathered from all over Russia. Wherever he stood, they say, and set up his easel, he would, before quitting for the day, stoop down and take a handful. This he'd carry home to Moscow and add to the pile. Whether this story is true or not, no one, now, seems to be sure. But I'd like to think it is. I'd like to think of him at peace, surrounded by the soil of his beloved adopted land, the earth of the hard road along which he travelled a pillow for his head and a bed for the weary powdered dust of his bones.

Born into a wealthy intellectual Jewish family, Boris Pasternak had always intended to become a composer. Discovering, however, his musical talent to be slim, he settled on writing as a career. Principally a poet, he helped, with the publication of *Doctor Zhivago*, to give voice to the growing dissident movement. Following the novel's international success, he became such an important figure it's often claimed that though Stalin wished to have him shot, he never quite had the nerve to order his arrest. Awarded the Nobel Prize for Literature in 1958, he was forced on pain of exile to refuse it by the Soviet authorities. Two years later, having retreated to his dacha at Peredelkino, Boris Pasternak died.

'Did my daughter tell you he once visited the university?'

Professor Rodianova, father of Aleksandra, the girl I'd met on the train from the airport, was a thin man with a close grey beard. He had an academic's pallor and a tall man's natural stoop.

'Did you speak to him?'

'No,' he said. 'I was just a lowly teacher. But I saw him. I remember thinking how pale he looked with his white hair. Of course, I didn't know – no one knew, I suppose – that he was dying of cancer.'

At his wife's call, Professor Rodianova rose from his old leather chair and indicated the way to the dining room. 'And did you know,' he said, as we moved along the narrow hall towards the sound of voices, 'people used to say that Stalin once had him on a list for deportation to Siberia but then crossed him off.'

I said I'd heard the story but had always doubted it.

The professor smiled. 'They *said* Stalin had found out he was working for the CIA.'

'Do you believe it?'

'No!'

'Then what about his being afraid of a mere writer? Do you believe that?'

'No,' said the professor. 'But he *was* frightened of America – that perhaps the arrest of Pasternak was the only excuse they needed.'

Later, after the meal had been eaten and we were sitting once again in his study, I told the professor a story I'd once heard about the American poet Robert Frost: how, before Kennedy's inauguration at which the poet was to deliver a specially written verse, an FBI agent – not recognizing the old man – had checked his trouser pockets for bombs.

'And what did he say?'

'Frost? Well, they *say* he told the FBI man that if he touched him once more he'd take a swing at him.'

A knock on the door. Aleksandra Rodianova entered the study. She was carrying a thick winter coat. 'Here,' she said. 'Mother says Nikolai won't be needing it any more.'

'My son,' said the professor. 'He's in Ghana. Building a school with his university friends. So take it, please.'

'No, I can't.'

'Nonsense.'

'Really . . .'

'Then borrow it. You can return it on your way home.'

Aleksandra held out the coat. I took it. It was heavy with the weight of the animals that had once and long ago worn it.

'It'll keep you warm where you're going,' said the professor.

I slipped the thing on. I put my hands in the pockets.

'When do you start?' he said.

My fingers found something smooth and cool, flat at one end, pointed at the other.

'On the road?'

I turned it around in my fingers.

'Do you know where it begins?'

'Begins?'

'The Vladimirka.'

A bullet. I was sure of it.

'Well, no,' I said. 'Not exactly.'

I turned it some more.

'Should I show you?'

'Would you?'

'Tomorrow,' he said. 'I'll take you on my way to the university. Tonight you must rest. You can have Nikolai's room.'

And so I did. That night, my first in Russia, I sat for a while half-reading *Hard Times* (the only English-language novel I could find in the room), then writing up my notes at the desk by the window. Far away across the city the lights of the Kremlin were burning. My notes completed, I lay back on the bed and considered Nikolai's bullet. I turned it round and round in my fingers. The shaft was silver-coloured, the rest brass and hinged at the top. This – the pointed bit – I flicked over with my thumb, igniting as I did so a feeble yellow flame.

B urning well even when wet, the silver birch is perhaps
the most useful of all the earth's trees. A pioneer tree,
it will rapidly colonize open ground, especially when that
ground has been cleared of all life by a fire. Paper can be
made from it and a strong and bitter beer. Birch tea is to
some a delicacy. Worshipped during Green Week,[1] it has
for centuries been a spiritual guardian to the people of
Russia and that nation's national tree. In millions, the silver
birch encircles the capital like a vast, uncountable army.
Napoleon called them *those damnable trees*, while, until the
eighteenth century, such woodlands provided shelter and
an unending source of heat for the region's Slavic peasants.
The ring around Moscow was a cradle, enabling civilization
to flourish. Relentless, unwavering, the birch is the Russian
aspiration made real.

'Do you see it?'

We were standing, the professor and I, in Red Square,
our backs to the vast GUM department store (once the

---

1 Also known as Holy Trinity, Green Week is a celebration of the land's
fertility, during which female ghosts are said to swing from the branches
of birch trees, their influence being so malign that all must guard against
their wicked ruination of the soil.

resting place of Stalin's wife but now the home of Armani and Calvin Klein), our faces set towards the Kremlin and Lenin's mausoleum. The square is so vast that people say should a man lie flat on his stomach and consider the horizon beyond the cobbled ground he'd be able to see the very curvature of the earth.

'Right here. This is where your road begins.'

The professor was looking down at the ancient cobbles. 'They say all roads lead to Rome,' he said, 'but they all leave from Moscow. Stalin's favourite epigram, so they *say*.' He turned me by the shoulders, facing me north-east, towards the Voskresenskiye Gate.

The wind picked up as we walked across the cobbles, Lenin's tomb to our left, the red-painted State Historical Museum before us.

For centuries the traditional entrance to Red Square and thus to the heart of the ancient city of Moscow, the Voskresenskiye – Resurrection – Gate and wooden Iveron Chapel (complete with miracle-working icon) beside it were demolished in order to make way for the parades of heavy weapons that became such an iconic image both of Soviet military might and the expensive bravado that finally finished the regime. Rebuilt in 1994, it once again stands guard over the large bronze plaque that marks kilometre zero of the Russian highway system.

'Well? Make a wish!'

I stood on the centre of the plaque and made a wish. That done, I stepped away. We started walking back under the gate. An arm found my shoulders. 'They also say,' said the professor, 'that anything that begins begins here.'

'And do you believe that?' I said.

He stopped. Once, he said, as a young man, no. As a young man he'd believed in neither fate nor luck nor God. To him, everything, as a young man, had been within man's gift to change. Now, though, it was two out of three. 'It was luck,' he said, 'that made Aleksandra's mother take the metro when she did and select the carriage that brought her to me, and the will of God that made our wishes on that plaque for a daughter to come true.'

'And fate? What about that?'

He shook his head. He pulled up the collar of his coat as the wind from the Urals whipped hard across the cobbles of the square. No, he said, not fate. Fate, he said, was just faith without God.

'Is that a bad thing?'

'To know everything – to have everything explained – is a prison. There's nowhere to go. Nothing to explore.'

'So God exists only as long as man's ignorance.'

'No. God exists as long as man believes in the possibility of the impossible.'

'A paradox, then, and consequently unsolvable. You prove the existence of God by proving the ignorance of man.'

'Precisely.'

'But where, then, is faith?'

The professor shrugged. Faith, he said, was like the bows on an old lady's hat – pretty to contemplate but of no use whatsoever.

I shook my head. 'Now you've lost me,' I said.

The professor smiled. 'Now you know what it is to be a Russian,' he said.

The winter day was darkening as we crossed the square towards Lenin's mausoleum. A broad, squat, angular building of dark red brick set in the shadows of the huge Kremlin wall, it's the place on top of which – from Stalin's time on – the leadership stood every May Day to watch and to be seen as the most spectacular and offensive examples of the vast Soviet arsenal trundled by. In a paradox quite spectacularly Russian, those placed closest to the Soviet leader were deemed to be those with the greatest influence; this influence, however, could prove fatal. Close and the power of influence is yours; *too* close and you're a threat and as likely to be separated from your life as you were to be airbrushed out of the ceremonial photographs.

I mentioned that I really should go in and take a look. 'Will you come?' I said.

The professor shook his head. No, he said, he would not be accompanying me. He had a faculty meeting at the university; besides, what more is there to see of something you've seen a hundred times? We shook hands and agreed to meet up on my return. I watched him walk away. Halfway across the square he paused, turned and walked back. 'I almost forgot,' he said. He fished around in his pocket for something.

The gift was a small box about half the size of a cigarette packet. The image on the front was that of a long snowy road bordered by birch trees heading into the distance, there to disappear. So thickly lacquered that it caught the lighted sky and seemed to glow as if with the force of life itself, it contained, on opening, a small folded piece of paper on which a name – Pavlik Mikhailovich – then a number had been written in a neat, sloping hand.

'A student of mine,' said the professor. 'I've told him to expect you.'

I didn't know what to say. I folded the paper.

'Although you may not thank me. It does get very cold where he is.'

'Where is it?' I said.

'Siberia,' said Professor Rodianova, puffing out his cheeks as if the mere sound of the word were enough to make a man's testicles freeze and all thought of exploration evaporate as quickly as snow in a heatwave.

'Thank you anyway,' I said, and for the second time that day I watched him turn and walk away. This time he didn't pause. This time he just kept walking until he sank beneath the earth's shallow curve and was in time gone from view.

'Last week we did St Petersburg. The week before we did Scotland. Hey, are you a Kiwi?'

I shook my head and turned away from the group of dentists from Cincinnati. At the metal detector I raised my arms for the pale young recruit in a uniform and an oversized cap. He patted me down and nodded me through. I walked briskly along the path beside the high Kremlin wall, keen to beat the dentists to the corpse, not wishing to hear again how everybody knew it wasn't really *him* at all but a waxwork facsimile, the original having rotted years ago from the attentions of an overzealous embalmer.

I moved away, continuing the slow shuffle around the low-lit glass-protected coffin.

As any man's body seems diminished in size by the absence of life, so does the body of Vladimir Ilyich Lenin. He lies in a dark suit – having lain here since the day of his death in 1924 – one hand on his chest, the other under cover of the shroud. For a while joined by the corpse of Joseph Stalin until the latter fell out of favour and was removed, his head is yellow-tinged, and if he were alive you'd say he was ill. You'd say how foolish so many were to be so duped by one man. But that, of course, would be to reckon without a messiah's burning light or the hunger of the crowd looking on.

That evening I stood once again on the brass plaque before the chapel that was the centre of Moscow (and so the centre of Russia) and threw a bunch of unwanted coins over my shoulder. Standing there in the centre as the old women whose livelihood it was to gather the coins crept out of the shadows like the thieves that had rifled the evening bodies at Borodino, I closed my eyes and made a wish in the fast-fading light. I opened them and looked around. I thought then about all I'd seen so far and tried to imagine what there was to come.

Years in the darkness; lives run out in a bitter, frozen landscape. How can those of us who haven't suffered such a fate understand what it means? How could we possibly know how it feels? The answer is we cannot, and thank God, for if we *could*, if we *could*, so to speak, *be there*, then we, like *they*, would be gone, as vanished as they from the world in all but the memories of the dwindling number of mourners left behind.

The next morning, heading north-east through the city with the wish I'd made for Max still in my head and the piece of his robe neatly folded in the bag on my back, I'd paused in a square whose name, still, to so many means terror, torture, exile and death.

'Forty roubles.'

I foraged around in my pocket and pulled out a bunch of notes. Just the name of the place – Lubyanka – made me nervous.

Having studied my passport and considered a list of names on a clipboard (officially, tours of the Lubyanka Museum are by appointment only; however, the gift of a few hundred roubles can, it seems, bypass this hard and fast rule), the uniformed man behind the glass partition

71

punched out a small, rough, oblong ticket of the sort I'd last seen thirty years ago at the Twickenham Odeon.

I moved on as directed. I looked back. The man was smiling like a spy – as if he knew my fate and knew it to be bad. I turned back and walked on.

Lubyanka.

If only, I thought, the walls could tell what they'd seen. But, then, who could stand to listen if they did? I stuffed the ticket in my pocket and headed without delay for the door at the end of the narrow high-ceilinged hall.

On 30 October 1990 an organization which calls itself Memorial erected a monument of remembrance to the victims of the Gulag on Lubyanka Square – the 'disappeared' whose voices can no longer be heard. Founded in 1989, Memorial is a civil rights organization that offers financial and legal assistance to survivors of the Gulag. Eloquent in its simplicity – a single, jagged piece of stone hewn from the site of the Solovki prison camp on the White Sea – the commemoration stands before the monumental complex that was the Lubyanka prison. People come from all over what was once the Soviet Union in order just to stand before it in silent contemplation, as mute in the face of the memory of such terror as a man will stand mute before a sea so vast and so powerful that there is nothing in his memory with which to compare it. Some touch the stone as if to do so will bring them closer to a lost brother or cousin or mother or friend; others try to chip off a trophy with the blade of a penknife, for which offence they will be, if apprehended, carted off – this with a terrible, seemingly unrecognized irony – to the building that has long dominated both the memorial and the square.

Lubyanka.

Some names have a resonance that reaches far beyond the borders of a nation.

'Ticket, please.'

I passed the grubby thing over; with a look of sullen gloom, the guard on the door took the ticket, tore it and returned the stub. He pointed to another door. Feeling the pressure of eyes in my back, I walked on.

The door opened on to a small courtyard, across which stood a building made of grey stone that has, since Andropov's ascension to the role of KBG chief, housed the museum.

The son of a railway worker, Yuri Vladimirovich Andropov rose with great speed through the hierarchy of the Communist Party, achieving the leadership of the KGB in 1967. Instrumental in crushing the uprisings both in Hungary and Czechoslovakia, and numerous other dissident organizations, he became Soviet leader in 1982 following the death of Leonid Brezhnev.

My guide Fedot was waiting for me at the door.

'Your name, sir?' he said.

I told him.

Another clipboard, another list.

He nodded. I was, he said, to follow him at all times. He would, he said, answer questions at particular times. He paused then, as if waiting for something – confirmation perhaps that I'd heard the terms of the deal and that I understood my part in it.

Another nod, and this time I'm sure his eyes narrowed – or was it just me? Did everyone in the building look shifty – or was it just the place and its terrible reputation? 'We go,' he said. And so we did.

For over 500 years the prison on the square (its name is one that many Russians still hesitate to use, for fear that to do so will put a hex on their lives) has stood – and indeed still stands – at the centre of what was and still is the most widespread and effective of the world's secret services. More populous at its height and woven more intricately into the fabric of society, particularly during the latter stages of the cold war than any other (with the exception of its bastard child, the East German Ministry for State Security – or Stasi – which, at its height, employed, covertly or overtly, one in six of that nation's population), it has served, under different names, governments of every hue, from that of the tsars to the Communists to the government today of the Russian Federation.

'Can I ask you a question now?' I said.

We were standing in a dull and gloomy room (the last of several), around the walls of which was a series of glass-topped display tables. These contained, as had the similar tables in the previous, similar rooms, artefacts – code-books, pistols, letters typed or handwritten in browning, fast-fading ink – belonging to employees of the service, among whom were several heroes of the Soviet Union.

Fedot nodded.

'Well, I was wondering,' I said, 'why he did it – Andropov, I mean – why he created this place?'

'The museum?' Fedot frowned, as if considering this question for the very first time. 'Well,' he said at last, 'you see, people don't like to be secret any longer. First Secretary Andropov knows this. So he makes the museum. To be not secret.'

'But he was head of the *secret* service.'

'Yes.'

'Which can only exist – only work – if it's *secret*. And yet you say he believed at the same time in being open – in not having any secrets.'

Fedot smiled. 'First Secretary Andropov believed in telling only some secrets.'

'But not all?'

'Of course not.'

'Why not?'

Fedot shrugged. There was, he said, no need. In a society as open now as Russia, all that it was necessary to know was already known.

'But who decides what should be known?'

He dropped the frown. With a gentle hand he steered me on to the exit and beyond. That, he said, no hint in his voice of either humour or irony, was a secret.

They used to hold a disco once a month in a room above the Lubyanka Museum. The sounds of Sister Sledge, of Earth, Wind and Fire and Kool and the Gang had been known to spill out into the dark Moscow night and to drift, no doubt, if the weather allowed it, across the roofs of this mock-baroque building and across the square, there to fade like Cinderella in the first light of dawn. Who was invited to attend these dances was – as with much else – kept strictly secret, as was the real purpose of such events. Some believe they were simply an excuse for a knees-up, while others believe they existed (and had existed for many years, indeed since the days of Burgess and Maclean) simply to make new recruits from the West feel at home. Today – officially at least – there are no such parties (but then officially there never were) and no longer any prisoners held without trial in the Lubyanka's cells. Those who claim to still hear at night the same anguished cries they'd heard in the 'old days' before glasnost and perestroika are dismissed as cranks – as people stuck in the past, those unable or unwilling to move on.

Kurskaya is one of six mainline terminals in Moscow – and, with its stained metal girders, artless graffiti and broken windows, the only one to have nothing whatsoever to recommend it. Of the six it's the newest, and consequently, in a way most splendidly Russian, the only one due (in 2011) for complete demolition.

I'd been sitting on the platform for an hour, waiting for the train that would take me east on a route running parallel for a while with the motorway they call the Volga (itself all that remains of the first stage of Isaak Levitan's – and indeed Joseph Stalin's – Vladimirka Road), when a tall, wiry man, smartly dressed, sixty, maybe seventy, came and sat down beside me. For a while he said nothing; he just sat staring out – at something or at nothing. Then he raised his arm and pointed to the track. 'That way's east,' he said. He turned. 'Are you going east?'

'Vladimir,' I said.

'Ah.'

'You?'

The man, he said, had business the next day in Suzdal. He turned and offered his hand. His name, he said, was Anatole. His business, he said, was shoes – shoes and trains, although the latter, he admitted, were really just an interest. 'I saw Kasparov on the St Petersburg Express once,' he said. He nodded. 'Such a smart man. Such shoes.'

I asked him how he'd learned to speak English so well. It was, he said, all down to his daughter. His daughter had been a teacher of English and German at a school in Odessa on the Black Sea. But then she'd been killed – run down in the street by a black marketeer who'd not even stopped to see if she was alive; he'd just gone on driving like a maniac, hitting an empty school bus on his way.

'I'm sorry,' I said.

He nodded. 'Kasparov,' he said. 'He would have done something.'

'Done something?'

'About such men. He would have emptied the streets of such people. He would have been strong. Not like Putin.'

'I thought Putin *was* strong,' I said. 'I thought he wrestled bears with his bare hands and went white-water rafting.'

The man beside me shook his head. 'Putin?' he said. 'Putin is a bandit. Putin is a little man. Not like Kasparov. Kasparov is a big man. But people don't like big men any more. Stalin was a big man. Strong.' He turned his head away. 'But here is the train.'

I glanced down the line. There was nothing to see or hear.

'Wait,' he said. 'You'll see.'

And then, in a moment, there it was – first the sound, then the sight of the Vladimir train. I looked at my watch; the train was eight minutes late. Anatole saw me looking. In the old days, he said, a man would be sent to the Gulag for such a crime.

'Seriously?' I said.

But Anatole said nothing. He stood up. What with the sudden noise of the train – the hissing and squealing of brakes and the slamming of doors – I can only assume he didn't hear me or perhaps – given how everything in his world had, it seemed, changed and not for the better – didn't care to.

The Russian steppe north-east of Moscow is lightly watered country covered thinly with shrubs and grass. Oases are abundant, as are gullies and deep river valleys. But first you must break out, like a prisoner forcing a lock – break out of the ring of birches and leave the wretched, unmended blight of squalid commerce behind you. Only then will you begin to feel it – gradually at first, of course – and only then will the vastness of the steppe spread before you, endless and rough-hewn, a country, it will soon come to seem, without end.

But first you must escape, as – thanks to drink and drugs and the terminal ennui that is their closest friend – so many in this rich land fail to do.

With Anatole snoring loudly beside me (his head had dropped and sleep overcome him as soon as the train had ground and wrenched itself free of the station and the rhythm of its wheels had taken over), I pressed my nose to the window and looked out at the grim, ruined landscape of broken-down buildings and the rusted husks of old machinery. There was nothing to see but bleakness – what colour there had surely once been in the advertising hoardings and bloated, rusting cars having drained from them long ago, leaving them sickly and bleached like corpses.

I pulled the postcard of Levitan's *The Vladimirka Road* from my pocket. The gallery shop and London and home seemed an age ago now – an age away from that slow, stinking train and the rain clattering against the windows as hard as if it were hail and soaking the land of Levitan and Kuinzhi, Shishkin and Sarasov on such a darkening afternoon as this.

I turned the card over.

The Vladimirka Road. Isaak Levitan. 30 August 1860–4 August 1900. A telephone number scribbled in red ink, a note to remember to buy onions at the shop.

I turned it back and was studying it for what seemed like the millionth time – the old broken track and the distant copse of trees and the milepost standing dark and spindly like a lone forgotten sentry – when Anatole snorted loudly and raised his head, as if he sensed something was about to happen that was not to be missed. He blinked, bleary-eyed, and, just as he did so, the wheels of the train hissed and squealed and the brakes bit hard and the train drew slowly to a stop. I peered out. There was nothing to see now but rain – an afternoon as gloomy as wintertime at dusk.

Anatole wiped the window with his hand, his fingertips squeaking with the moisture.

'What is it?' I said.

'Dal,' he said. He shrugged. 'Or maybe this time just the rain.' The rain, he said, was always bad there. Every day at the same time it rained so hard it stopped the train. He pointed, the tip of his finger stabbing at the glass. A hunched figure was crossing the tracks, moving awkwardly as if he were in some way disabled, then climbing with difficulty up the shallow bank. The figure was bare-headed, the rain bouncing off the top of his head like tiny marbles.

'Who's that?' I said.

'Dal.'

'Dal? You know him?'

'Of course.'

'So what's he doing?'

Anatole nodded, as if something unheard – a question of only moderate importance – had been settled. He turned away and, with a weary sigh like that of a father whose son has repeated yet again the same foolish mistake, he sat down. He wiped his face with the palms of his hands, then laid them to rest on his bony knees. He looked up. Leonid Dal, he explained, always got off at the same place every day. Though he lived several miles away, it was closer than using the station at Orekhovo-Zuyevo and walking back. Cheaper too.

'But what about in the summer?' I said. 'What does he do when it doesn't rain and the train doesn't stop?'

The train shifted, then started creeping slowly forward.

'In the summer he jumps,' said Anatole.

'But isn't that dangerous?'

He shook his head. The Gulag, he said, had already taken one of his legs – so what else had he to lose?

In a while, with the train once again under way, Anatole settled back into his sleeping. With his head once again hanging forward and rocking with the movement of the train, he started breathing slowly and heavily, and soon his breathing turned to snoring as the worldly burden of consciousness slipped away.

I sat back and closed my eyes. I felt tired, suddenly, but sleep wouldn't come. I took out my notebook, turned the pages at random (settling for a moment on a page of poets' quotes), reading until my eyes grew heavy and my limbs numbed by the train's gentle rocking. Again I closed my eyes. This time sleep came, drawing over me like a warm and gentle tide.

Russia, the poet Pushkin told a friend (this according to my *Writers' Guide to Russia*), was born – like any child – of two parents. The first was the land, a father built of colossal strength, poor but abundant; the second – the mother – was the people: generous and all-embracing but weakened by a crippling, debilitating sentimentality. Consequently, their child was born a mix of contradictions – something, the result of such a gene pool, that you can't help but see to this day.

For example.

Before you leave Moscow, take your life in your hands and, with your back to the ageing Olympic stadium, cross the four-lane Olimpiyskiy Prospekt a mile or so north of Red Square, then head through Ekaterininskiy Park along the edge of a once-elegant but now dilapidated artificial lake towards the rear of the Armed Forces Museum of Russia. Then pick your way around the perimeter until you get to the children's playground. Here, looming over the brightly coloured swings and creaking roundabouts and polished slides like a monster's sharpened claws, are the barrels of several abandoned and rusting T-34 tanks, the nose cone of a Mig-27 and the shaft of what had once and not long ago been an intercontinental ballistic nuclear weapon of the type once pointed at Washington and London.

According to Nataliya Markova, a local news reporter (whom I'd met quite by chance in the Armed Forces Museum's tiny – and almost entirely empty – cafe), in the last three years alone, three children – all regular visitors to the playground – had been taken ill with suspected radiation sickness. This sickness, it was believed (though not, of course, officially, for officially such sickness does not exist in Russia as it had not existed in the Soviet Union), came from the weaponry so casually stored at the rear of the museum. According to Nataliya, an inquiry, though promised by the Mayor of Moscow, Yuri Luzhov (a colleague in the United Russia Party of both President Medvedev and Prime Minister Putin), had yet to appear.

I asked Nataliya what she thought was going on – whether she believed there was some sort of cover-up. She shrugged. Had I not seen, she said, a matryoshka doll – the doll inside a doll inside a doll? Yes, I said. Of course. She gave another shrug then, as if to say, *Well, there you are, then.* And the children? I asked. Still sick, she said, but alive. And their futures? She shook her head. They would die young, she said, and be forgotten. She shrugged, a look of great sorrow drawing over her face. Except, she said, in the eyes of God it would be as if they had never lived.

Anatole awoke as the train slowed – this time for the station at Orekhovo-Zuyevo. He gathered his things from the shelf overhead, then, to the sound again of hissing brakes and the banging of doors, we stepped down from the train. He shook my hand and offered me his card. This I took; he wished me luck.

'Will I need it?' I said.

He smiled but said nothing. It was as if such an answer – such a silence – were answer enough.

I found a seat on the platform and sat. In a while the train hissed, a bell clanged. The train groaned and moved on and soon was gone. The station, soon abandoned by those with homes to go to and loved ones to greet, grew quiet. I looked up at the lowering sky and caught the briefest of glimpses of the moon as it raced to hide its face behind the clouds.

A patent granted for the first roller coaster, the death announced of Jumbo the elephant, the arrival in New York of the Statue of Liberty. All this, and, in the small Russian town of Orekhovo-Zuyevo that straddles the Vladimirka Road, the women's weavers' strike of 1885, which led to what historians routinely describe as Russia's first piece of democratic legislation.

And – that month – no moon rising.

Blood moon down.

Despised even by other women for their strident defiance of their sex's traditional position of subservience, they left their looms idle and gathered in the town square, demanding bread sufficient enough to ensure at least survival and working conditions at least equal to those of the lowliest of beasts. Arm in arm they stood, as loyal, they said, as any other to the tsar (to exist without a tsar, they said, was as unthinkable as to contemplate a life without God) – although the tsar, they said, should know of the harshness of their lives. They were mothers, after all, and, as such, guardians of the future.

The men laughed, the older boys spat. It was the moon's forgetful absence, the men said, that had drawn them to such wild, irresponsible actions.

But, arm in arm, the women made their way to the road, set their faces to the south and marched. They marched, singing as they went, unaware as they did so that other women elsewhere – and men too – would be ready to join them, so desperate were they also and so exhausted by the harshness of their lives, and that – as a consequence – the great strike of 1885 was about to begin.

'Is this it?' I said. 'Where they started?'

'Yes,' said Yelena Revnik. 'This place precisely.' Vice-Principal of the Orphanage for Mentally Defective Children three miles west of the town square in the village of Krasnaya Dubrava, she's a tall woman and thin – thin enough to make you think of her bones and how frail is even the strongest of human bodies.

'And did they make it to Moscow? Did they see the tsar?'

'They arrived in Moscow, yes.'

'And the tsar? Would he see them?'

'Some.'

'Not all?'

'Not the Jews. The Jews were arrested and sent away.'

'For being Jews?'

'And for being troublemakers.'

'What about the others?'

'The others? They were given something to drink and to eat and told to go home. *Things would be different*, they were told.'

'And were they?'

'Yes. But not for many years. Not until the Revolution.'

We were standing on the street corner outside the town hall. A light snow was falling. Before us was the road that had once been the main route from Moscow to Vladimir and beyond. I asked Yelena whether, when the tsar had sent the

Jews among the marchers to their exile, it had been along this road that they'd come. She said yes – that many of them had been marched past their own houses, the women weeping and calling out to their children, the men not daring to look up from the road lest the sight of their home removed from their hearts the last of their will to survive.

'And did they,' I said, 'return?'

Yelena nodded. 'One.'

'One?'

'Spartak Davidenko. But everyone said he was a spy – that he'd been sent back to record what people said and what they were thinking.'

'And what happened to him?'

Spartak Davidenko, a furrier, she said, disappeared.

'Was he murdered?' I said.

Yelena Revnik shrugged, as if to say *Who cares now – after so long?*

We stood a while longer.

'Where does it go?' I said.

'Go?'

'The road. Where does it lead?'

'Siberia,' she said. 'Though to most it led to death.' But then she smiled – but a smile so weary that it could have been centuries old. 'So shall we go?' she said.

I nodded. We walked together in silence through the snow to her car.

Everything in the world – even God's mercy, it seems – is relative, approximate, contingent. A woman, starving, leaves her children behind and takes the road south towards salvation. When she returns, the road – the same road, but now heading north – is the way towards imprisonment and death. Breathe the fierce freezing air of the steppe one day and its sharpness will revive every part of you anew; take a breath on another day and your children will be born dislocated from the world, mute as the trees that rise above the vast fields of wheat.

Yelena says that, when she first arrived at the orphanage, it was difficult to think of the children as children: they seemed more like sullen and secretive ghosts.

Everything is relative, approximate, contingent.

The Orphanage for Mentally Defective Children in the small town of Krasnaya Dubrava is a collection of low, squat, ochre-coloured buildings whose best days were a long time ago. Once a stable (until the Revolution the land had been part of a vast, grand estate), there is accommodation now for approximately one hundred children, most of whom are so lost to the world of telephones and email that they might just as well have been the children of the age of steam and plough. Chronically underfunded and due for demolition, it had itself been retreating from the world and would surely have been nothing now but a strange and bitter memory had not a spark been ignited at the foot of a reactor and an explosion so bright so lit up the night that a man, people said, could have seen it without squinting from the surface of the moon.

'We're here?' I said.

She turned the car off the track and switched off the old, rattling engine. 'When I first came here,' she said, 'I was seven years old. I had nothing, and this was my home. I hated it – the cold, the voices at night.'

'You were an orphan?'

She shrugged. 'Are we not all orphans in the end?' She started the engine. 'Are your parents alive?'

No, I said, both were dead.

She turned to me and smiled. 'Then welcome,' she said.

The orphanage was blessed (by God or man's criminal incompetence) with its greatest harvest – and therefore its survival – in the years following the disaster at Chernobyl nearly a thousand miles away. Many children born deaf or mute or blind or uselessly slow-witted were simply abandoned, while others were housed in draughty former barracks; some – the lucky ones – were brought to this place along the poorly made road by mothers and fathers, grandfathers and grandmothers, who themselves were as shocked and silent as the children who lay huddled on the back seats of dirty smoke-spewing cars or on the council buses that would pause a half-mile from the hospital and make the children walk across the broken, rutted ground.

'Do you know,' said Yelena, 'what it means?'

We were standing in the draughty hallway, the sound of children close at hand.

'What what means?'

'Chernobyl.'

I shook my head.

'Black grass. It means black grass. Some of the old people believe – believed long before the explosion – that the land on which they built the reactor was always meant to be the site of the beginning of Armageddon. In old Russian, Chernobyl means "wormwood", the name of the bright star that would one day signify the beginning of the end.'

'But we're still here,' I said.

'Yes,' said Yelena, 'we're still here.'

The sound of voices rose – a crescendo that was met by the ringing of a bell played over an ancient sound system – and suddenly the hallway was filled with children. They were young and older, tall and short – and all very thin and very pale. But there was life in them, and some were even laughing – though not all. Some stood quietly, watching, though, with many, where their focus lay was difficult to tell.

Yelena Revnik clapped her hands; the chatter and noise of the children abated. She addressed them firmly, looking from one face to the next, her words brusque, kind, and to me, of course, impenetrable. The children had the look in their eyes you'd surely find in the eyes of baby penguins if placed by careless fate in the care of an eagle: needful, scared – but above all loving.

In her office, Yelena showed me photographs of the place as it had been. Once grand, the stable had been a temporary home to the mounts and grooms of aristocrats and well-to-do people – both Russian and from overseas. Even the tsar himself, she said, spent a day once at the big house, from where, on his favourite horse, Jascha, he'd gone hunting for fox and wild boar.

She closed the album and put it back in the low drawer.

Later, in the car going back to Orekhovo-Zuyevo, where Yelena had business with the town council to conclude, she told me two stories – one concerning Catherine the Great, the other the great Count Leo Tolstoy.

First, this.

Catherine the Great (1729–1796), easily the most influential of any Russian leader before her reign or since, was both a harsh and a sentimental empress. Although she had no particular love for them as individuals, she is said to have seen the plight of the peasants as an indicator both of the health of the nation and the extent of her own Christian charity. To this end, she would often takes rides into the countryside with her most favoured courtiers, where, on many occasions, she would be delighted to find, in the distance, row upon row of small but neat peasant houses. Thus satisfied, she would in time then return to her palace, delighted at the 'state of all things'. The fact that the 'houses' were fakes (mock-ups built of light wood and painted with some care) neither she nor her courtiers ever mentioned. They looked like houses and that, to Catherine the Great, was all that mattered.

And second.

A wealthy aristocrat, the great writer Leo Tolstoy always craved recognition as a man of the people. With this in mind, he ventured out on several occasions into the hinterland of his great estate, determined that he would live like a peasant and learn the peasant ways. On one occasion he bought some pigs, but he found that the pigs stank and kept him awake at night with their incessant snorting. So, wishing them dead but not having the guts to slaughter them, he decided instead to just let them starve.

'And did they?'

Yelena nodded.

'And Tolstoy? Did he ever try again?'

She shook her head. It was, she said, too hard. And anyway, stuck in a hut with no ink and no paper, how could he finish *War and Peace* – with all those counts and princes and emperors?

I stood on the roadside and watched her drive away – watched her until the sound and the smell of her old car had gone.

The day was cold and getting colder. The trees in the far distance were turning a rich, dark vermilion. I stood and waited for a car to come along. I couldn't stop thinking about Tolstoy and his pigs and how Max would have laughed, while all the time shaking his head in despair at the world.

The Russian Orthodox Church (or Orthodox Christian Church of Russia) believes a man should wear a beard as a sign both of manliness and, more profoundly, of his closeness to God. God, after all, wore a beard – so surely, also, as a mark of respect, should man.

After a journey spent rattling around in the back of a gas bottle delivery-man's truck and a night in a hostel where the bugs were as big as the palm of my hand (or so it seemed in the dark dead of night), I'd woken with the fierce need to be clean. Following a shower in water so cold that it was like (I imagined) being battered with grapeshot, I'd walked the two miles into the centre of town and sought out the local barber.

The barber (himself a man with a beard quite as wild as Charles Darwin's) shook his head – not refusing to shave me but just curious as to why I should want him to.

'My wife doesn't like it,' I said. 'And neither do I.'

'Your wife?'

'She says it makes me look older.'

The barber looked around. He said he saw no wife. 'Is she a witch?' he said.

'A witch?'

Witches, he said, could see everywhere and everything.

'She's at home,' I said.

He shrugged. Witches, he said, would seek out and inhabit a man without a beard. A man without a beard, he said (this with the obvious approval of the man in the other chair who was there, it seemed, just to have his bald head polished), was like a lion tamer who, despite having mislaid both his chair and his whip, still insists – with more courage than good sense – on stepping into a ring full of wild and hungry beasts.

'She works in a garden centre,' I said.

In other words, he said, such a man was a fool.

With a shake of his head, the barber fetched a bowl, a towel and a cut-throat razor. He cocked his head as he stood behind me, frowning, clearly giving me the chance to change my mind.

'It's itchy,' I said.

'Itchy? What is itchy?'

Slowly, like a gunfighter, I raised my hand and scratched my cheek.

He nodded; I nodded. He narrowed his eyes; I narrowed mine.

'OK,' he said.

I could feel my heart thumping.

Solemnly, he set down the bowl and the towel. I opened my guidebook, quite nonchalant and unperturbed. *The Lipna Murders*, I read. I glanced up. The barber nodded; I nodded back. Then, with the glinting of metal in the harsh overhead light, he glanced at the bald man by his side and slowly opened the razor.

At eleven o'clock on the night of 22 February 2003, Sasha Levodkin and his nephew Sergei Gretusov set off from their home in the tiny town of Trud. They were carrying a selection of knives and hammers. They walked for two hours across the hard moonlit land until they came to the Vladimirka Highway. This they crossed, unseen by a soul, then scuttled down the bank on the other side. They were heading for another small town, Lipna, and to the house of Tanya Varasova, a woman who, they said, had cast a spell on them and had made their lives unendurable. Wild, half-human beasts, they said, came to visit them at night, and they'd wake in terror, their eyes on fire.

They had no trouble finding the house. They were led to it, they said, by a spirit – the same spirit that had told them that their intentions were righteous, and that Tanya Varasova, for her part in the ruination of their lives, deserved to die.

So, lifting the latch and easing open the unbolted door, they crept like thieves into the house. But they weren't thieves – and, besides, there was nothing in the house worth stealing. Having been poorly built, the house now was rundown, with paper peeling off the walls and a garden gone many years ago to seed.

Sergei Gretusov knew the layout of the house well. A woodcutter, he had the previous year met and – despite her lazy eye and rather distant nature – taken a liking to Tanya Varasova. They had gone out together, sometimes walking in the woods, sometimes just sitting holding hands on the sofa. In time, such activity had bored Sergei Gretusov – not so Tanya Varasova. She was in love with her new friend, and made it clear that she wished them to marry. Sergei Gretusov, however, did not want this, and when he made his feelings clear she, he claimed, put a hex on him and his best friend, Sasha Levodkin, whose influence she blamed for Gretusov's change of heart.

When they entered the house, the two young men found that not only was Tanya Varasova present and asleep, but her sister and her sister's children were there also. All was peaceful, the children sleeping with that depth and completeness peculiar to the young.

The two men looked at each other. Then, with a nod, they raised their knives and hammers and began their night's work.

When they'd finished, one of the women – Tanya's sister – was dead, and four of the five children were critically wounded. Three of these children would later die of their wounds. As for Tanya Varasova herself, she suffered several severe hammer blows to the head, though she survived. That she never spoke again is seen by some as, of course, evidence of the effect of the attack and the consequent terrible trauma. To others, however (and such people, in a town such as Lipna, are much easier to find), her survival and subsequent silence are evidence of something far less prosaic: proof, they say (and they will shrug their shoulders as if such proof were, of course, entirely unnecessary), that she is, after all, most certainly a witch, and one with powers that cannot, by man alone, be defeated.

'So you look now?'

I opened my eyes and looked at myself in the mirror. A week's worth of beard had gone; my skin was once again smooth – not a nick, not a single trace of blood.

I asked the barber about Tanya Varasova – whether, after four years, she still lived in the town. He nodded. She could be seen, he said, most days, walking alone in the forest; sometimes, in summer, she would lie on the grassy incline by the highway, her face turned towards the sun.

'And the men,' I said, 'were they arrested?'

He glanced at the bald man beside him and shrugged.

'You don't know?'

'They found a book,' he said. 'In the Varasova house.' It was a book, he said, about magic – black magic.

'So do you think she's a witch?'

Another shrug, another glance at the bald man. The bald man said something I didn't catch. I asked him to repeat it.

'He said Baba Yaga,' said the barber. He spun the chair and removed the towel from my shoulders. He stepped back. I didn't move. He sighed. 'What do you want?' he said.

I wanted to know, I told him, about Baba Yaga.

He shook his head.

'Why not?'

The bald man stood. He was taller than I'd guessed he'd be and sturdy, like a man who'd spent his life on the land. He looked me straight in the eye and started jabbering something in Russian. Then he left the shop, closing the door hard behind him.

'What did I do?' I said.

The barber was folding his towels.

'Was it about this Baba Yaga?'

He crossed to the door, opened it and stood by it. It was clearly a demand more than an invitation.

I paused in the doorway. 'What happened?' I said. 'With your friend?'

Nothing. A shrug.

'If you don't tell me what I did wrong,' I said, 'then how can I be sure I won't do it again?'

The barber sighed. He was frowning hard and seemed to me to be deciding something. He glanced out of the window at the bleak, run-down street, then closed the door.

He flicked the lock and pointed to my chair. He solemnly drew down the faded yellow blind.

In Russian folklore, Baba Yaga is a fearsome witch with iron teeth who flies through the forest on a broom of silver birch. Whenever she appears a wild wind begins to blow, trees creak and moan and leaves wheel around as if possessed. Travelling with her faithful servants, the three horsemen she calls My Bright Dawn, My Red Sun and My Dark Midnight, she seeks out the godless and those with evil thoughts and turns those evil thoughts into spells. These she delivers in the dead of night, anointing the unfortunate sleeper with a touch to the centre of the forehead of long, pointed fingers. She is evil – but worse than that: she is evil, but once was wise, and knows all the weaknesses of wisdom. When not delivering spells, she searches the forest for someone humble to share her burdens – a girl, she says, a virgin, one with the mark on her forehead. In such a way, through such a succession, Baba Yaga will never die.

When I left the barber's shop the air was cold – especially so on my clean-shaven face. I remembered what a climber friend had told me once: that a woman would climb Everest only when she could grow herself a beard, thus sparing her face the sharp and bitter cold.

'Can I get a bus here for Vladimir?'

The bus stop was rusting, the seat missing slats. Despite the barber's certainty, it seemed unlikely that a bus would ever stop here again.

The old man beside me said something I didn't understand. I turned away and stood, waiting, blowing on my hands and stamping my feet. After a day of walking and fighting the cold, I felt exhausted and quite dispirited, and all I really wanted to do was go home.

When it came, the bus was noisy and filthy. I took a seat by a grimy window and watched the town's bleak streets, its broken-down houses and overgrown yards slip away. I was glad to leave. As we approached the highway, the evening sun rose, golden like a promise of good things to come. I looked at my map. Vladimir, next stop. I gazed out and back at the last of the town, then into the depths of the forest that was gradually replacing it. The forest was dark and deep. I closed my eyes and thought of Tanya Varasova and wondered if she was wandering through the trees tonight or maybe lying back on the grassy bank and looking up at the stars.

The October Revolution of 1917 was bad news both for bees and for the art and science of Russian bee-keeping. The exodus from the countryside left thousands of log cavities suddenly unattended, and the inhabitants within prey to the unhelpful attention not only of bears (with which the forests were plentifully stocked) but also the ravages of the harsh extremes of climate. Bees – though, of course, ignorant of Marx and his ludicrous dreams of an equitable society – died as a consequence of the fight for democracy just as much as did the men with the red flags on the battlefield or those wide-eyed dreamers manning the barricades.

Imagine, if you will, a queen bee.

I pointed at the hole in the tree and tried to do just that. 'There?' I said. 'In there?'

The man, whose name was Karp (he'd given me a ride on the road to Vladimir, but first, he'd said, there were errands to do), who had been a policeman in St Petersburg, had returned many years ago to the forests north-east of Moscow as security officer at one of the largest state-owned queen bee-producing bee farms in the whole of Russia. Now, all thoughts of security discarded, the bees were his life and their welfare his only concern.

He pushed my hand aside and thrust his own into the trunk of the tree. Huffing and puffing and becoming increasingly red-faced, he pushed more and more of his arm into the hole, as if he were a lover attempting to steal, without the benefit of words either written or spoken, the heart of the woman of his dreams.

With a cry of victory, he at last withdrew his hand. 'There,' he said, and, uncurling his fingers, exhibited with some pride what to me looked like a palmful of old, rotten wood shavings – but which were, in fact (so I have since learned), the remains of an old pre-Revolution hive. He held the bounty up and invited me to smell it. In my memory, now, it carries the faint scent of honey, like the morning following a storm carries still the faint scent of rain.

His work in the sector completed, we walked back to his pickup. As he started it up, I tried to ask him where all the bees were. He frowned. I buzzed, flapped my arms, held up my hands, empty palms uppermost. 'Ah,' he said, nodding. Then, starting the engine and revving it up (so producing a toxic cloud of foul black smoke), we set off back through the forest and up to the highway. We paused on the verge. Hunched over the wheel and leaning forward in order to check out any oncoming traffic, Karp turned the knob on his tape player and soon Karp and I were heading off down the highway, an old cassette tape of Rimsky-Korsakov's *The Tale of Tsar Saltan* blasting out high and loud and Karp singing along, every now and then – at moments of great drama – striking the wheel with his tightly clenched fist and calling out to passing motorists the great composer's name and the fact that, like Karp himself, he was a native of the great city of St Petersburg.

During one of the opera's quieter moments, I tried to share with Karp the only thing I knew about the 'Flight of the

Bumblebee's composer – the fact that, all his life, he'd been an officer in the Imperial Russian Navy, ending up as the inspector of (naval) military bands. To illustrate this, I drew a battleship beneath the bumblebee on a page in my notebook and tapped the thing vigorously and quite uselessly.

'Yes! Yes!' he cried. 'Rimsky-Korsakov!'

I nodded and smiled.

As the day's light started fading and the dusk rolled in like a fog across the fields, we drove on, Karp singing until he at last fell silent and there was nothing to hear but the pickup's growl and clatter and the voices in our heads of our own separate thoughts.

The pickup slowed. The traffic was bad. Karp stuck his head out of the window and shouted something; this was met with other shouts and the blasting of car horns. There were flashing police lights up ahead.

The traffic moved slowly, three lanes squeezing into one as we cruised single-file past the scene of the accident. There were two vehicles, one – an old Russian IZH saloon – upside down on its roof, its driver's door staved in, the other, a small truck – an old farm vehicle, perhaps – nose down in the ditch beside the highway. A body was lying on the verge covered in a blanket; standing over him, as if guarding him, a pale, thin-faced policeman was smoking a cigarette. Behind him, a man was lying unattended on a stretcher in the back of an ambulance.

Karp clucked disapprovingly and shook his head as we passed by. Then, soon, the single lane once again became three, and all that had gone before slipped quietly into the darkness.

Karp dropped me where the road split east and west. He was heading west to a bee farm that was closing down and had drones going cheap. I thanked him and watched him go.

The land beyond the highway was dark blue and black now, the lights of a city I took to be Vladimir spread out on the horizon like a necklace. I stood and waited, my thumb out. Cars passed me by, some blasting their horns, voices spilling out now and then, harsh and visceral. During a lull in traffic (the cars were growing fewer as the minutes and hours passed by), I dropped down and gathered a handful of dirt from the road. It was cool on my palm and between my fingers. I thought of Isaak Levitan and his wanderings along this road. Had he ever been here, I thought. Had he ever perhaps stood where I was standing? I looked around me as a car approached, slowing down, half expecting to see the tall, thin ghost that had so disturbed Maria Chekhovna. But there was no one. Just the night and the road and the flickering yellow headlights of an oncoming car.

Go hitch-hiking in Russia and everyone will tell you you're mad. You will, they say (with the absolute certainty of ignorance), get your throat cut or, at the very least, be held against your will by a band of Kazakh bandits until payment is received of some outrageous ransom.

While, of course, this may be so, for every one of them there is a Karp or a Yegor, the latter at the wheel of an old Kamaz truck that even he detested. To change direction even slightly, he had to grip the wheel with both hands and push as hard as he could on the wheel's central spokes, while every time he touched the accelerator the cab rose and fell alarmingly, as if it were barely secured to the rest of the truck.

But Yegor, so he said, was a man on a mission of love – so what should he care about the state of a truck or its contents of Israeli oranges?

'Yes, absolutely,' I said, trying to smile as the cab rose and fell and – with both hands for the moment off the wheel – he leaned across me and, from a pile of old rubbish on the dash – bits of paper, old coffee cups, a Dynamo Moscow football programme – fished out a picture of a stout, moon-faced woman in a short fur coat and shaggy boots.

'Agata,' he said, beaming broadly.

'Your wife?' I said.

'Wife? No!' His wife, he said, was in Moscow. His wife, he said, was living with his brother. He shook his head, as if the situation – though familiar – still perplexed him.

I asked him if Agata knew he was coming. He nodded. He grinned. Agata, he said, would already be cooking. I looked again at the picture, at the short, stout woman with the boots and the coat and flushed and jowly face.

Agata will already be cooking.

I smiled and looked out of the window. What exactly he meant by this I tried not to imagine.

He dropped me at the M7's Elektrostal/Noginsk exit, a short walk from a service station and a bus that would take me along the road as far as Vladimir. He was heading, he said, north to Noginsk and then on to Sergiyev Posad and thence in his old Kamaz truck to wherever the lovely Agata was waiting.

They say the Vladimirka is the road of death – a place of exile and of suffering, a ribbon of evil that cuts through the heart of the nation. Over centuries, they say, millions have travelled it in chains and in boxcars and, of those millions, only a handful ever returned.

Of course, this is true: there are witnesses too numerous to dispute it, the bones of too many corpses left abandoned by the roadside with nothing more to do than to turn into dust.

But there is life too on the Vladimirka Road. Every spring, tiny blue and yellow flowers push up between the cracks in the slowly warming asphalt, and every July and August families travel north to the cool of the western steppes, while amateur painters, devotees of Levitan, of Shiskin and of Arkhipov, set up their easels and squint into the sun and try to capture summer's harsh and fleeting beauty. But the seasons move on and winter returns through the slow, creeping conduit of autumn, and the road again freezes and the days grow shorter and the sun sets early on the camps of the north – mostly deserted now – and the summer road returns to the road of bitter memory, the crooked finger pointing north and east towards the Arctic, its frozen, broken surface swept by the bitter winter winds.

The road of death, people say.

The road back to life, say others.

Take the case, for example, of Leonti Krabka.

According to the archives of the Vladimir Bee-Keepers' Association, Leonti Krabka, when, having served six years of an eight-year sentence of hard labour in a camp at Omsk in Siberia for the crime of having spoken critically of Joseph Stalin's conduct of the war, he was released in 1954 (the year following the generalissimo's death), was promptly sentenced to a further term – this time in internal exile, for a period not exceeding the remainder of his life. Never, he was told, should he attempt to leave his native land. His native land was now his home and his prison.

Following his release from the Gulag (but while he was still, of course, under arrest, still a criminal, therefore, and therefore not allowed by law to own even the scrappiest piece of land), Leonti Krabka made his way back to Moscow along the Vladimirka Road, his intention being to return to his former work on his parents' bee farm north-east of the city. However, things were not, on his return, as he'd left them so long ago. In his absence, both his father and then his mother had succumbed to the typhoid epidemic of the previous year, and the farm, left unattended, had fallen into complete disrepair. Of the once many thousands of bees, only corpses now remained – mounds of silent husks where once had hummed the glorious and deafening buzz of life.

For ten days Leonti Krabka wept, mourning not only the loss of both his parents, but also, of course, the loss of what he'd hoped would become his livelihood. In time, though – being a man strengthened both in body and in spirit by the brutality of his treatment, his tears dried and his gaze was set forward. Having survived the Gulag, Leonti Krabka would not, he determined, become a man buried by aimless despair. Instead, he set to work burning the corpses of the abandoned bees and repairing the hives, and, drawing on the goodwill of neighbours who offered him goods with which to barter in return for a slice of future profits, hour by hour and day by day he returned the place to a state of good order. When this was done (after many months of back-breaking work), he travelled to Moscow and bought his first bees, including two dozen queen bees, the largest and most fertile of whom he christened Nadhezdha, in memory of the second wife of Joseph Stalin, whose brutal treatment of her led to what many historians believe was not suicide at all, but murder.

Today, the Krabka bee farm is the seventh largest in the whole of Russia, a producer of honey that can be found on the breakfast tables and in children's sandwiches from Rio de Janeiro to Reykjavik and Rome. Though Leonti himself has passed away (an easeful death, people say, as befits a man who had suffered so), the farm itself, on his death, was bequeathed into the hands of his children who, every year on the anniversary of his arrival at the then-broken-down and neglected farm, hold a tasting contest in his honour. For this, people come from all over the district (some even come from overseas), while some, like me, are guided there by simple good fortune.

I tipped back my head and let the smooth golden liquid run down my throat.

'So what do you think?'

It was as thick as syrup and twice as sweet. I couldn't help smiling.

Avram Krabka was studying my face – as if mine was the only opinion that mattered. 'Is it good?' he said.

Yes, I said, it was good. He nodded and, with the solemnity of a priest or a prizefighter's trainer, took my hand in his and raised it.

'Yes?' said a voice from the group of perhaps fifty onlookers.

'Yes!' Avram Krabka replied, his voice echoing out around the arched underground vault. 'Next stop England and Her Majesty the Queen!'

I swear the taste of that honey is still on my tongue as I write these words – as it was, still, on my arrival a few days later in the city of Vladimir – and I cannot help but think now what Max would have made of it, how delighted he would have been that something as sweet as Leonti Krabka's honey should exist in the world – a sweetener born directly from the bitterness and death of the Gulags.

They numbered – those terrible places – close to 500 (some say more, for definitions vary, as the fickle tides of Russian politics ebb and flow) and were scattered like shrapnel scars across the great barren unpeopled land of what constituted the greater part of what was then the Soviet Union. They were large – some indeed by any measure vast, catering with great ingenuity to the misery of thousands – while others were smaller and more intimate, more bespoke; but they were all, from the ice-bound north to the arid southern steppes, prisons unlike any other. Though the tools of their cruel trade were familiar from camps the world over – the unspeakable torture, the starvation, the arbitrary and capricious punishment – they had one thing about them that other such places couldn't claim.

Isolation.

Complete and utter.

Take a man or a woman or a child from his or her family (and take him, with no warning, as, unawares, he sets down his cup or pauses in his ploughing to consider the sky and what the changes in its colour may herald), deny him any contact with those left behind him (or even the chance to look back) and then take him to a place as far away and as foreign as the surface of the moon and all but a few will be broken by the endless nothingness, the spirit of all but a few – what remains of it after such a journey – draining away as if through the soles of their bare feet to be lost for ever in the bitter, stony soil. And even then, should a man break free, what good will that do him if he finds himself a thousand miles from the nearest source of heat, a thousand miles from the chance of conversation – a thousand miles in which a man could go mad with nothing and no one to observe but a Siberian eagle that flies so high and distant that his eyes can observe the very curve of the earth, and the ease of whose flight, in any case, seems to mock a man's faltering footfall?

No good is the answer. For isolation and abandonment have the power, when used well, in tandem and with gusto, to break a man in spirit and heart just as a pistol, when fired with skill, has the power to penetrate the flesh and break a man's bones.

So, 500, then, the number of camps.

But the numbers go on, multiplying with bewildering speed, thus:

One million, six hundred thousand men, women and children perished in the camps – so say Soviet records, less scrupulously kept than their Nazi equivalents. But say another number and that could be true too – for who knows (*nobody*, is the answer) how many died years hence as a result of their treatment, or chose to cauterize memory's bloody wounds with vodka or a rope or the wheels of a fast-moving train?

The scale of destruction, then, was unimaginable – except, it would seem, for the corrupt imagination of one man.

Stalin, of course. Always Stalin.

He was a great man, you hear people say almost every day in Russia. *He kept people safe. You knew,* they say, *where you were.* These people – though he had three biological children (one an alcoholic, one a suicide who killed himself at Sachsenhausen, one – a daughter – who fled to America in 1967) – are no less the consequence of such a grotesque paternity than his own. In their millions they still exist and are only slowly dying – those for whom the darkness is filled with the ghosts of *strada* and Prince Vlad and the bloody, brutal grip of the Mongol invaders. They still jump, these victims, at the mention of Ivan, as if he – the first tsar – were fifty miles away but every day growing closer, his bloody sabre in his hand, and in their dreams they still see him standing bare-headed on the frozen Moscow River, or his hands running red with the blood of his own murdered son, and when they close their eyes at night there he stands, Boris Godunov, murderer-in-chief, the man for whom slavery was the peasants' natural state – and on and on through the Romanovs and the nation's dragging westwards until the peasant-slaves had nothing more to lose than their poverty and their chains, and so they rose, a rabble-horde, guided both by their thirst for bloody revenge and the words of Vladimir Ilyich Lenin, the greatest Red charlatan of all.

Even now, though discredited and even the subject of jokes,[1] this clever little man – Stalin's great mentor who became his greatest threat but who had the good taste to

1 In 1967 the government minted a new silver coin showing Lenin, arm aloft. That he was pointing to eleven o'clock soon became a much (though quietly) repeated joke – eleven o'clock being the time the vodka shops opened.

die and so leave the field early and for others – still stands, striding out on a plinth across a thousand town squares, untouchable still, his shadow still casting a lethal gloom across the cobbles. That he didn't live to see the dread results of what he'd started, of course, made the possibility of recantation void, and the fact that he died when the child was a hope-filled squalling infant, long before it grew to full and monstrous adolescence, perhaps explains his cold and stony presence still in so many hearts and homes. *He would have changed things*, you hear people say. *He would have known what to do.*

But the dead are dead – merely passengers now, whispering and plotting in the back of the car.

All but one, that is. Only one man, it seems, in Russia has really beaten death.

Stalin, of course.

Always Stalin.

Dead or alive, he's still the backpack full of stones, still the spy in the corner, still watching and listening as a man and his wife lean over the carrycot and whisper in the ear of their easeful sleeping child what they know to be true but fear to say out loud in the queue for a Filet-O-Fish or a Big Mac and fries.

'His body is dead,' a man would tell me sotto voce as, some days later, I waited in line to buy a cheap winter scarf, 'but his spirit lives on in the camps.'

'Really?' I said.

He nodded; others around him nodded too.

'But the camps are closed,' I said. 'Aren't they?'

I turned to look at those who'd raised their voices in agreement, but not one would meet my eye.

The camps are closed.

I moved away; paused, turned back. Dark eyes in sallow faces were watching me. They followed me until I had gone from their sight, and it struck me in that moment how far I had to go – in miles, in language, in my journey across the hinterland and into the heart of Stalin's blighted land.

Once the glorious, gilded capital of the vast medieval Russian Empire (and for so long the location of the nation's largest and most sensitive air force base), the city of Vladimir is a city now of factories and cathedrals. Once, long ago, at the centre of a golden age of spirituality and learning, its sacking and burning by the great Mongol hordes left it for ever thereafter in the shadow of cities further east.

Today, sitting on the banks of the Klyazma River, Vladimir gleams in the sun on the days when the sun can be seen through the factories' thick acrid smoke. The smoke, people say, is the challenge of the godless, its slow, creeping progress a blight on the purity of man's eternal soul. They *also* say that the man who sells the paint to the man who paints the walls of the Cathedral of the Assumption (a building, even on the worse, most foul-smelling days, quite extraordinarily, ethereally white) has the nation's most secure employment.

It was to this – the once Mother Church to the whole of Russia – that I was pointed on the morning of my arrival, a morning of such spiky-sharp cold that I had to wrap Aleksandra's brother's thick coat tight around me and fold in my new CSKA Moscow scarf in order that I not (or so it seemed) freeze.

Once inside the cathedral, my guide, Anna, suggested I consider Rublev's frescoes – particularly his icon of the Trinity. 'Here,' she said, 'with this most beautiful of paintings, the artist has gathered the Father, the Son and the Holy Spirit and placed them with our mother like a child is placed in its mother's womb. You understand?'

I looked at the picture – at its blues and golds and the curious figures with their strange, twisted necks – then back at her. I understood, I said – all but the mother thing. Wasn't Mary the mother of Jesus – and where was *she*?

Anna smiled and raised her hands, indicating with an elegant sweep the entire length, breadth and height of the cathedral. 'This is our mother,' she said. 'The Mother of all Churches. Here we are safe now from the Khan and his murderers. Here we are protected.'

In the light of such certainty I looked again at the picture and wished again that faith was something you could find just by seeking it. If only, I thought, the need for peace was enough; if only the knowledge of God's absence in your life was enough to negate that absence. But it isn't and never will be. It seems that if you don't have faith, no amount of searching for it will help you find it; like cancer or a talent for the piano, it has to find you.

We stepped outside. The sky was white now, the ground hard as stone. 'Will it snow, do you think?' I said.

Anna looked up. She had a scar on the side of her neck. 'In perhaps one hour,' she said.

'An hour?'

It was the kind of scar I'd once seen on the neck of a man who'd tried – and failed – to hang himself.

'Perhaps.'

I wanted to ask her about it, but, of course, could not. Instead, we stood in silence for a moment, looking out across the city towards the smoke-spewing factories on the banks of the icy river and the winding ribbon of the Vladimirka Highway heading ever east.

After a while I mentioned the prison – how I'd read that it was here in Vladimir that the American U2 pilot Gary Powers had been held. I wondered if people in Russia still knew about him.

'Of course,' she said.

'So they know that it's because of him that the band is called what it is?'

'Of course.'

Wasn't it unusual, I said, for young people to care about history?

Maybe, she said, as we made our way down the steps, but not in Russia. In Russia young people were interested in these things. She paused. 'Do you know that Bono came here?' she said.

'To Vladimir?'

'To Vladimir, yes. He visited the cathedral and sat in the cell of Gary Powers.'

I asked if she'd seen him.

She nodded. He'd spoken, she said, about freedom. He'd stood on the steps in his strange coloured glasses and spoken about Nelson Mandela – how a man in a cell should always have a canary.

I asked her what she thought he'd meant.

'Hope,' she said. 'A person always needs hope.'

She paused at the bottom of the cathedral steps and turned – an action I imagined she'd performed a thousand times. 'Will you look now?' she said.

The Cathedral of the Assumption was as white as stripped bone, its golden minarets gleaming like newly minted coins.

I thought of Max and wished he could see it, and wondered exactly where and when his own kind of faith had found him.

'Do you like it?' said Anna.

It was something I'd never asked him and now never would. 'It's beautiful,' I said.

'People say it was made of God's frozen tears.'

'And the fire I read about, the one set by vandals – it didn't melt them?'

She shook her head.

God's tears, she said, are eternal – as eternal as His love for His children. She pulled off her right glove and held out her hand. We shook. Her hand was warm and tiny in mine. The tour over, we said goodbye. She turned and walked away. As she reached the end of the street, she paused and looked back. She held up her hands, palms upwards, and smiled, just as – as if cued by the distant bell marking the hour – the first idle snowflakes of winter started falling.

He was born on 17 August 1929 in Jenkins, Kentucky, to a family of mixed European, African and Native American ancestry – a Melungeon heritage he shared with Elvis Aaron Presley. While the King, however, abandoned his studies and hitched a ride with his guitar to the bright lights of Memphis, Francis Gary Powers did not. Instead, he studied hard and, following graduation, entered the United States Air Force with a pilot's commission.

'You cannot sit. You are a prisoner.'

I stood up.

The cell into which I'd been gently nudged by the end of a fake warder's baton measured about eight foot by six. There was a metal-framed bed with a thin mattress and coarse blanket, and a high barred window.

The door slammed shut. The peephole flipped up.

I sat.

Ten minutes, they'd said. Every visitor is allowed ten minutes. I looked at my watch and started counting. What I'd thought would be amusing was suddenly less so, for a cell, they say, will steal the contents of a man's soul as surely and swiftly as a pickpocket picks the pocket of a fool. I stood up; I sat down. The walls and the stone bench were clammy to the touch and porous, the low ceiling having buckled in the centre as if beneath the weight of the judgement of God or – perhaps worse – of Generalissimo Joseph Stalin.

I pulled out my guidebook for distraction. I turned the pages to the mark and read: *Following his shooting down by a Soviet surface-to-air missile battery on 1 May 1960, and his subsequent arrest and imprisonment as a spy, Gary Powers spent twenty-one months of his sentence at Vladimirsky Central Prison – the same prison (and, indeed, the same cell) once occupied by Stalin's own son, Yakev.*

And now, temporarily, me.

I squinted at my watch. Three minutes, four.

Later, long after his release, he told a priest in Oklahoma City how he'd contemplated suicide.

I looked up at the ceiling again, then away. I stood, reached up and gripped the bars of the window. As with all prison windows, it had been built too high for an inmate to be able to see anything but sky: a familiar torture, of course – that of allowing a man to watch birds flying free, so reminding him every day of his own incarceration – beloved of jailers from ancient times right up to the blight that is Guantánamo Bay.

I eased myself down.

Seven minutes.

Today there were no birds – just the city's grey immobile sky and the slow fall of snow with its whispered threat of winter.

Exchanged after twenty-one months of his sentence for a KGB colonel caught spying in Washington, Gary Powers returned to America not a hero but a man who, in the eyes of the Pentagon – though not a traitor – had proved himself less than the military ideal. Not only had he failed, on his discovery, to activate the U2's self-destruct mechanism (which many years later was found to have been faulty and now resides in a glass case at the Armed Forces Museum several hundred miles away in Moscow), but he had also allowed himself to be captured. This, in the eyes of the old soldiers at the Pentagon, was unforgivable. What, for heaven's sake – those senior men on the board of inquiry wanted to know – was the purpose of a suicide pill if not to be used in circumstances such as these? Having chosen to live (and later to be forced to 'confess all' in a Soviet court), he had chosen, they determined, the path of disgrace.

I rapped on the door. 'Can I go now?' I said.

Nothing. I sat down and waited some more.

Having left the USAF and, following a period spent as a test pilot for Lockheed, Gary Powers took a job as a helicopter-borne traffic reporter for a California radio station, and died one day, at the age of forty-seven, when his helicopter quite mysteriously (for such an experienced pilot) ran out of fuel and crashed.

At last a key rattled in the door. The door opened inwards. The guard stepped back. I took my chance and slipped out. I watched the guard close the door and lock it.

'Is there anybody still here who knew him?' I said.

Georgiy Listev shrugged. He said maybe some of the old ones might have seen him.

'Could you ask for me?' I said.

'I will ask,' he said. He turned and set off down the hall, his boots squeaking on the high-polished floor, the keys – as big as pantomime keys – on his key ring rattling and jangling on his belt.

A philosophy and social policies student at Vladimir State University for the Humanities, Georgiy Listev spends his nights working in a factory assembling Nike running shoes and his holidays working as a 'guard' at the Education and History Wing of the prison. Four days a week, he leads tours of the public part of the building (the rest of it – the majority – is still a working, high-security prison, containing, among many others, those accused of the Beslan massacre), each tour culminating in a visit to the cell once inhabited by Gary Powers. Here, following a mock denunciation and the passing of a sentence of life imprisonment with hard labour, the 'prisoner' is 'persuaded' by the end of a baton to enter the cell, where he'll spend the first ten minutes of his sentence behind lock and key.

Later, I was standing in the former exercise yard when Georgiy found me. None of the old men, he said, had actually met Gary Powers – though all, of course, knew who he was.

And do they know, I asked him, that the CIA – the people who sent him to fly over Russia in the first place – were convinced when he came home that he'd become a double agent? Or that some people in America think the government had him killed for that very reason?

'Killed?' Georgiy Listev seemed genuinely surprised. It was the sort of thing, he said, that would have happened back then in Russia – not in America. To most Russians, he said, America was a place of safety – somewhere where you could say anything and nothing bad would happen to you.

I asked him if he thought that was still the case.

He shrugged. He had a cousin, he said, who'd visited Baltimore with the university. On his second day in America his cousin had been attacked by a gang of black men who'd taken his watch and his laptop and stamped on his head so hard that they'd cracked his skull. He'd had to spend a month in hospital before they said he could come home.

So, I said, wasn't that an example of a bad thing happening?

He shrugged.

'And yet you'd still go?'

He nodded. He'd go tomorrow if he could.

'So why don't you?'

'I have a family,' he said. 'A mother. A father.'

'So?'

He frowned, clearly astonished that I could suggest he should be so selfish.

'Wouldn't they want you to go – if they knew it was what *you* wanted?'

He shook his head. He couldn't leave, he said. His parents would starve.

'Starve?' The word sounded arcane, absurd.

He nodded. His mother was old and couldn't work. His father had been an engineer but had damaged his arm in an accident and couldn't work either, and what with the state benefit going down every year, without him they'd soon, he said, have barely enough money for bread. Without him, he said, and his days at the prison and the nights he spent working in the factory, his parents would starve and he, their son, would never be forgiven – neither in this world nor the next.

The history of Dynamo Moscow Football Club seems to the casual observer so utterly unlikely that one can only conclude that it must, of course, be true. It is true, for example, that, following the Revolution of October 1917, the club, which had been up to then no more remarkable than, say, Crystal Palace or Millwall, became, following its adoption by the Cheka (the Russian secret service, fore-runner of the KGB), the most powerful and feared team in the land. Tackles that opponents would have previously thrown themselves into without fear of the damage they might do were suddenly avoided, and referees' decisions – once vehemently disputed – were accepted with a meek-ness born of fear. Everyone knew that the boys from the Interior Ministry were not to be messed with – unless you fancied a transfer to a faraway league where the only foot-ball played was in the snows of Siberia in an exercise yard thick with ice that even the heat of summer would never entirely melt. Frowning and squinting at the screen behind the desk in the hotel reception, Dimitrii tapped some more on his computer keyboard. Behind me, the lobby was fill-ing up with members of a Japanese tour group – all thick coats and cameras and itineraries so thorough that having to stand behind me and just *wait* must have seemed almost too much to bear.

'Is it football you would like?'

I'd said it didn't matter – that I'd just like to see a game of something.

Dimitrii shook his head. He could find only basketball.

'Fine,' I said. 'When is it?'

Another tap-tap. His face fell. 'Yesterday,' he said. He looked up. So anxious to help, his failure to do so seemed to sit on his shoulders as a heavy, painful burden.

'It doesn't matter,' I said. I smiled.

And then it struck him. 'You like football?'

I said yes, of course.

Tap-tap-tap. He looked up. The smile was back, the burden of failure suddenly lifted from his shoulders. He spun the computer around. 'You see?' he said, jabbing at the screen. Dynamo v. Spartak, it said, then something more.

'What's that?' I said.

Another frown. 'It means, I think – how to say? – little ones.'

'Little ones?' I said. And then I got it. 'You mean "youth teams"?'

He nodded.

'And it's today?' I said. 'In Vladimir?'

'Close,' said Dimitrii.

Behind me, the Japanese invaders were growing anxious, their plans slipping ever further into chaos. Dimitrii glanced over my shoulder, then back at me. He leaned forward. I leaned forward to meet him. 'Don't forget,' he whispered. He paused, again flicking his eyes over my shoulder.

'Forget what?' Though I expected some strange revelation, all he wanted to do was to offer some advice about singing.

'Singing?' I said.

'Always sing when they sing,' he said.

'Who's they?' I said. 'And sing what?'

Dimitrii cupped his hand to his mouth. 'The Garbage Boys,' he whispered. He moved back. He nodded.

'Absolutely,' I said, and I promised there and then that on no account would I for one fail to join in when the Garbage Boys of Moscow started singing.

The All Russian Commission for Combating Counter-Revolution, Profiteering and Corruption (Cheka for short) was the bastard child of Vladimir Ilyich Lenin – the only means by which his great popular people's revolution could control and terrify the people and so be sustained. Its work involved murdering political opponents, putting down workers' strikes and peasant rebellions, and overcoming the frequent mutinies suffered by the newly democratized and now hopelessly inefficient armed forces. Forerunner of the KGB (and of the current FSB), the Cheka's brief was simple – to crush any form of dissent: to imprison, torture, rape and murder anyone and everyone who might possibly be considered a threat to the great and glorious experiment that was Communism. No one was to be spared. The old, the young, men, women, children, the weak-minded, the strong-minded – all were available for sacrifice at the hands of Comrade Lenin and his thugs.

In short, that is, the people would pay for their freedom with their blood and with the innocent lives of their children.

Three hours later I stepped off the bus and into the bleak hinterland of the city of Vladimir's Torpedo Stadium. The skies were grey, as if reflecting the cracking concrete of the car park, which was scattered with mostly old cars, the

stadium itself hopelessly rain-stained and plainly shoddily constructed. Owned by the Vladimir Tractor Company
('Where the Enterprise World Continues to Progress in
Enthusiastic Tractors'), it looked as though it would, at any
minute, achieve the distinction not managed by its predecessor – that of falling down on its own with the aid of
neither dynamite nor wrecking ball. Indeed, like so much
in Russia, it appeared to have been built out of spare parts,
not a single one of which was fit for purpose. Somehow,
however, the thing was still standing.

I had to circle the place twice before finding the ticket
office. It was in the end a plain, unmarked, grubby window
in the shadow of the main stand.

The woman behind the counter was so fast asleep she
looked dead.

I tapped on the glass.

'Da?'

I turned. A man with a box of pale, sour-looking oranges
was staring at me harshly as if the woman behind the glass
really *was* dead and I, clearly, was responsible. I pointed to
her and then to the stand. I tried to remember the Russian
for ticket but, of course, could not.

The man put down his box. He nodded, indicating I
should follow him.

We walked along behind the main stand. The place
smelled of damp and urine and rotting concrete. From somewhere there were voices, now and then the shrill sound of
a whistle.

'Dynamo?' I said.

The orange man shrugged. He turned a corner, towards
the sound of the voices. I followed him up a shallow incline
that split the main stand in two.

He paused at the top. He was out of breath. He pointed towards the pitch and the two dozen young men – every one of them skinny and as pale as if they never in the normal run of things saw the sun. They were chasing a ball across a pitch close to frozen, their breath coming thick and heavy like the smoke from a power station. They were surely no more than sixteen or seventeen years old, half of them dressed in the blue shirts and white shorts of Dynamo Moscow, the other half in red and white.

'Dynamo,' said the orange man. He folded his arms and rocked them to and fro as if he were carrying a baby.

I nodded. 'Youth team?' I said.

He shrugged.

'And the others?'

The others, he said, were Spartak. He grinned and slit his throat.

Despite the freezing weather and the lowliness of the game, the crowd was somewhere between two and three hundred. Though they were mostly dressed in blue and white scarves and hats, there were a few in red and white. These were huddled together in the opposite stand, the glumness of their faces illustrating not only the biting cold but also the fact that their team, Spartak Moscow (whose nickname 'the Meat' reflected their Soviet-era owners, the People's Union of Collective Production Farms), were already, after only half an hour, calamitously five goals down.

I made my way along what had once been a running track and climbed the steps towards where the majority of the Dynamo fans were sitting. I smiled as I drew nearer, receiving nothing in return but a blankness, as if – far from being foreign or in any way interesting or worthy of even the most cursory attention – I scarcely existed at all. I selected a seat, a dozen or so away from my nearest neighbour – a fat man in a blue Dynamo shirt who either didn't feel the cold or had been sitting there so long that he'd died and just not been removed. I turned to watch the match, half an eye on the supporters beside me. I couldn't help wondering when the singing that Dimitrii had warned me about would start.

The city of Moscow has a dozen or more professional football clubs, although only four of them – of course, as elsewhere in Europe, the most generously funded – have ever made even a modest impact beyond the borders of the Russian Federation. While Dynamo has the backing of the Ministry of the Interior (something that they consistently deny – which, of course, being spies, they would) and Spartak the butchers and meat-packers, CSKA Moscow (Central Sports Club of the Army) can thank the Ministry of Defence for its creation, and Lokomotiv Moscow – unsurprisingly – the Socialist Union of Railway Workers.

'Hey.'

I turned to find the 'dead' man not only alive but holding out a half-bottle. 'You English,' he said. 'Drink.'

He shook the bottle.

I reached across and took it. The bottle was unlabelled, the liquid within blue-tinged like petrol. I smiled at the man; he urged me on. The English, he said, drank vodka like Russians.

I raised the bottle.

This he'd seen, he said, on TV. Particularly, he said, the fans of Manchester United and Arsenal. They were animals, he said. He smiled, the description clearly intended as a compliment – just as, on the pitch, a skinny boy in blue hit

Dynamo's sixth goal and the crowd (including the dead man) rose as one.

Unseen, I lowered the bottle. Two things were immediately clear. One, it wasn't vodka, and, two, it had the blue tinge of petrol because it *was* petrol.

'You like?' My neighbour was grinning at me, his face flushed both from his consumption of heavily leaded four-star and his team's wholesale slaughter of the butcher-boys from Moscow.

What war couldn't do, or famine – or even the monumentally vicious pogroms of a series of bloody tyrants – alcohol and its bastard fellow travellers is achieving, it seems, with ease.

Russia – or, perhaps more accurately, the Russian people – are, it seems, thanks to drink, disappearing.

With levels of (booze-fuelled) male impotence and female infertility rising and a national birth rate, as a consequence, steadily falling, the demographic future of Russia looks bleak indeed. Alcohol now, not religion or its replacement, socialism, is the opium of the people. In Russia today, the majority of the people who drink (and that *is* the overwhelming majority) drink not to complement their food or to enhance a communal, socializing experience but to anaesthetize themselves against the cold, the disastrously high levels of unemployment and the hopeless grind of poverty – and against the sheer intimidating distances that can separate one man or one woman from the next.

And nothing, it seems, can be done to halt the steady march of drink's demon army. Mikhail Gorbachev tried to ban it, but hadn't the power to defeat those for whom the profits to be made were too high, while his successor, Boris

Yeltsin, with his stumbling and snoozing and erratic behaviour, was no help at all in the fight. Even Vladimir Putin, the former KGB director and arch teetotaller, is known to enjoy the occasional glass of whisky.

Half-time and the man with the sour-looking oranges made his way across the icy pitch to the centre-circle. Gathered around him and noticeably shivering, the twenty-two players and three officials took what succour they could from the near-frozen fruit. As they stood around, stamping their feet, trying (and clearly failing) to get warm, the Dynamo supporters to my left started singing, their rough voices sweetened with alcohol and gasoline:

> We are the boys from the Ministry,
> The Ministry, the Ministry,
> We are the boys from the Ministry,
> Fuck with us and we'll skin you alive.

Neither the Dynamo players nor their Spartak rivals seemed to notice the singing; perhaps the words were too familiar, or maybe they were just too cold to care. Either way, with the referee's whistle blowing for the start of the second half, the voices beside me grew silent. I glanced over. From my place a little way off, I could see that at least half of them were sleeping, most probably – almost certainly – drunk.

The Russian Academy of Services Hotel about a mile or so from the centre of the city had once been the de facto home of the Vladimir Communist Party. Across the road from the Party's offices, it was to the hotel (a place open only to Party officials on official Party business) that delegates would retire at the end of the day and where the real horse-trading would begin. Accompanied by jugs of vodka, alliances would be made and broken and the fates of men and women and even children decided.

I ordered a glass of wine and sat in a chair by the window. In times past, from where I was sitting, the Vladimirka Road had apparently been clearly visible – a roughly paved road heading north and a little east. Party officials would sit where I was sitting and watch with satisfaction as their outmanoeuvred rivals (along, often, with those rivals' wives and children) were hustled and harried away towards an uncertain fate, the only certain thing about which was the bitter cold to come and a life lived in fear of the Gulag's random justice.

The wine when it came was from a Rostov winery; the grapes came from vines planted over a century ago by a pair of brothers from Bergerac in the Périgord region in south-western France. A deep red wine, full of fruit, drinking it in such a place seemed extravagant – decadent almost – a reminder of my other life at home.

I finished my glass and ordered another. I looked out at the street. Dusk was falling, the evening traffic building. At the crossroads, a woman was struggling through the snow with three small children, all four of them bundled up like yeti against the cold. The street lights clicked on, yellow against the white of the snow. The second glass of wine finished, I ordered a third, then a fourth. There may have been a fifth and even a sixth. This and so much else about that night I can now no longer remember.

All I *do* remember is opening my eyes in the early hours of morning and, adrift for a moment in first waking's strange confusion, wondering what I'd done to deserve such a wonderful, fortunate life – and how long it would be before the boys from the Ministry would appear in their dark-windowed limousines and take it all away.

'Only from up here,' Chekhov wrote in his story 'Fortune', 'is it possible to see that there is another life in the world beyond the silent steppe, a life not concerned with buried treasure and the thoughts of sheep.' From high up in the highest dome (there are five in all, all golden) of Vladimir's Cathedral of the Assumption you can certainly see what the playwright meant; standing so high up above the sprawling city you can see as far as it's possible to see without running out of world. From so high up, it really is possible to believe in that life beyond the steppe – that life beyond the everyday – that can turn the most ordinary of men into the most reckless and fearless of explorers.

Men like Mikhail Babushkin, famous thrower of paper aeroplanes (as a child, from this very dome) and – more famously – polar aviator and twice Hero of the Soviet Union.

When Babushkinskaia station, part of the Moscow metro's northern Kaluzhsko–Rizhskaya line, opened to much fuss and fanfare in the spring of 1978, a great deal was made, of course, of the life and untimely death of the man after whom it was named. He was – this Mikhail Babushkin – speaker after speaker reminded those invited to the ceremony, though a hero, particularly and especially a *Soviet* hero, a man the manner of whose great courage and dauntlessness in the face of terrible danger made his achievements uniquely *Soviet* achievements. 'Never forget,' the (Soviet) Minister for Transport declaimed, 'that not only were Soviet pilots the first to fly, but also the best and most respected around the world in the art and science of flying.' That the first of these claims was certainly untrue (let us not forget the Wright Brothers and those twelve little seconds on the beach at Kitty Hawk) and the second contentious at best was, of course, immaterial. The Minister knew (as all did and *had* to in the Alice in Wonderland world of Soviet politics) that all that would matter in the end was the claim and not the truth – as long as that claim was sustained. Repetition, he knew, can make a man come to believe every time what he knows to be untrue – to have faith in something for which not only is there no proof, but evidence, indeed, to the contrary.

Standing at the top of the very dome where legend has it Babushkin himself stood, it's hard for any man who was once a flight-obsessed boy not to try to do as he did.

So.

Alone, and with the wind whipping hard around the golden onion-shaped dome, I folded my own paper plane as best I could with near-frozen hands, held it up, aimed it, paused a moment and then let it go. Out it went, serene and purposeful, heading for the distant horizon, until – suddenly caught in the vortex of the bitter swirling winds sweeping down from the Arctic – it spun out of control and crashed somewhere out of my sight, unwitnessed and unmourned.

I began the long walk down – always the price of a momentary thrill.

'You're searching for something?'

I was looking, I explained, for my plane.

Dressed in the shadowless black of a priest, the man would either, I was certain, reprimand me for indulging in such a childish activity or help me look.

'I'm sorry,' I said. 'You must get people doing this all the time.'

He nodded. His frown deepened. But then he smiled – for he too as a child and as a man had been a soul in thrall to the mysteries of flight. He would, he said, help me look.

So, as if in accordance with some prearranged plan, the man I would later discover was Father Bohdan from Bucha, fifty miles north-west of Kiev, and not Russian at all but Ukrainian took the left-hand half of the frozen, snow-covered neatly manicured lawn that stretches out westwards from the cathedral, and I the right. Of course, the chances of finding my little white aeroplane in such a vast and snow-covered landscape were practically nil, and in the end, though such odds had not deterred him, we had to admit defeat and abandon the search.

Father Bohdan shrugged. He was smiling still. He held out his empty palms.

'Thank you anyway,' I said.

'You know Babushkin?' he said.

I said yes, though only what I'd read in the cathedral's own slim guidebook.

'You like the English?'

I didn't know what he meant and it must have showed, for he told me then that the translation of the guidebook's Russian original into English had been his responsibility. He'd spent a year at a language school in Oxford, during which, as well as studying English, he'd become engaged – though they'd never married – to a girl from Milton Keynes.

I mentioned (as everyone does) the town's famous stone cows. He nodded, though his thoughts were clearly elsewhere. I asked him then how come he'd known enough English in the first place to warrant its improvement. Again he smiled, his solemn thoughts, whatever they'd been, drifting off. 'How did I learn?' he said. 'Would you really like to know?'

'Of course,' I said.

'Come, then,' he said, and he turned and strode out across the untrodden snow towards the car park that in summer could accommodate perhaps a thousand cars but which, on that harsh winter's morning, was temporary home to just one.

The car was an old Mercedes saloon of a drab olive green and rusty around the edges. Though any shine it had once had was long gone now, the seats were still leather – a reminder both of past affluence (not their own, Father Bohdan explained, for they'd bought the thing third- or fourth-hand from a plastics importer in Kiev) as well as present, rather more modest, circumstances.

Father Bohdan slipped in beside the driver, while I took the rear bench seat. He twisted around. 'I'm here for you to meet my father,' he said. 'Father? This man I found flying aeroplanes from the cathedral.'

In the mirror, the father smiled. 'Ah,' he said, just as his son had done. He twisted in the seat, offering a thick weathered hand. His face was his son's face, only thirty years hence. 'English?' he said. I said yes, and he told me how, during the war, he'd flown a Hurricane and had been shot down by a pair of Messerschmitt 109s over Murmansk. Only recovered in the 1980s from its grave deep down in a farmer's field, what was left of the plane was now in storage at Kiev's Museum of the Great Patriotic War on the banks of the Dnieper River – all but the tail fin, with its hand-painted red star, which was now an exhibit at Brooklands Museum near Weybridge in Surrey.

'When you see the plane now,' I said, 'what do you see?'

'What do I see?' The old man shrugged. 'I see a foolish young man with no thought of death. A young man with no thought of the family death would deny him.'

'My father was a hero,' said Bohdan proudly.

His father shook his head. He was, he said, no hero. Not like Babushkin. Babushkin, he said, without a thought of his own safety, had flown north across the Arctic time and again in his old Poliarkov R-5 biplane in search of the stricken steamship *Chelyuskin*.

I asked him if the great man had found her.

'In the end, yes. She was stuck in the ice. Slowly being crushed. So he landed his aeroplane on the ice, and the rescue of the sailors began.'

'And so Stalin gave him a medal.'

Bohdan's father nodded. His medal proclaiming him a Hero of the Soviet Union was, he said, one of the first ever given.

'What happened to him?'

'Babushkin? He died.' Bohdan glanced at his father. 'In a crash. And now he's buried in the Novodevichy Cemetery in Moscow.'

'With Chekhov. And Levitan.'

He nodded. He glanced again at his father. The old man looked suddenly tired, as if thoughts of the past had exhausted him.

'Is he still a hero – this Babushkin?' I said.

'To some. Not to all.'

'Why not to all – if all he did was save lives?'

The old man looked up, caught my eye in the mirror. 'He spoke up,' he said. 'About what he saw. Some people didn't like it. Even now they don't like it. Even today. They say he should have kept his mouth shut.'

'About what?'

'He saw what the government said didn't exist. He saw all the people who didn't exist – people who they said had never existed. He saw them – the hopeless and the starving heading north along the road to the camps. From the air, he said, they were like ants, each following the other to the poisoned nest and death. And then he died.'

'How?'

'They said his plane crashed. They said he lost his way. And then they said he ran out of fuel. It was like they were saying, "Whatever you want to believe, it's true!" Everything but the truth, of course.'

'My father is certain of some things,' said Bohdan. 'Things that cannot be proved.'

The old man huffed. 'Like God, you mean?'

Bohdan sighed. It was clearly an argument they'd had many times before – one that it seemed likely would never be resolved.

'I'm just saying he was a good pilot and would not get lost, and that he was too honest a man for Stalin to let him be. So he killed him, like he killed so many others. It's sense. Only a fool would deny it.'

Bohdan turned his head away and looked out of the window. His face, in profile, had a look of the American actor Edward Norton.

'They should make a film,' I said.

'Of Babushkin?' said Bohdan.

His father huffed. 'They should tell the truth is what they should do.'

Looking for a moment so terribly weary, Bohdan closed his eyes.

'They should tell the truth about that whole gang,' said the old man. 'Not hide it like Putin. Not make people long for what was never real and anyway was paid for with suffering.'

Bohdan opened his eyes. 'Why did we come here today?' he said. 'Was it not to visit Matrushka?'

The old man shrugged, conceding.

'Well, it's nearly five o'clock. So we should go.'

'Matrushka won't mind if we're late. How could she mind?'

Bohdan opened his door and stepped out. I did the same. I followed Bohdan towards the cathedral across the snow-covered grass. He paused, glanced back, let me catch him up.

'Who's Matrushka?' I said.

'Matrushka was my father's wife. She died on the way to the Gulag at Vorkuta, after my father was shot down. They said he was a coward or a spy. Stalin said it. He said the wives of cowards were cowards too and whores. So he sent her to the camps, but she never got there. She died on the Vladimirka Road and they left her there. My father thinks – *knows*, though he can't know it – she was one of those people Babushkin flew over. One of the people he talked about.'

'Is there any kind of marker?'

He shook his head. 'No one knows where she's buried.'

'Then why here?'

'This is where they were married. This is where they were happy, before everything changed.'

I looked back at the car. The old man was standing beside it now, looking out into the distance, perhaps northwards – who knows? – towards the road and the Gulags of the Arctic and all that had gone before.

Later that day, as I boarded the night train for Kovrov and Nizhny Novgorod, I thought of the old man and his son heading back in their car to the town in which they lived. As the guard blew his whistle and the train started moving, I thought of a line of Pushkin that I had read in the museum that had once been the great poet's home. *The lie which exalts us is dearer to us than a host of truths.* I closed my eyes. In the eye of my mind, then, I saw the old man again, leaning back against his car, then Babushkin flying high above the stark and frozen land. The train shuddered, hissed, stopped then moved again. I thought of Matrushka standing, frozen, on that long-ago road, shielding her eyes against the blinding white of snow, watching an aeroplane growing larger then smaller, until all trace of it was gone as if it had been just a mind playing tricks, as if it had really been nothing more than a dream.

I half-woke in the early dawn, drifting in half-sleep, my dreams of Max and our long summer days on that endless Red Beach up at Warkworth dimming but slowly until – for the moment at least – all memory of the past was gone, and all that was left was a hard slatted bunk that bit into the flesh on my back and the narrow compartment's thick toxic heat.

I turned over. The other three bunks were empty, the distant sky beyond the train's grimy window rising pink and orange. I pushed myself up. My clothes were wringing with sweat, the heater above the window going full blast. I reached up, feeling for a way to turn it off – but there was none. I tried the window. The window was sealed shut. I felt suddenly queasy and in need of air.

The corridor too was deserted, the train rattling so hard (despite being, surely, the slowest train known to man, taking most of the hours of darkness to cover a distance of perhaps 300 kilometres) that not a rivet, it seemed to me, could possibly withstand such shaking. I made my way to the end of the carriage. Easing open the connecting door, I was met with a blast of sharp freezing air – a reminder (as if such were needed) that in a place and at a time such as this

147

any warmth not hazardous to a person's general health was still half a year away and that winter in Russia really does (as they say) have the patience of a yak but the teeth of a ravenous wolf.

An hour later I was sitting alone in the buffet car, writing up my notes, when a voice overhead announced what I assumed was our imminent arrival. Outside, open frozen fields had given way to the first scrubby signs of human encampment, while, far away, on a horizon that could have been a thousand miles distant, the first signs of the city rose up – tower blocks blunt and bitten like short stubby fingers, winter-grey against a colour-drained sky.

If it wasn't for the fact that the city of Kovrov (which sits north-east of Vladimir on the banks of the Klyazma River, surrounded by the most beautiful forest of pine) produces more pistols, mortars, tanks, guns for shooting tanks, guns for shooting aircraft, and all the bullets, shells and explosives that without which all the above would be useless, then the city's splendid, grand, blue and white, spick and span station would be just like so many others in the region – run-down, overlooked, left to peel in the summer and shiver in the long northern winters. And without them – the guns and the station – I wouldn't have stepped off the train on that crisp early morning with a handwritten list of names in my hand. Copied from the archives in Moscow, the names – six of them – were of those men and women who, on a similar morning over sixty years ago, had been surrounded in the waiting room by a band of Beria's Cheka and then shot in the head, one by one, all pleas for mercy having been, of course, ignored.

I looked around me, searching for the plaque that only a year ago had been unveiled by Kovrov's mayor following the reading of a dedication written by no less a person than President Medvedev himself. I found it in the far corner – a solemn grey tablet, the names etched in the stone alphabetically:

Lev Abram, *exiled.*
Anna Bulganin, *exiled.*
Maksim Gerashchenko, *exiled.*
Egor Kalanta, *exiled.*
Dimitrii Kliuchevskii, *exiled.*
Vera Zalygin, *exiled.*

Let the names of these six men and women, the President had said, *stand for the millions who died as a consequence of criminal activity.* Suitably ambiguous (was this 'criminal activity' referred to that of the victims' – 'crimes' for which they'd been exiled – or the state-sponsored 'crimes' of Beria's dreaded secret police, the descendants of which still exist today?), the President's words were greeted with polite applause, a small curtain drawn aside, and the ceremony concluded with the voices of a local Cossack choir singing songs both devotional and secular. Among the guests looking on were (aside from the mayor himself) other dignitaries and a selection of local people, among *whom* – the latter – were the top men from the Degtyarev factory (the city's largest employer), the place in which – ironically or perhaps merely coincidentally – the guns and bullets with which the victims' lives had been ended had been made. Most strikingly absent from the guest list were any relatives of those victims. None was present as none had been invited. Even after more than sixty years, it seems, the stain of spurious guilt remains, even down the generations. Even after so long, it seems, the theft of a cow, the telling of a joke, an unavoidable lateness for work will not be forgiven and the grotesque absurdity of their being sent into exile down the Vladimirka Road not properly and finally acknowledged.

This duty done, I crossed the echoing waiting room and studied the street-map on the wall. I searched without success for the biggest and best known of the city's arms factories. I ran my finger down the index, comparing the strange Cyrillic letters with those in my guidebook.

Nothing.

I checked again. Again, nothing. I recrossed the empty hall and approached the ticket window. I bent down, peering in.

'I'm looking for the Degtyarev factory,' I said.

A large man in the khaki uniform of the Russian National Railways was eating his breakfast at a table some way from the window. I thought perhaps he hadn't heard. I asked him again. Again, nothing. I paused for a moment, then tapped on the glass. He looked up; his eyes were pale and rheumy.

I later learned from the *Book of Thanks and Remembrance* in the town hall that he'd lost his sight during the Russian war in Afghanistan, the victim of a mujahedin roadside bomb. That both the explosives used and the small arms with which his unit had been attacked following the initial incident had been produced in the factory somewhere in the very town from which he'd been dispatched for his two years' national service seemed to me far beyond any irony. Surely, if any further evidence were needed of mankind's utter failure, then such a story as this is it.

He heaved himself up from the table and made his way to the window. He said something that sounded a little like the place I was looking for.

'Yes, that's it,' I said. 'Is it far?'

He unbolted the glass partition and opened it inwards. Reaching out a hand, he gestured to the left, then again. I thanked him; he nodded, withdrawing his hand. He closed the partition and returned to his table.

It was still early, the tramlines glinting in the light, not a soul about from one end of the broad street to the other. Like the station itself, all the buildings were white and clean – as if a cloth had been taken to them in the moments before I'd arrived. Even the snow – as yet undisturbed – did nothing to break the perfection of the scene. All was quiet. I started walking. As I crunched my way down the road, I couldn't help thinking how terrifying it would be to be suddenly blind – how forbidding to suddenly find yourself in a world where there was nothing all around you but darkness and nothing before you but never-ending uncertainty of an old and broken road.

Amongst Degtyarev's most famous products was the type-28 machine gun. Armed with bullets fed from a fast-spinning drum that was said to remind all who saw it of a disc spinning around on an old-fashioned record player, it was said, also (in concert with its more famous cousin, Kalashnikov's AK-47), to have slaughtered more soldiers in the field than any other machine gun before or since. From the Spanish Civil War to the genocide in Somalia, it has killed untold millions and maimed and made orphans of millions more, while still being known – quite inexplicably now – in some quarters by the nickname given it by the Finnish Winter Army in their brave but doomed fight against its Russian inventors.

Emma.

A nice name for a gun.

For reasons now as lost as its ice-bound victims, they called it after a once-famous (and famously mournful) waltz – some say because it reminded them of home and other, better times, while to others, some say, it represented a sort of brutal conductor – that it was the orchestrator of a brutal dance of death played out before an audience in three-quarter time.

Walking briskly in order to keep warm, I took the first left as instructed, then on and on, until the buildings' stunning whiteness started fading and was gradually replaced by a dullness and shabbiness that seemed to increase the closer I drew to the factories.

I stopped on a street corner. People were starting to emerge bleary-eyed from their houses and their single rooms, greeting each other in their gruff early morning voices, some glancing up to the sky as if trying to divine its intentions, while others – those with worries more urgent – preferred just to keep their heads down. I wondered how many of them were heading towards some brightly lit factory and a day spent assembling mortars for the army or packing copper-cased, boat-tailed, armour-piercing bullets into boxes of a thousand – and whether they knew or cared where those boxes and those bullets might end up.

I walked on, drawn along by their slow, sweeping tide.

The Degtyarev Joint Stock Factory was opened in the spring of 1917, just in time to supply an Imperial Russian Army crippled by poor leadership and unrest in the ranks, an army – like the nation itself – on the verge of complete disintegration. From then until now it has, with great and unlikely efficiency, produced the weapons used to overthrow the tsar, equip Stalin's bands of thugs in their murderous interwar pogroms, fight a war in the far east against the Japanese invaders and a war of attrition in the west against the Nazis. Democratic governments have been toppled with the aid of its bullets and guns and mortars, and the cruellest and most ludicrous of regimes sustained. Along with its brothers in arms, it made possible the great socialist disaster from which a third of the world is barely even now recovering. *Give me a gun*, said Lenin, *and I'll give you a thousand votes.* The Degtyarev gave him a million, and there was, as a consequence, no need of a ballot then for three generations.

I stopped at the heavy iron gates. The guard shook his head. The vast yard behind him was deserted now, all the workers inside at their lathes or assembling, boxing up or making ready for shipment.

I pulled out my letter of introduction from the trade attaché at the embassy in London. The guard scanned it, then, indicating with a raised palm that I should wait, stepped into his dung-coloured Portakabin. A moment later a metal door beside the big gates clicked open.

'Hello? I didn't think you'd get here.'

'No? Why not?'

Andrei Baikov shrugged. A cheerful man with an engaging smile and manner, he took me aside and dropped his voice. 'Well, it's not exactly Moscow,' he whispered. He grinned. 'Is it?'

No, I said, it wasn't Moscow. But it *did* have a splendid white station.

Baikov frowned. 'Does it?' he said.

'You haven't seen it?'

He shook his head. All he'd seen of the place so far had been the factory itself and the road from the airport at Nizhny Novgorod.

'Then you must let me be your guide,' I said.

He grinned. 'Excellent!' First though, he said, I must let him be mine.

The factory was vast – more a *collection* of factories than a single one. In addition to weapons of all kinds, they made lawnmowers and – of all things – sewing machines. For every anti-aircraft gun they turn out, they produce on average three sewing machines. According to my guide, there is scarcely a single clothing manufacturer from Mumbai to Indonesia who isn't in possession of a Degtyarev machine: they're cheap, he said, and reliable – which was more, he said, than could be said for the average Russian worker.

'Really?' I said.

He nodded in a just-between-you-and-me kind of way, so embracing me with his prejudice against anyone less fortunate than himself.

I asked him what it was like making bombs for a living – whether the thought of how they would be used kept him awake at night.

'Awake?' he said, still grinning.

'So do you always know the end user?'

I thought of the child soldiers with their huge dark eyes whose pictures I'd seen in the *Guardian* and the *Sunday Times Magazine.*

'Of course!' he said. 'We're not gangsters. We supply only those who meet the general standard.'

'What's that?' I said. His grin was starting to annoy me.

He said something then about protocols and international agreements. He assured me most earnestly that the Degtyarev was a company that had never once been touched by the merest suspicion of scandal or been affected by the slightest hint of corruption. But I was no longer listening. As he went on, all I could see were the faces of those children – their still-growing bodies scarcely bigger than the weapons they were carrying, the distance in their mournful eyes so great that no amount of love could ever now breach it.

That afternoon I went in search of a present for my son. I found a store on Abelmana Street, a few yards from my hotel. 'I'd like something for a boy,' I said. A boat, perhaps, or an aeroplane – something small, easy to carry.

The girl in her smart uniform smiled. I followed her across the store to the toy department. 'Here,' she said, indicating the shelves with a sweep of her arm, obviously proud of the selection. But then the smile dipped. 'Forgive me,' she said, 'but we have no guns.'

'No?' I said.

She nodded. After Beslan, she said, they were known to be a danger.

'Even toy guns?'

Yes, she said. Even toy guns. But then she brightened. 'But we have many ships!' she said, selecting from the shelf a 1:600 plastic model of the battleship *Bismarck*.

The next morning, while waiting for my bill to be printed, I asked Gregor on reception how easy it would be for a stranger like myself to buy a handgun. He leaned forward, a broad and knowing smile on his face. 'You want bullets as well?' he said.

I like to think he was joking.

Sitting both on the slow-flowing Klyazma River and the Vladimirka Road, midway between Kovrov and the closed city of Nizhny Novgorod, Gorokhovets is currently home to nearly 15,000 people. Although this number varies, of course, with every birth and every death – and includes men and women of all talents and accomplishments – one son of the town will for ever be remembered above all others.

His name is Standartenführer Stirlitz.

I consulted my map. Having been off the bus from Kovrov for only ten minutes, my ears were still ringing from the noise of the thing (halfway along the road I'd looked out through the grime of my window just in time to see something dark and cog-shaped spin out from underneath) and my stomach was still queasy from the exhaust fumes that seemed to be being fed (like those on the night train to Kovrov) back into the bus as much as out and away. I sat down on a bench beside an ill-kempt, potholed road. The road was lined with stunted trees that had once, presumably, given the place a lighter, more optimistic air.

I turned the map around, trying to place where I was. The man's birthplace could really have been anywhere, so many of the streets having names so similar that to tell them apart was impossible. Some of the streets, in fact, had no names at all.

Arina from the tourist office was just leaving for her lunch when I arrived. She said she would take me to the Stirlitz birthplace – and so she did, her tiny bird-like frame (she was seventy years old, she said proudly) all angles and points and her heels clipping sharply on the uneven cobbles until we were standing before the very house in which Stirlitz had been born. It was here, she said, that his statue would stand.

'It's definite, then, this statue?' I said.

She nodded firmly – which in Russia, of course, I'd come to learn meant certainly no more than a possible maybe.

'Are there people who don't want it?'

Despite her age, Arina Nemirovich-Danchenko had a sprightliness about her that would have been remarkable in a woman a good deal more youthful. She shrugged. Such people, she said, were selfish and ignorant. Did they not want the tourists and money that such a thing would gener-ate? Did they not want better schools for their children? Did they really want a hospital with more patients than beds? No, she said, it would come – the statue – whether such people wanted it or not. Although he'd never really existed, Stirlitz, she said, was a saviour, and everyone should be thankful. Without Stirlitz, she said, the town of Gorokhovets would by now be nothing more than a home for drunks and ghosts.

Filmed in 1973 at the Gorky Film Studios in Moscow, *Seventeen Moments of Spring* was a twelve-hour mini series based on the novels of Yulian Semyonov. Widely popu-lar throughout the Soviet Union, and concerning the adventures of the KGB spy Stirlitz and his work at the heart of the Nazi empire, the making of the series, some say, had been ordered by Yuri Andropov, then head of the real KGB and later General Secretary of the Communist Party of the Soviet Union, with the intention of 'realigning' the poor (but accurate) image of the Russian secret service.

On the way back to her office in the council building, I asked her whether she believed it – that Andropov had been responsible.

Again Arina shrugged. As the sister of a widow of the Gulag, she wouldn't, she said, put anything past Andropov and his thugs. Anyone, after all, who could send a young man to his death for the 'crime' of speaking unfavourably of the decision to invade Afghanistan in 1979 was certainly capable of such a thing.

'He spoke out?' I said.

She nodded, a darkness drawing over her at the memory.

I asked her then what she knew of his experiences in the Gulag. She sighed. All she knew, she said, was what her sister had read to her from the three letters he'd smuggled out in the pocket of one of the inspectors who'd once employed his father in the train yard at Nizhny Novgorod. Aside from the personal declarations of love (which were, of course, private), she said there really hadn't been much. We stopped to cross the road. She turned. In that moment she suddenly looked her age and more. 'What can you say about snow?' she said. 'What can you say about feeling abandoned and hopeless, when you've said it already? Nothing. So in the end you say nothing. You pull your coat in and bury your head. You wait like a tortoise for spring.'

'And yet he's still a hero to you, this made-up Stirlitz, even though Andropov may be responsible for making him so famous – the same Andropov who was responsible for the death of your brother-in-law?'

'Of course,' said Arina. 'Stirlitz was a good man and a brave man. A man of principle. And when they said he was born in our town, we knew he was special – and so were we.'

I asked her what she thought he'd have done – this Stirlitz – if he'd ever met Andropov.

If he'd have ever met Andropov, she said, her eyes narrowing like a spy's, then he'd have known, she said, nodding, exactly what to do.

I looked at Arina's weathered face, expecting to see there some evidence of irony – or at least mischief. But there was none: she was serious.

We were standing at the traffic lights in the small square, waiting while a big truck carrying chickens rattled by. It was here that, as a child, Stirlitz is supposed to have felt the first pangs of love for a girl in a baker's shop with dark brown plaited hair. When at last the noise but not the smell of the chickens had cleared, Arina told me she had something to give me – a souvenir. When I asked her what it was, she shook her head. 'Come with me,' she said.

The lights changed; we stepped out. Once on the other side, she stopped. This time she touched my arm, as if she'd just remembered something so distant – a memory so fragile – that any further movement might send it fleeing again from its temporary place at the front of her mind. 'Yes, there was something,' she said, as if in answer to a question.

'Something?'

'In his letter. The last one. I remember he said being sent to the Gulag had made a real Communist of him – what with everyone having to work together and think of each other if anyone was going to survive – and how he wished he could tell Andropov, just to see his face. That and how he'd finally been released from his belief in God.'

I asked her if his faith had been strong before his exile.

Arina raised her shoulders as if to say who knows? 'Every Russian carries faith on his back,' she said, 'whether he believes in God or not. It's just there like the mud on your boots or the dirt under your fingernails.'

'But it can be shed,' I said.

'Shed?'

'Lost. Put down and never picked up again.'

She thought for a moment, then nodded. 'Yes,' she said. 'But the cost is high. To willingly make yourself an orphan is to let go of the hand of the past – to just let it drop – and without the past to guide us, how do we know where to go?'

That depends, I said, on the point of it all. Whether or not you think there *is* a point.

'To life?' she said.

I said that maybe the point of life is living.

She shook her head. No Russian, she said, could bear to live like that. For a Russian there must always be something more – something better ahead, an answer to the riddle. Had I not visited a Russian church? she said. Had I not seen how a Russian, when he prays, prays with his eyes open?

I nodded. It's true: this had struck me. I'd noticed it in St Basil's on Red Square – the eyes of the faithful wide open and fixed on the gold and blue icons, while the choir of four bearded men sang plainsong, a mournful invocation stripped of all harmony available, for 400 roubles, on a CD in the gift shop.

'Then you understand.'

I nodded again and said nothing. I didn't like to admit that, at the time, I'd thought the staring of those praying little more than further evidence of what – even after so short a time – I'd come to see as a people made so suspicious of their fellow citizens by a state built on secrecy and lies that even in the moment of prayer they were still keeping watch and expecting betrayal.

Arina sighed, as if she was somehow aware of my thoughts and was saddened by them.

'No pews either,' I said, for no reason other than to fill up the silence.

Arina Nemirovich-Danchenko nodded. She took my arm and squeezed it, as if our difference in ages excused everything. She smiled, and much of that difference slipped away. 'Give a Russian a seat,' she said, 'and he'll never get up again!'

I covered her hand with mine and we walked on, turning at last into the street dominated by the pale stone council buildings. We climbed the steps while a pair of security guards, each with a hand on his holster, did their best (successfully) to appear menacing.

My souvenir of Kovrov was two-fold. First, a matryoshka doll, containing a selection of Russian leaders from Lenin to Medvedev (excluding, among others, both Andropov and his protégé Gorbachev), each one smaller, of course, than the last, until the smallest – Vladimir Ilyich Lenin – was about the size of my thumbnail.

My second souvenir was a DVD – or, rather, a series of six – a box containing the entire twelve-hour run of *Seventeen Moments of Spring*. 'You can see for yourself,' she said, 'if what the Nazis thought of him was true.'

'Which was?' I said.

Arina said something incomprehensible in Russian.

'In English?'

'In English,' she said, 'I believe it means moron. You know moron?'

I nodded, thinking suddenly of my old maths teacher, Mr Phillips – the Welsh Windbag – who had many times used the word to describe me, his worst-ever pupil.

We said goodbye outside Arina's office. I thanked her and shook her hand. Before I turned away, I asked her if anyone knew where her brother-in-law was buried. She shook her head. Such a thing now, she said, was something only the wolves would ever know.

That evening I stood in the office of Pavel's Car Hire. The office was a mobile home decorated with pictures of Michael Jackson and Madonna. Pavel himself a short, sweaty man with twice as many rings on his fingers as he had fingers and a permanent disbelieving scowl on his face.

'You have licence?'

I pushed my licence across the desk. He glanced at it with infinite disdain.

'You have money?'

I said yes, I had money.

'Well?'

'Well?' I said.

'So you want a radio?'

I said yes, a radio would be nice.

Sighing and with a shake of his head, he pulled open his desk drawer and fished around for what I assumed would be a key.

Twenty minutes later, when the deal at last was done and I'd reluctantly been allowed to rent a car, I was sitting at the lights, still somewhere in town and trying to get out, when a moose appeared on the pavement beside me. It lowered its head and considered me with one huge, dark, watery eye, so close that I could see myself in it. The lights changed; I ground the Lada's gears and lifted the clutch. As I slowly moved off, I glanced in the mirror. There were thirty of them – maybe more – all tethered together. I watched them grow smaller in my mirror until they were gone. Moose. Although it was true, it seemed at the same time quite ridiculous and something that only a small boy like my son would ever be likely to believe.

In June 1439, during the barbarian invasion of Russia, the Monastery of the Holy Trinity at Yellow Lake in the forests outside the town of Semyonov in the district of Nizhny Novgorod was destroyed and its half-dozen resident monks – 'Old Believers' for ever at odds with the modernizing will of the Orthodox Church – cast out with instructions to leave Yellow Lake. Failure to do so, they were told, would mean their death. After several weeks of wandering, the monks ran out of food. A moose then appeared. Racked with hunger, the monks decided to slaughter it; however, it being then the first of the three-day Fast of the Holy Apostles, their leader forbade it. Instead, he cut off its right ear. The beast was then released. God, he said, would provide.

For three days the monks wandered along the road heading north, troubled with doubt – the result surely of the disorientating effects of hunger. Then, on the third day, at dusk, the moose with the missing right ear returned to them, presenting itself as if commanded to do so, for slaughter.

Taking the road east out of Kovrov, I drove along the road the monks had walked, my thoughts of home – of my son Joel and his Royal Canadian Mounted Moose soft toy – all the time interrupted by the bunching and rattling of the old

Lada's wheels as the road beneath them grew worse with every mile.

A sudden *thud* and the sound of something dropping and dragging. I pulled over.

Thanks to rivets already loosened by untreated corrosion, a part of the left wing had dislodged itself just below the lights and was hanging down. I tried to push it back up, remembering as I did so Pavel's fearsome scowl, but it would not stay. So, instead, I pulled what was left of it off and laid it in the boot on top of an old bag of tools, a plastic jerrycan and a stack of old and yellowing newspapers.

The Road of Bones that was once one road is now many. What was once one route, along which thousands travelled by car and by truck and above all by foot, is now several shorter stretches, one town or city connected to the next by road (local road or highway and everything in between) or rail, so making each part of the way north and east different both from that which came before and that which is to follow. Once scorched on the land, a scar, indelible, though it's faded now, it's still there if you look, alive beneath tarmac and rails, a trail of bones buried just beneath the surface, a chain of voices which, though distant now, can still be heard by those willing to listen.

Voices like that of Leszek Arbatov, whose crime was to hesitate when ordered to shoot his brother who'd been convicted of cowardice during the siege of Leningrad; voices like those of Alexander and Nicholas Vlascov, twelve-year-old twins found guilty of subversion on account of the imperial echoes of their names; voices like that of Osip Danilovichi, a weaver from Kursk, who dared to speak out about the rape of German women during the battle for

Berlin by his fellow Red Army soldiers and who, as a consequence, was raped himself: these voices and thousands, millions more hang in the air if you stand by the roadside or on the edge of the tracks and wait and listen hard enough.

And there are more – thousands of voices, voices without number.

Voices like that of Jörg Kleinmann, a German Jew, whose marker (a rare thing in itself) had clearly been recently tended (there were flowers tied to the body of the cross no more than a few days old) twenty yards from the roadside where, by the pale light of that early morning, a broken wing had caused me to stop.

I eased myself down the bank and dropped to my haunches.

The name was neatly carved, the dates (1921–1944) also.

According to the National Historical Archives in Moscow (whose records, though woefully incomplete, can sometimes throw up the most remarkable of stories), Jörg Kleinmann had been a Soviet citizen (naturalized through having married a Russian girl of whom no records remain) whose work as a designer of sets for several theatres in Moscow came to an abrupt end when, like millions of others, he was called up for service in the Red Army, charged with the task of defending the motherland against what all referred to as the unprovoked and quite outrageous attack of Hitler and his Nazi armies. This he did willingly and, during battles before Moscow, proved himself so valiantly devoted to the cause that he was recommended for a medal. However, before such an award could be considered, he was captured by a unit of the Waffen SS and – despite his naturalization – found guilty of treason and sentenced to be shot. Before the sentence could be carried out, however, the SS unit was itself overrun by forward units of the advancing Red Army, and Kleinmann was liberated – only then to be rearrested (also for treason) by the political commissar attached to this liberating unit. Quite clearly a spy (so they said) and a traitor to the motherland, Jörg Kleinmann was sentenced to a life of exile, to which end he was sent on the long walk north-east. That he never made it, that – so weakened and dispirited by his experiences and the casual brutality of his treatment – he stumbled and fell and died on the side of the road is clear now for all to see, thanks to a simple cross twenty yards from the road and a small bunch of flowers placed in remembrance by an unknown, anonymous hand.

I stood a while, a mourner at a grave, and tried to imagine how it must have felt to have been so abandoned by those whom you'd been so willing to serve. But, of course, I could not. To really know such a thing – such a terrible betrayal – you have to have been there – you have to have been him. Only by walking, they say, in another man's boots will you feel the stones that dug into his heels or feel the pinch of old leather as it tightens with the freeze of late autumn, so gripping your flesh with the first claws of winter.

His details noted in my little brown book, I climbed the shallow bank, unlocked the car and got in. The car started first time and for this I was grateful (you can spend too much time contemplating the dead, feel the grip of their fingers sometimes on your collar) – especially so when the heater that would soon enough fail bled the cold from my hands with its feeble, stinking warmth, so making the road to Nizhny Novgorod seem – despite its condition – positively luxurious, at least when compared with the road as once it had been and the journeys made along it by others in other, bleaker times.

For so long known as Gorky (after the writer and pal of Joseph Stalin), the city of Nizhny Novgorod is the fourth largest in the Russian Federation. Until recently a closed city, access to which was denied to all foreign nationals and those Russians who were neither resident there nor employed at one of the many military installations, today – though a visitor will often still require a 'special' visa – you are free to leave the M7 motorway (which replaces now a part of the Vladimirka Road) at Lenina Prospect in the centre of the city and explore the place at your will.

Ask at any one of the four tourist centres for information on the city and you'll be directed to the GAZ factory car plant or the Perchersky Ascension Monastery or perhaps the art gallery, with its grand collection of Russian landscapes. You will not be referred to the works of Paul Robeson, for whom the city was once a temporary home. No statue of *him* stands on the banks of the Volga – though it should, for he was truly a much greater socialist than Stalin's friend Maxim Gorky, in whose honour there *is*, of course, a statue in a park named after him and for whom there remains great official reverence. Ask about Robeson and you will be met with a shrug. His story, however, is a story of the road and one that should be told.

Paul LeRoy Bustill Robeson was born in April 1898, the son of a church minister, a descendant of plantation slaves. Though enough to swamp most men's ambition – especially a black man in America's racist south[1] – his low beginnings failed to prevent him growing into a man of such strength and such conviction that the segregation of one man from another was wrong, that there was, towards the end of his long life, scarcely anywhere in the world that hadn't been touched by his sonorous voice and its mellifluous message of love and of freedom.

Standing in a tiny store in a bleak-looking street, I flicked through the CDs in a tray marked *America*. And then there they were – three Paul Robeson albums, three more in fact than I'd really expected to find.

The first two – *Paul Robeson sings 'Ol' Man River'* and *Songs for Americans* – were compilations and pretty familiar. The third CD, *Paul Robeson Live at Carnegie Hall, May 9th, 1958*, was by far the most enticing.

I asked the young man what he knew about the singer. He was pale – the young man – with bad skin, and was clearly a stranger to daylight. He glanced down at the CDs on the counter and shrugged. The man, he said, was a slave.

'Did you know he came here?'

'In Nizhny?'

'Yes,' I said. 'In 1934, he came to Russia to meet Joseph Stalin.'[2]

---

1 Only the second African American to study at Rutgers University, Robeson then studied at Columbia Law School, and then in Europe, before his career as an actor and singer took off, thus giving him a platform for what were considered in America his 'socialist' then 'Communist' ideas.
2 During his second visit to Russia, Robeson accepted the Stalin Peace Prize – an award that delighted his detractors back in America, who used his apparent endorsement of Stalin and his methods to stifle much proposed humanitarian legislation at home.

He shook his head. No, he said, he didn't know. His skin looked in places translucent, and sickly. Touch him, and he looked like he'd crumple.

Paul Robeson, I said, had come to Russia in search of the equality so glaringly absent for the black man in America. He came to see for himself this wonderful place that everyone was talking about – this new, brighter, Communist world where everyone was free and no man lived in chains. He had come, I said, to see this workers' paradise.

'He believed in Communism?'

'He wanted to.'

'Why?'

'Because of what had happened to black people in America. He thought it was maybe a better way to live. He thought Stalin was a great man – that he cared about the people.'

Again the young man shrugged. It was, he said, all too long ago to matter. It wasn't the same country – not *his* country. It wasn't, he said, *his* history. Not any more.

'Then what is?' I said.

He looked around him, at the rows and rows of second-hand CDs, at the Yes and Genesis and Paul Young posters Sellotaped to the walls and across the ceiling. 'This is all I have,' he said. 'And when I leave, I will burn it down.' He turned away, started rummaging through a rack of Russian metal CDs. Finding the one he wanted, he held it up before me. The band was KAOS, the CD *Scorched Earth*.

'So where will you go?' I said.

Another shrug. 'Maybe America.'

'Why?'

'The land of the free,' he said. He smiled; his teeth were unexpectedly white. He picked up the Robeson CDs. I thanked him and left the shop. Back in my shabby hotel room, I took the discs out of their cases. They were perfect, unscratched, undamaged by experience. I turned them in the light. In a place so grey, the colours that the light drew from them seemed wonderful and magical – as strange and unexpected and quite as out of place as the young man in his shop or, indeed, a black man in all the whiteness of Russia.

Siberia, people say, is always there and always watching. It stares, yellow-eyed, they say, like a lean Arctic wolf and – like an Arctic wolf – it waits until you're too far from home to ever make it back safely before pouncing, sharp-clawed, in time colouring its white coat red with your blood.

Standing that evening on the banks of the Volga, huddled up against the Arctic cold and looking out across the vast and darkening water in my thick borrowed coat, I thought of Paul Robeson – the voice of the Volga if there ever was one – and imagined him standing where *I* was standing, his face set to the north and to the east, his eyes catching, perhaps with the memory of other eyes in other times, a chain of lights strung out and moving slowly across the hard, inhospitable ground – a caravan of misery, of loneliness and despair – perhaps a thousand human souls, each of which – though aware of his fate – is unaware of his terrible destination. With the certain uncertainty of a man who knows the gallows but not the life or the darkness thereafter, they trudge on and he watches them until the lights have gone – until, in his mind, they are subsumed into the earth – so much blood, so much bone – like millions, half the world away, before. Is it too ludicrous and fanciful to think he might sing to them – cast that great thunderous voice of his out in solidarity across the land that had made them and to which they'd now returned?

Perhaps.

Suddenly bitten by the cold as if by that wolf, I turned away from the river and wound my way through the city's broad and dark outskirts towards those lighted streets at its heart and something warm to eat and something to drink that would neutralize my home thoughts as effectively as the cold had numbed my hands.

I passed the record store. It was all shut up now, though – I was pleased to see – not yet burning. I cut around the empty open-air swimming pool and across Nizhny's own Gorky Park and paused for a moment at the statue dedicated to the famous writer of that name.

Aleksey Maksimovich Peshkov was born in the city in 1868, the same year that saw the birth of Nicholas, future Tsar of All the Russias. Orphaned, he wandered the country as a young man, in time working as a journalist, for which work he took the name Maxim Gorky. By nature a socialist, he opposed the tsarist system,[1] a position that drew him into the orbit of Vladimir Lenin and the Bolsheviks. In 1932, following lengthy periods spent abroad – both in exile and travelling on behalf of the Communist Party – the new leader, Joseph Stalin, invited him to return home to Russia. Now, resting his left elbow on a pillar, his head is raised as if what concerns him lies not at hand but in the barely discernible distance – or as if he were searching for what had once been so certain to last for ever but which now was as ancient as a long-ago affair. While many admire the statue, finding in it a reflection of a man's strength and virtue, to me his

1   And it opposed him, the tsar himself revoking Gorky's election to the Imperial Academy of Literature.

expression is that of a man who, though much fêted for the breadth of his vision, knows himself, in reality, to be a timid man – a man for whom only others have, in the end, the strength of his convictions.

In a while I moved on, leaving Gorky behind me and the weeds that are already reclaiming the stone plinth on which he stands, and turned into a restaurant and bar inexplicably called the Red Balloon, grateful for the warmth and a chance to pull away at last from the grip of the past.

I ordered a beer – something Russian, I said.

The girl brought me a Guinness, brewed in Dublin.

I sat and watched the families – eight and ten to a table – and envied their loud, easy talk. For company, I pulled out my map, tracing with my finger the route of the Vladimirka Road through the city. Once beyond the city walls, and having crossed the Oka River, it heads east and a little south towards Kstovo, shadowing the Volga until that city's LUKOIL-Nizhegorodnefteorgsintez oil refinery rears its blackened head above the horizon.

In a while I folded my map and eased back in the chair. I was so weary I could have closed my eyes and slept. I kept myself awake by writing my notes. I wrote that what was now Freedom Square had once been Prison Square, and that Andrei Dmitrievich Sakharov, nuclear physicist, dissident and human rights campaigner (and winner of the Nobel Prize for Peace[1] in 1975 which he was forbidden to receive in person) had had Nizhny Novgorod chosen for him as the location of his internal exile. The grim brown tower block on Gagarin Avenue in which he spent seven

1 Embarrassingly for the authorities, Sakharov had previously been awarded the Order of Lenin, the Stalin Prize and the Lenin Prize, as well as having three times been named as a 'Hero of Socialist Labour'.

years under constant surveillance and harassment from the KGB is now a museum containing, among so many other far more important things, a pair of his battered old slippers. They sit there beside his desk, still shaped by his heels and his long narrow toes, as if their owner has just stepped out for a moment and would, at any moment, return.

I closed my notebook and finished my beer. The waitress asked me if I wanted another. I said no. She smiled a shallow, mechanical smile.

It was dark in the street now, the mercury falling fast. I pulled my coat around me, looking left and then right. I could go either way and no one would know or stop me. I could walk and keep walking. But I would not – for there were things to see in Nizhny that I had yet to see. Instead, I thought again of the millions who had taken the road and how few of them had ever returned. For them, freedom had been a currency withdrawn; as for me, I still had far more than I knew how to spend.

In the spring of 1961, racked with feelings of loneliness and paranoia, Paul Robeson attempted suicide in a Moscow hotel. Unsuccessful (due in large part to the CIA's regular, secretly administered cocktail of drugs), he returned to the United States via London where, at the Priory Clinic, he was given his ECT treatment.

On his eventual death from a stroke on 23 January 1976 at the age of seventy-seven, the American newspapers – those kings of hypocrisy – that had for so long hounded him and were in large part responsible for the decline of his health that had once been so robust now, of course, eulogized him, calling him 'a great American' and a 'beacon of freedom'. It is, consequently, surely the abiding irony of Paul Robeson's life that a man whose whole existence had been dedicated to the pursuit of freedom and justice for those too weak or disenfranchised to fight for them themselves was at every turn denied them himself by those supposed to guard them, and that, in the end, the only freedom he was ever granted was the bitter, final freedom of the grave.

I pulled off the road and into the GAZ plant's vast car park.
I switched off the engine, grateful for the sudden absence
of the engine's awful clanking. Even after driving for no more
than twenty minutes, it was difficult to believe that, though as
streamlined as a house brick and as friendly to the environ-
ment as a pocket-sized nuclear reactor, the Lada – in English
'Glorious Spring' – 1200 had been for many years the best-
selling car in Eastern Europe. One of the few cars *available*,
of course, it was cheap but certainly not cheerful, the earliest
examples having a tendency to fill themselves up with exhaust
fumes which, if a driver were exposed to them for long enough,
would cause him to become, first, light-headed and, second,
delirious – this latter condition perhaps accounting for the
maker's insistence that 'to own a 1200 is to make big smiles'.

I eased myself out and stretched my arms and neck. My
back was aching, a queasiness creeping up from my stomach. I locked the car and crossed the car park, making my
way through the lines of gleaming Volga saloons.

The man I'd come to meet was dressed in a sharp suit and
a striking red tie. He held out his hand and smiled. It was,
he said, *extremely interesting* that I should arrive at the GAZ
factory in a Lada.

I glanced back towards the vast plant car park. I asked him how he knew.

Assistant Head, at thirty-two, of GAZ (in English, Gorky Automobile Plant) International Public Relations, Gennady Shervud smiled. He flicked his eyes up to a camera in a corner of the reception's high ceiling.

'You were watching?' I said.

'Yes,' he said. 'After Tolyatti, everybody is watching.'

I nodded, thinking at once of what I'd read about the attack that morning in my guidebook.

At ten minutes after eight on 31 October 2007, a bomb exploded on a commuter bus in the city of Tolyatti[1] in the south-western corner of the Russian Federation. Ten people died – three children among them – and eighty were injured, many seriously. Although terrorist groups from the north Caucasus and Chechnya have often been cited as possible perpetrators, those most likely to have been responsible are generally considered to be rival gangs associated with the motor industry.

Gangs like the Lada Boys, whose record of threats and intimidation and extortion – and even murder – is second to none.

I asked him if it was right that the violence in the industry was as bad as people say.

He shook his head. The industry, he said, was peaceful.

'And the people who planted the bomb at Tolyatti?'

'Terrorists,' he said. 'Not workers. Here at GAZ people work and are happy to feed their families.'

---

1 The city is named after Palmiro Togliatti, leader of the Italian Communist Party from 1927 to 1964. Togliatti was a staunch supporter of Joseph Stalin until the latter's death, when, like Beria before him, he changed his mind and denounced the generalissimo's crimes.

'And you?' I said. 'Do you have a family?'

Again he shook his head. He would, he said, be married in four years – maybe four and a half.

'How do you know?'

He frowned. To Gennady Shervud, such a question was obviously absurd. Clearly, if a man such as he set in train a plan and a date for its successful completion, nothing – neither acts of God nor those of fickle man (nor even, it would seem, the vagaries of romance) – would get in the way of that plan. He would, he said, make his choice soon. Then, as if I were a soul of modest intellect who really knew not what he was saying or, indeed, where he was going, the palm of his right hand found the part of my back between the shoulder blades and, with the firm but gentle ease of a ballroom dancer, guided me with some purpose across the floor towards the lifts.

As we rose amid the lift's gentle hum, I asked him about himself. As if speaking from a card, he told me that he had spent four years in Flint, Michigan, studying the American automobile business before returning to Russia and rising to his present position. He was, he said, the proud owner of the ninth Volga ever built. Did I want to know about the plant, he said then. I said of course, and off he went.

The plant, he said, had been built in the 1920s as a co-venture with the Ford Motor Company, many visiting American engineers and skilled workers deciding to stay after the plant's completion. He told me much more, of course – stuff about output and profits and exports to China – all of which was clearly a source to him of much genuine pride. What, of course, he *didn't* tell me was that – having been forced to surrender their passports, and deeply mistrusted by Stalin – the American engineers and workers who'd been so instrumental in building the plant were in time sent north up the Vladimirka Road, singly and in groups, where they died in the Gulags, the whereabouts of their corpses remaining for ever unknown.

As the lift's progress slowed, I asked him what the city had been like before people like me had been allowed in.

He looked at the illuminated buttons.

'Do you remember it?' I said, unsure as to whether he'd heard me.

The lift pinged; the doors opened.

I was clearly being told with the benign firmness of a nanny to mind my own business.

So, of course, I tried again. 'Tell me,' I said, 'did the people here in those days *feel* cut off?' We were walking down a heavy-carpeted hallway that ended in a floor-to-ceiling window through which could be seen, I imagined, most of Nizhny – a grey cityscape punctuated here and there with the Orthodox church's gleaming domes.

Gennady stood at the window. I stood beside him. Peering down, it seemed like an awfully long way. He sighed. 'A long way,' he said, as if reading my thoughts.

'Yes,' I said. I felt suddenly uneasy. Below us stood row upon row of newly made Volgas – three-quarters of them saloons, the remainder estates.

Gennady cleared his throat. There were things, he said, that it was best not to discuss.

'Like what?' I said.

Gennady said nothing. I asked him if he'd heard of Paul Robeson. He shook his head. 'Do you see it,' he said, 'how wide is the River Volga?'

I said yes, I could see it – and it was indeed wide. It was, he said, the most powerful river in the world, making, through its dams, enough hydroelectricity to power the whole of Moscow. It was the kind of power they could only have dreamed of in the old days. In the old days, he said, it was like they had windmills, whereas now, of course, only China has more nuclear power.

'Is that a good thing?' I said.

He shrugged. 'For us, yes.'

'And for the rest of the world?'

He turned. His face was pale, impassive. The rest of the world, he said, was not their concern. The rest of the world should look out for itself. Russia was Russia and would no longer be dictated to by America and her allies. Putin, he said, was a strong man who would shake things up – deal with all those who would sabotage all that had lately been built.

'What will he do?' I said.

'Do?'

'With the saboteurs.'

He shrugged and turned down the corners of his mouth as if to say *Who knows, who cares?*

We shook hands at the lift. I thanked him for his time. A bell pinged; the doors closed and I descended. Soon I was back in the car park. Standing beside my old rented Lada, I looked up, trying to find the window at which Gennady and I had been standing, but could not. All the windows looked the same – all shiny, all clean, all utterly blind.

Running down from the walls of the Nizhny Kremlin to the banks of the Volga River are the wide wooden steps built by German prisoners of war. Local people will tell you that, if he stands on its highest step with his back to the rust-red Kremlin wall, a man with the eyes of an eagle, standing on the shoulders of a bear, will be able to see where the snows of Siberia begin, and where – as a consequence – all civilization ends.

Not possessing, however, the eyes of an eagle and only the shoulders of a naturalized Australian to stand on, Siberia, for me, remained undetectable.

'I can see a lot of trees,' I said.

'Trees? Is that it?'

'And a road. A highway. Must be the M7.'

Stephane Herr, half-French, half-English but since 1985 one hundred per cent Australian, shook his head. Half an hour previously, he'd approached me for a cigarette. Failing in this (I don't smoke), he'd suggested going down to take a look at the river. 'Right, that's it,' he said. 'Get down. I can see a fucking *road* anywhere.'

He bent forward; I jumped off. We made our way down the steps to the banks of the river.

The longest river in Europe, the Volga – like the Ganges or the Thames or the mighty Mississippi – carries with it the ever-moving restless spirit of a people, part midwife, part mother, as it winds its sinewy way through both the history and the daily, living toil of a nation. It is both what it is and what it stands for; it both preserves and endangers. Judging not, it flows democratically, blindly, for all – for the fisherman, just as it flows for the saint.

For the fisherman and the saint – and for the murderer too. For men, indeed, like Arek Bebekian who, one night, backed his mustard-coloured GAZ-24 estate carefully down to the water's edge and – having eased up the rear door – dragged the weighted-down body of his beloved wife of twenty years across the mud and stone riverbank and into the dark and oily waters.

Bebekian, originally from Armenia, was eventually arrested and found guilty of his wife's murder. He claimed in his defence that his wife, who was suffering from terminal cancer, had asked him to release her from life. The truth of this will never be known. He was sentenced to life imprisonment, his sentence to be served in a Siberian prison.

'Did you know,' I said, 'that thanks to Stalin and his great reforms, so much grain was taken from the villages and towns around here and sent to cities like this that people were forced to eat grass and cats. And dogs.'

'Look at that,' said Stephane. He was squinting, pointing at something upriver.

'And each other,' I said. 'They were forced to eat each other.'

He turned back to the river, pointing at the bank. Perhaps a quarter-mile away, a man was pulling a wooden dinghy with a rope, straining hard. The dinghy, sitting low in the water, was stacked high with what looked like potatoes. It could have been a scene from two centuries ago.

I looked at Stephane. I wondered if he was thinking what I was thinking. 'You know what that man is?' I said. He shrugged. 'That man is a genuine Volga boatman.'

'So?'

He'd not heard of the song, and so I told him. I told him that the famous 'Volga Boatman's Song' (made famous in the West by Paul Robeson's magisterial 1958 recording) was inspired by Ilya Yefimovitch Repin's painting, *Barge Haulers on the Volga*, on exhibition at the Russian Museum in St Petersburg.

We watched in silence, then, for a while as the man with the dinghy approached, drew level, then started moving away. Soon he had gone.

'Hey, you know what you were saying,' said Stephane, 'about them eating each other?'

'Yes,' I said. 'What about it?'

'Well, I was thinking, if a person decided to eat himself, how much of himself could he eat, do you think, before he was starting to eat the bit that was doing the eating?'

I shrugged. I had to admit that it was a question that I had never in my whole life considered.

There was a time – twenty years ago now – when a visitor to Kstovo could take a boat all the way along the Volga from Moscow. This was, in good weather, a pleasant enough journey, interrupted, perhaps, by a short stop at Nizhny for a turn on dry land and, perhaps, in summer, something sweet and cool to drink. The boats in those days were frequent (though unpredictable) and the tickets cheap and – being state owned and run – they ran, of course, at a heavy financial loss.

The roads, on the other hand, were wretched – crumbling and pitted and lethal to all but the most robust of cars.

But cars run on petrol.

And petrol comes from oil.

And oil – though always abundant by Western standards – with the advent of perestroika and the slow, creeping hegemony of the market, soon became a commodity whose worth in foreign currency was quite staggering.

The town's main employer, LUKOIL ('Always Moving Forward!'), has approximately two per cent of global oil reserves and is responsible for four per cent of global production. It's a vast concern – a dozen plants in Nizhny Novgorod Oblast alone, beside the main refinery – and vastly profitable. Placed like a beating heart in the centre of the Russian Federation, it has thousands of shareholders who follow the share price every morning in their papers, unaware (or uncaring) that the paper on which those figures are printed is, because of the destruction of forests necessary for the production of that oil, itself a fast-diminishing resource.

This was half on my mind (the TV news that morning had led with a story that had seemed to be about logging and some sort of protest) when I pulled on to the hard shoulder and drew up before the two rather downcast-looking hitch-hikers.

They were a boy and a girl, Luka and Irina, both in their late teens or early twenties. They were heading for Kstovo and the protest. As we pulled away, back on to the highway, I asked them what exactly the protest was about – what exactly they were protesting *against*.

'Capitalism,' said Irina. There was no defiance in her voice – no fear of ridicule. She was simply sure of the rightness of what she was doing.

'So it's a bad thing?'

She turned and considered me sharply. 'Do you mean capitalism or to protest against it?'

'Isn't capitalism freedom?' I said.

'To do bad, yes,' she said.

'And good.'

She huffed. 'You sound like Putin.'

'Is that bad?'

Luka leaned forward. He was a thin boy, pale-faced, and had a blankness in his look I found disquieting. 'Putin is a fascist,' he said. 'He stole all the oil and now it costs the people to use it.'

I looked in the mirror, and for a second I saw myself lying still by the roadside, my head surrounded by a slowly widening halo of blood.

We drove for a while, not speaking.

'What's that sound?' said Luka, perhaps ten – maybe fifteen – minutes later.

I listened. All I could hear was the rattling of the car. I glanced at Irina. Her eyes were closed. 'It's just the car,' I said.

Luka shrugged. We drove on.

With Nizhny Novgorod creeping east and Kstovo creeping west, soon, thanks to the gradual, insidious spread of factories and the housing projects necessary to house those factories' employees, the latter will cease, as an entity, to exist, becoming just a district of the former. It seemed to me, as we drove along, an example of the way things seemed to be going all over the world – the drive to turn the planet into nothing but an oasis of steel, glass and concrete. I mentioned this to Irina. She nodded. The trees, she said calmly, as if she were describing their colour or the fact of the loss of their leaves in the winter, were dying.

I glanced in the mirror. Behind me, Luka leaned forward. Everyone knew, he said, they were – the trees – first poisoned with chemicals and then, when they were weak, cut down to 'save' others from catching the same sickness.

'That's terrible,' I said. He sat back, staring hard at my reflection, as if something in his mind – an important question – were, as yet, undecided. Yes, he said, of course it was terrible. He scowled. I looked away. Irina sighed. Her eyes were red.

'What's wrong?' I said.

Nothing, she said. She was just tired. Then, quite out of the blue, she told me her father was sick – as if this explained something and everything. It was cancer, she said.

'Is he having treatment?'

She shrugged. Treatment, she said, was very expensive, and the only one who could help – their mother – was dead.

'You have brothers and sisters?'

'One brother,' she said.

'Where's he now?'

She glanced over her shoulder. Her brother, she said, in a voice shot through with a seam of great tenderness, was asleep in the back of my car.

From the top of the Ferris wheel in Kstovo's Freedom Park you can see, on a clear day, pretty much the whole sprawling, ramshackle city and much of what surrounds it. You can see the factories with their chimneys belching out smoke so heavy with toxins that it barely seems able to rise through the air, and you can see (the drift of that smoke allowing) the scars on the land, pale like the flesh of a newly shaved cat, where once there were forests but where now there is nothing but oil rigs and the wastefulness and blight that are always their companions.

And you can see, of course, the progress of the road as it winds ever north-eastwards, further into Siberia and the land that even now and even for Russians is a place of mystery that holds, still, all the romance and terror of the furthest frontier. The 'Sleeping Land', they call it, implying with that name a life and independence that will surely cause it, one day, to awaken like some kind of giant – a great voracious beast measured against which all of man's deeds will come to seem as nothing. Rich with resources as yet barely touched, the majority of this vast land, which stretches all the way from the Baltic Sea in the west to the Pacific Ocean in the east, is so hard of climate and to man so inhospitable that only those who were given no choice but to do so made their homes there – the unwanted, the dangerous, the outspoken, the criminal – those whose fate was to be cast out and forgotten and the fact of their lives expunged from the history of their nation.

All this and more you can see on a clear day from the old Ferris wheel.

'So what will you do?'

But the ride on the rusting wheel lasts only so long, and soon the bar is lifted and you step out, legs unsteady, and drift back down into the early evening crowd.

Irina shrugged. Beside her, her brother was staring up at the sky as if he saw something there that required his attention.

'Will you go home?' I said. 'After the protest.'

Yes, she said, they would go home. They would care for their father and watch him die.

I said that surely there must be some help available – some kind of state-funded treatment. She said maybe, but for that you had to wait. Sometimes for years. And besides, the cause of their father's sickness wasn't recognized by the State Funding Board, because everyone knew that the cause was asbestos – breathing it in over so many years – but for the government to recognize this would mean banning its use, and banning its use – as everyone else had done – would mean tearing down much of the housing that surrounds Moscow and St Petersburg and so many other towns and cities. People, she said, would have nowhere to live – and having nowhere to live is worse than living in a place that in the end might kill you, isn't it?

'Is it?' I said.

'You have a house,' she said. 'It is easy for you.'

There was really no answer to that except to confirm it. Yes, I said, it was easy for me, and when, an hour later, I stood at the gates of the fairground and watched the two of them make their way through the crowds and out towards the ravaged land beyond the city, I couldn't help thinking how fortunate I had been to be born where I was and so be able to step into and observe the lives of others – and to be able to do so always only for as long as I could stand it and always, of course, with the luxury to hand of the means of escape.

Travel it in the autumn and the Vladimirka Road will take you through a vast and changing landscape that seems all around you to be wrestling to the death late summer's retreat, while the lowering sky seems to roll and twist like the darkest of seas, all the time angry with the threat of the north.

And all the time the road rises unconcerned, then falls with the valleys, carrying its cargo of ghosts and broken souls.

Souls like that of Nadezhda, who sold herself for drink to a chemist from Warsaw – a man who, once done with her, sold her again to the boys from the Ministry, who tried her on a Tuesday and whose fate, by Friday, was exile to Siberia and the bitter endless cold that would kill her on what would have been her twenty-third birthday; souls like Iyurii, who grew his own potatoes in the rough, stony earth and distilled his own vodka from which he made not a single rouble's profit (not a bottle left the house and not a drop was consumed anywhere but in his kitchen), but for which 'profiteering' he was sent, as a consequence, to the camp in distant Tomsk on the say-so of a young man whom he'd raised from a baby as his son.

These souls and so many others – thousands and millions, many of whom will be for ever now known only unto God – will crowd you and bustle you if you let them, each one pregnant with the saddest, most wretched of tales, each one of them heavy with longing and regret heavy enough to drive a living man earthwards, there to sit with his head in his hands and weep.

Ask anyone about Cheboksary and they'll tell you a story about beer. As a consequence, if you didn't know otherwise, you'd think, from what people say (many of whom have never, of course, been there), that the streets there are awash with crowds of staggering drunks, and that the Volga, on the southern bank of which the city stands, runs not with water but with light, red or semi-dark Chuvashia beer.

I give you a Cheboksary joke:

A man goes into a bar and orders a Yantar – a strong local beer – and a lemonade chaser. He comes back the following day, complaining of a terrible hangover. This time he orders a Yantar, but with a Coke chaser. The next day he returns with an even worse headache. 'What'll you have?' says the barman. 'A Yantar,' says the man, 'but forget about the chaser – it seems to be giving me a hangover!'

It was noon, and I was standing in the lobby of Cheboksary's famous Museum of Beer in the company of Abram, a Russian Jew from Archangel, and one of its part-time curators.

'It's a funny joke, yes?' he said.

Yes, I said, it was funny, all right, and I gave it my best shot at laughing. I'm not sure he was satisfied – but, anyway, we walked on, continuing the tour.

'So you like Russian beer?' he said.

We were standing now in front of a glass case containing some kind of wooden contraption that did something to
hops or barley – pressed them (I think) or anyway performed
a function that was vital to the production of beer a hundred
or (maybe, I can't now remember) six hundred years ago.

I told him how, in a bar in Nizhny, when I'd asked for
Russian beer, I'd been given a Guinness.

'Did you drink it?' said Abram.

Of course, I said. I was thirsty.

Abram shook his head. It was clear from the pinched look
of distaste on his sallow face that in his view I was obviously not only unappreciative of his native land's humour,
but so feeble into the bargain that I might just as well have
been a girl. I asked him if he thought I should have sent it
back.

'Of course!' he said.

'And should I maybe have called for the manager and
asked that the waitress be disciplined?'

'The manager? Yes!' The thought of such decisiveness
pleased Abram greatly: I could see my stock rising. I may
not have done the right thing, but at least I knew what the
right thing was.

'So what now?' I said ten minutes later as we neared the
end of the tour.

'Now?' said Abram. 'Now we drink!'

Of course. I should have known.

We drank for nearly two hours, Abram and I, sampling
sixty-seven different beers. Although most were Russian,
there were others from Georgia and the Ukraine and still
more from the smaller republics. Although I'd like to report
that each beer carried with it characteristics of the place and
people from which it had sprung, I cannot. Perhaps, to start

with, there'd been differences in taste, colour and texture (and to an expert like Abram each of these did seem to speak of their origins); after a while, though, all distinctions had blurred and one had come to seem scarcely different from the next, until by the end – by the time I was sinking the sixty-seventh sample (what it was and where it had come from I no longer have any idea) – all I could think of was lying down and maybe sleeping, or at any rate trying to stop the world swirling in such a wild and nauseating way.

It was late afternoon when I woke. I was lying on an old sofa in one of the museum's back rooms. I tried to sit up but a voice behind my eyes forbade it. Instead, I lay back down and let my eyes close again.

The second time I woke, Abram was standing over me, his face spread wide in a smile. 'How are you?' he said. I turned my head left and right. Something was banging inside my head. Despite this, I tried again to sit up, and this time I made it. I stood, unsteady. I had to get some air. I said goodbye to Abram and stumbled out of what I assumed was the museum's back door.

With Abram and the museum behind me, I set out straight, heading for where I was pretty sure I'd find what my guidebook refers to as the city of Cheboksary's second great wonder – a place of serenity where even the most careworn would find peace.

If, being wooden, the museum is in large part the colour of beer, then the Artificial Bay in the centre of the city is, being water, the colour, of course, of the sky. At that time of the year, when the snows of the north are creeping ever south and the bitter Arctic winds, so bracing to the white wolves that still creep down at night to drink from the slow-flowing Volga, can scour your face and scrub it clean with one stroke, the Bay is, for the most part, deserted, the cafes – so busy in the summer months – closed and boarded up. Where, in summer and spring and on into the autumn, people would stroll arm in arm as if they were in Paris along the paths that border the Bay's still waters, and children would sail boats with their fathers and complain that the new term at school was advancing too fast, now, in winter, only the geese – shortly, themselves, to leave on the long trip to Canada – seemed to appreciate not only the great effort made to reclaim the land only recently derelict, but also the further effort made to then dig a big hole in it and fill it up with water.

I paused at the monument to Vasily Chapayev, trying – and, of course, failing – to make any sense of the Cyrillic inscription. Who he was I didn't then know; how extraordinary was his story I would only later discover.

I stopped an elderly woman and tried to describe the lake with my hands. She scowled at me, uncomprehending. I stabbed at the freezing-cold air, my patience with myself for barely speaking a word of the language close to exhausted.

At last the old woman nodded, raised her hand and pointed, and that was good enough. I walked on, passing a grand theatre set back on a rise from the street and a bus station that was eerily silent. I turned; the old woman was still watching me as if she thought I was sure to do something extraordinary. Not wishing to disappoint her, I stopped and flapped my arms like a bird; not a thing about her changed. She could have been made of stone.

At first – as I was expecting to see it – I thought the river was the Bay. It was only when a tanker filled with oil edged into view that I knew it was not. I sat down on a bench and watched the tanker moving slowly through the water that seemed as thick and slow as the ship's cargo. The craft made no sound as she drew closer, then passed by, and when she had gone there was nothing left behind to prove that she had ever been there.

It was too cold to sit, and so I stood. I walked on, turning over in my mind as I did so what Abram had said about his family.

The Zaslavsky family had lived for generations in the city of Kirovsk, thirty miles east of St Petersburg, until, following the assassination of Alexander II on 13 March 1881 (there was a widely held belief that the Jews had been responsible), they had, with a thousand other families, been expelled and sent west into a newly created Jews-only area known as the Pale of Settlement. Here, on the borders with Germany and Austria–Hungary, they lived in conditions so poor that the child mortality rate reached fifty per cent and a man's life expectancy was no more than forty. It was only with the German invasion from the east of 1914 and the wholesale fleeing of the Pale Jews into the Russian interior that the Settlement ceased to exist; then, with the Revolution of 1917 and the rise of the Bolsheviks and Lenin's 'spirited defence' of Jewish equality (which was, of course, a typical sham, as he had no intention – despite the nominal formation of a Jewish section of the Russian Communist Party – of doing anything other than destroying their 'Jewishness' and subsuming them into the greater proletariat), the plight of the newly returned Jews improved. As a consequence of the Bolsheviks' supposed policy of inclusion, many Jews who had hitherto seen themselves quite rightly as an oppressed minority joined the army in defence of the government that they saw now as guarantors of their liberty against the forces of reaction still loyal to the tsar. These were young men like Abram's great-grandfather, who was wounded in September of 1919 at Lbishchensk, in the same action that took the life of Vasily Ivanovitch Chapayev,[1] whose daring escape across the river made him one of the most celebrated officers in the history of the Red Army.

Later, with the deep Russian night falling dense and heavy, I stood on the bank of the broad Volga River, wrapped up against the cold in my second-hand coat. In the distance, across the water, lay the Vladimirka Road running north and east, and a railway line beside it, the latter crossing the river a little to the north via a bridge now nearly 150 years old. The sky in the distance was orange and gold. I sat for half an hour, determined, despite the cold, to wait – as long ago I'd promised Max I would – until the next train to cross the bridge came along.

Half an hour.

Forty minutes.

My nose was frozen; I could barely feel my hands in my pockets.

Just then a shape – a wolf, I was sure of it – appeared on the far bank. I sat forward, squinting in the gloom, my eyes straining hard in the dusk.

Nothing.

Just the shadow of a shadow.

I held my breath against the cold and went back to studying the bridge.

---

1 So famous did he become that not only was the nearby town of Lbishchensk renamed Chapayev in his honour, but also several films have been made of his life. There is even a popular board game based on his wartime exploits.

On 3 January 1870, on the same day that, far away on America's East Coast, construction began on John Augustus Roebling's hugely anticipated and revolutionary Brooklyn Bridge, work also commenced on another project, this one altogether more modest – another bridge, certainly, but this one set to span not New York's East River but the Volga, so linking by railway the Chuvash Republic south of the river with the Mari-El Republic to the north and, beyond that, Siberia, with its endless white landscapes that, though so bitter in the winter and scarcely better in the short months of summer, have always attracted the most daring or foolhardy of men.

That a French building company had been charged with such a construction was lamented by many as being yet further evidence of the still-backward nature of the Russian working man, while some, of course – those men who sought to prosper from such an arrangement – thought otherwise.

One such man was Elyashiv Levitan, a Lithuanian Jew and teacher of French and German – a man for whom no distance was too far to travel if it meant the promise of work and food enough for his wife and two sons. Within a week of arriving, he'd found work as the company's translator, work he would pursue until the bridge was completed, when, gathering what few possessions they owned, he headed west with his family to Moscow.

On their arrival in the capital, the two boys – Avel and his younger brother Isaak – enrolled in the Moscow School of Painting, Sculpture and Architecture, a school open to Jews and sympathetic to the plight of the newly arrived poor.

During the autumn of 1875, Elyashiv's wife succumbed to the typhus that had claimed so many that year; then, two years later, with the death, also, of their father, the two boys were alone. They had nothing but their talent for painting

– that of the younger being greater always than that of the older – and nothing before them but poverty. They were Jews who had wandered far from their home, and, in so doing, the protection of a clan had been forfeit.

And then, at nine-thirty on the morning of 20 April 1879, in a faraway act that would, among many other things, change in time the course of Russian painting, Alexander Soloviev, a student and a Jew, stood on a Moscow street before His Highness the Emperor and Autocrat of All the Russias brandishing a loaded revolver. It is said that the two men – emperor and subject – considered each other with great interest – and then Soloviev raised his gun. The emperor closed his eyes. 'Ah, the Jews,' he said. He'd always feared them – feared they'd come for him, as once and long ago they'd come for Christ – and now, on the street in broad daylight on a fine spring morning, here they were.

But Soloviev hesitated and the moment was lost. With the emperor having fled, his would-be assassin was arrested, tried and executed. All of which would have meant little to the Levitan boys had Soloviev not been a Jew. But he was, and so were they, and they – like so many others of their kind – were suddenly guilty by dint of shared heritage and no longer welcome in the land that had so avariciously swallowed up their own. Contracts were ended and terms of employment gratuitously abandoned; restaurants and galleries and parks were closed to Jews, then cities made suddenly out of bounds. Many fled to the country – the Levitan boys among them – while many of those who chose to stay were arrested by the once-liberal tsar's vicious secret police and sent into exile along the Vladimirka Road. Thousands perished during the journey to Siberia, many drowning in the freezing waters of the Volga. Of those who survived, only to arrive in such a bleak and barren land, almost none lived long enough to return. Whole families died together, cast out into the ice-bound wilderness in which only the wolf was equipped to survive. Bodies froze where they lay and were seldom discovered; last words were uttered that not a living soul would ever hear.

'Is that it – Siberia?'

I squinted out across the river in the fast-fading light. The man beside me – a travelled man, a banker, he said, now retired and walking easefully along the towpath with his dogs, Pavel and Sergei – squinted too. 'Yes,' he said, 'that's it. Is it what you expected?'

'I don't know,' I said.

'You were expecting perhaps something different? For the land to suddenly look different?'

I said yes, I supposed I was.

'Close your eyes.'

'What?'

'Go on.'

I closed my eyes.

'Can't you feel it?' he said.

'Feel what?'

'The ice on the wind. Can't you feel how it bites like the sharp teeth of wolves?'

I nodded.

That, the old man said, was the beginning of Siberia. The beginning of the edge of the end of the world.

I opened my eyes. The old man was staring out, his eyes fixed hard on the furthest distance. I followed his gaze. The land beyond the Volga's far bank was vast, endless – the graveyard of millions, the birthplace of the long Arctic winter. He turned his eyes up towards the heavens.

'Do you see that star?' he said.

Again I followed his gaze. One star in the night sky seemed brighter than the others. 'What is it?' I said.

'It's their star,'[1] he said. 'The Tretyakovs. Pavel and Sergei.' At the sound of their names, the two dogs at the old man's feet sat up.

I had to admit I had no idea who they were.

The old man lowered his eyes. His smile had gone. He seemed suddenly troubled. 'I thought you said you were here because of Levitan. The Vladimirka Road, you said.' He shook his head. I was clearly, to him, suddenly an ignorant fool. 'If you're interested in Levitan,' he said, 'how can you not know of the brothers? Pavel especially. Don't you know that without him there would have *been* no Levitan, no *Vladimirka Road*? That without *him*, you wouldn't be here now, and I would be standing here talking to myself like a fool?'

I shook my head. If I needed to know, I said, would he tell me?

He shrugged. He sighed. But in the end he lifted his eyes and fixed them on mine. He would tell me, he said, on one condition.

'Which is?' I said.

That I would mention the boys and their star in my book. I said OK, of course. 'That,' he said, 'and one other thing.'

'Of course,' I said. 'Anything.'

He looked down at his dogs. They were sitting neatly, attentive. Would I, he said, mention them also? Would I say how he'd found them as puppies in a box, thrown out into the cold as if they were nothing?

1   The planet 3925 Tretyakov was discovered in 1977 by the Soviet astronomer Lyudmila Zhuravlyova. Ms Zhuravlyova is currently ranked forty-first on Harvard University's list of Minor Planet Discoverers.

'What are their names?' I said, though, of course, I could guess.

'It's *their* star too,' said the old man, casting his eyes up and out into the heavens. 'So will you do it?' he said after a while.

Yes, I said, I would, of course.

And now I have.

On 1 September 1860, close to the centre of Moscow, a large stone house – newly designated a school – opened its doors to its pupils for the very first time. An endeavour substantial enough to accommodate nearly 200 students, the Arnoldo Tretyakov School for Deaf Mutes was the brainchild of Pavel Tretyakov, a wealthy Moscow businessman and philanthropist, and his brother Sergei. Genuinely concerned for the welfare of the city's deprived and marginalized citizens, the brothers' Moscow school provided a meeting place not only for those who could neither hear nor see, but those whose exclusion from society had other, more overtly political causes. Among those invited to attend (and so tacitly invited to break his bonds of exclusion) was a young man reports of whose talents as an artist had – despite his distance from the city – found their way to the ears of the school's benefactors. He was, people said, a genius to be sure – a young man who, if given his chance, would place Russian landscape front and centre in the world of modern art, and in so doing inspire a revival of what had once been a source of great national pride. And so return the young man did, and such was his talent for depicting in paint on canvas the rural, timeless Russia that all felt they knew but few had ever really seen that he was soon in great demand in the very society that had once so brutally dismissed him from its presence. To entertain him at their soirées was delicious and dangerous – quite as wicked a thing as paying to observe an errant serf's execution or taking a working man as a lover. They vied with each other to sit beside him, revelling in the kudos that such a placement would bring. They squinted at his pictures, bathing in their calm mellow loveliness, choosing not to see (or perhaps being unable to see) the shadow of sorrow in which they'd been cast and ignoring (or simply choosing to not see) the sense of elegy within them for what had been lost and could never be regained. This loss, for Isaak Levitan, was nothing less than the loss of communion with nature, with the waters and the land and the vast, arching skies – an estrangement from the very soul of Russia herself. What others chose to see as nature abundant was for him a statement of absence, a record of a theft, a portrait of abandonment. *Why no people?* people say of his pictures. *They are gone*, he says. They were here – *there* (they left an hour, a month, a year ago) – but now they're gone. They trod the track that in time became a road; they built the church then abandoned it to God. They whisper their secrets from just beyond the frame; they stand on either side of you and behind you in the gallery. *How bleak*, they say, *how bleak, how bleak*. Once, by God's grace, they were with us; now all that's left of them are shadows, now all that's left of them are ghosts and their bones – bleached white – lying brittle and untended beneath the rich but poisoned soil.

* * *

The brothers opened the Tretyakov Gallery on 15 August 1893, in the heart of Moscow's Zamoskvareche[1] district. Beside their protégé Levitan, the gallery offered a home to the work of Ilya Repin and Valentin Serov, of Ivan Shishkin, of Arkhip Kuinzhi and Vasily Surikov and many more. Indeed, many of what would become icons of Russian landscape painting would first hang there, before, in time, touring the world, a portable diorama, both intimate and panoramic, expressing the very essence of what it is to be Russian.

Pictures like Repin's *Barge-Haulers on the Volga*, in which the painter acknowledges both the suffering – the *strada* – of the working man and the debt owed to him by the privileged classes, or Shishkin's *Midday*, in which man is both dwarfed and caressed by the land and the sky, so returning to his lost place in nature, or Arkhip Kuinzhi's *Moonlight on the Dnieper*, in which the moon and the river whisper like lovers in the dark Russian night, their voices heard only on a gentle midnight breeze.

And pictures like Levitan's *Vladimirka Road*, a seam of conscience seared across the land, a portrait of remembrance of lives so long gone now, a reminder, by their absence, of the men who have crossed it alone or with their armies, or travelled north and a little eastwards in their hundreds of thousands towards graves as yet undug, or, singly, southwards – those whom fate or good fortune had spared, only to burden them with the dead weight of memory.

The Vladimirka Road, the spine of Russian history.

---

1 Meaning literally 'Across the Moskva River', the Zamoskvareche district was once a bulwark against the Tartar invaders, then the city's industrial heart. Today, it is a series of gentle streets filled with brightly coloured houses and gold-domed churches.

To know Russia, said the painter, *you must first know this road.*

With the old man and his dogs gone and the Volga reflecting the slow-fading stars, I stooped to gather a handful of earth. I thought as I did (as I weighed the cold dirt in my hand) of the dead Levitan and how heavy must have been his wooden coffin. Had the mourners struggled, I wondered, as they'd borne it aloft before lowering it into the earth? Had they cursed him for his selfishness or celebrated the depth of his love for his homeland? And when all was quiet, when all the attendants had gone, had he risen – a ghost – and wandered off to join those the absence of whose voices he'd so strived to record?

I fed the earth into my pocket and stood up. Tomorrow I'd cross the river, heading for Kazan. Tomorrow, sleep and spirits allowing, I would walk my way into Siberia.

A restless night; an early waking; stars through a grimy window, seen fading in the day's first light. I lay on my back, warm beneath a mountain of blankets, listening for the day's first sounds. The sky was as pale as it ever was these days, a bloodless harbinger of the snowfall to come. I closed my eyes; the chatter of birds. I tried to sleep, but the last of sleep had gone.

I sat up. The last of my blankets was my borrowed coat; I reached into the left inside pocket and withdrew the page I'd taken from Nikolai Ilyanovitch's *Moscow Times*. I opened it out (the creases were fraying now, so often had they been folded and unfolded), lay back, held it to the light and read.

A native of Dushanbe, capital of the former Soviet Republic of Tajikistan (most southerly of the fifteen that had once constituted that nation), Dineo Banzan[1] was – as a Buddhist in a country that was and remains ninety-five per cent Islamic – a minority of the minority, and so, consequently, from the moment of her birth, vulnerable to the capricious intentions not only of the local majority but also those decrees emanating from the faraway powers in

1 The literal meaning of which is, appropriately enough, 'Mountain of Invisible Strength'.

Moscow. Denied a regular education, all that she learned, she says, came from her parents, whose teachings had, by necessity, to be learned in secret. They spoke of bondage and liberation – of how a starving man will sit before a banquet until he understands that food is what he needs, and how a rose is precious not in spite of its short life but because of it. She learned to see things as they were – not as she wished or believed them to be. She learned to accept that hers was a journey with neither end nor beginning – that *being* was enough, that her chains were of her own making and could be broken only with the giving up of desire.

But then, seeking more wheat with which to feed (and so placate) a hungry, restless people, the boys from the Kremlin descended on Tajikistan, took all that people had cultivated and enslaved and exiled all those whom the great and fearless generalissimo feared would one day seek vengeance. Men and women, Muslim, Jew, Buddhist and Christian: all were taken and with them went the means of the crops' re-emergence with the cycle of the seasons – a loss that would lead to the poverty and starvation of generations to come.

And Dineo? What of her?

For her, all there was was a life of slavery to be passed minute by minute and year by year in the bitter, freezing hell of the Gulag, with nothing but the strength of her youth and the teachings of her parents to sustain her.

But sustain her they did, and somehow she survived, and now she stares out from a page removed carefully from the *Moscow Times* – a much younger woman than she is today, even then, in her youth, neither angry nor pitiful. All she wants, she says (desire, she says, has not been totally vanquished), is acceptance that what was done was wrong

– that no one man should have the power of life and death over another, nor that the faith of one must ever be sustained against the aggressive disapproval of another.

I folded the paper and slipped it back into the pocket of my coat. Outside, the sounds of the day were rising – car horns, the muffled chatter of passers-by, the black dot of an aeroplane moving slowly in an arc across the sky.

I pushed back the covers, swung my legs out and set my feet on the cold ground. I thought once again of Max, and how I wished he could have read Dineo Banzan's story, and I was just feeling the slow familiar creep of sadness drawing over me when I remembered what he'd once told me. There is, he had said, no end to existence and no beginning, and he'd said that we float – all of us – on an ocean of merely being. Sitting on the floor of his empty, airy room, he'd told me then about the Buddha's last moments of earthly existence. Apparently, as his death approached, the Buddha had said the following to those gathered around him:

Be a light unto yourself; betake yourself to no external refuge. Hold fast to the truth. Look not for refuge to anyone but yourself.

A light unto yourself.

This, I thought again, was Max. His joy and faith had always seemed as if they came from within, and that they needed nothing else to survive and be sustained. Perhaps, I thought, the same was true of Dineo Banzan. Perhaps, for her – as, perhaps, for all of us – all she'd ever needed was already inside her, the life, the spirit, the reason for it all – perhaps they are all already there, both as permanent and fleeting as the joy to be found in the scent of a single summer's rose.

F ounded by the Tartars, the Siberian city of Kazan was that people's major stronghold in eastern Asia until the city was razed and the population murdered or dispersed by Ivan the Terrible. Only with the advent of Catherine the Great and her general emancipation of Muslims did the Tartars return.

I left the car near the entrance to the main municipal car park and posted the keys back to Pavel at his mobile home in Kovrov. Then, with my pack once again on my back, I made my way into the centre of the city.

Ask anyone who's studied Russian literature and they'll tell you that Gavril Romanovich Derzhavin was – after Pushkin – the nation's second-best poet. Whether or not this is true, he was certainly without peer when it came to social climbing. A native of Kazan, he deserted the city at the first opportunity and fled to St Petersburg, where he joined the army as a private. By the time of his death in 1816, he'd not only served a term as Minister of Justice but had – even more eminently – spent several years as Principal Private Secretary to Her Imperial Highness, Catherine the Great, Empress and Autocrat of All the Russias.

I stopped on Pushkin Street (there is no Derzhavin Street – a slight to the hometown boy if ever there was one) in order to ask directions for Kazan's famously beautiful Kremlin. The woman, all bundled up against the cold, shook her head and hurried on.

I discovered it in the end quite by chance – by turning a corner and simply finding it before me, a magnificent collection of white-painted buildings made not of brick but of the supple local sandstone. The centre of Kazan (which itself is the centre of the Republic of Tartarstan), it was built by command of Ivan the Terrible, a citadel so formidable that not once in all the centuries of sectarian bloodshed have the walls been breached – indeed, not once, or so it is claimed, has the blood of Muhammad's defenders stained the snow-white ramparts or the honour of his followers been compromised by defeat. On the contrary. So complete has been Allah's victory here that on 24 June 2005 the Qol-Särif Mosque – by some way the biggest in the whole of Europe – was opened in a ceremony attended by nearly 30,000 people, among them Mintimer Shaemiev, Tartarstan President.

I approached a couple of young men who were sitting on a low wall in the shadow of the Kremlin and asked them where they came from – if they were from around here and if by any chance they were Tartars. Sullen, saying nothing, the nearest one just looked to his friend. His friend, who was wearing a purple and green Portugal football shirt, turned down the corners of his mouth and shrugged.

I pointed to the Russian word for *Tartar* in my guidebook. Still nothing.

'You think they can read?' said a voice from behind me.

Feliks Ashavin was a half-Russian, half-Polish student of rocket engineering at the Kazan State Technical University on Karl Marx Street. He'd been following me, he said, for maybe an hour.

'Following me?' I said. 'Why?'

He said something harsh-sounding to the boy and his friend; as they turned sullen-faced and were clearly offended, I thought for certain there'd be a fight – and that it would be me who would, of course, suffer the most. Having never hit another person in my life, I braced myself for action.

But the moment passed. Perhaps seeing that I was either a master of some ancient martial art or liable to cry at any moment, the young men pushed themselves up and sloped off across the square in the general direction of the city's famous leaning tower.[1]

'Why?' said Feliks. 'Because I have to practise for the day I am captured.'

'Captured? By whom?'

'People who want to know what I know. What I *will* know.'

I asked him what it was he'd know that people would want to know so badly that they'd go to all the trouble of capturing him.

'Rockets,' he said. 'I will know all there is to know about them.'

'And if I captured you? Would you tell me everything you know?'

He shook his head as if the idea was quite genuinely absurd. To counter such a snub, I told him I'd once met Neil Armstrong.

'Neil who?'

1 The famously leaning Söyembikä Tower is believed by many to be the only remaining example of genuine Tartar Kazan; others say it was built by Ivan the Terrible in order to have a platform from which to witness the Tartars' mass execution. In other words, no one really knows who built it and no one ever will. That it leans, though, and will one day topple over is beyond dispute.

'The first man on the moon. At a golf club. In Walton-on-the-Hill.'

He shrugged. The moon, he said, was history. *He* was heading for Mars.

'He left his sunglasses on the table,' I said. 'I picked them up – didn't even *try* to give them back.'

Mars, he said, needed special boosters – and plenty of fuel. Did I, he said, have any money?

'What for?'

He said he wanted to make a bid for Gagarin's flight socks. They were two hundred dollars on eBay.

I glanced over Feliks's shoulder. The two young men he'd so casually dismissed were still hanging around, shooting mean glances in our direction.

'You want a drink?' I said.

'What about the two hundred dollars?'

'Let's get a drink first, eh?'

Feliks shrugged. He knew a place, he said, where a student could get served.

'OK,' I said.

It was called, he said, Gagarin's.

'Like the astronaut.'

He didn't move – didn't look in that moment as if he'd *ever* move.

'So will we need special boosters to get there?'

He scowled.

'It was just a joke,' I said.

By now, he said, it was probably three hundred dollars.

'Never mind,' I said. 'They're only socks.'

He turned and looked at me and shook his head as if *I* was the one that was just a little bit strange.

*   *   *

The city of Kazan was the route to the Orient, a place to buy spices from Persia and trade hardy steppe sheep for fine Indian silks. It was the beginning of the ragged end of Christendom and the first blue shadows of Islam half-blended together; a changing of the guard from one God to the next. For so long the scene of Soviet persecution (the city's dozen or so mosques having been closed down and turned into flats or, in one notably barbaric case, a slaughterhouse), it was only in the last twenty years – since that curse's lifting – that Muhammad's faithful followers could raise their voices in prayer without fear of the consequences.

From far off beside the city's vast and serene lake, the amplified call of the White Mosque's current imam spilled out through the cold, crisp air, reminding all the faithful of their duty of prayer.

Feliks pushed on a red door. The door was in a side street, the street shabby and unremarkable.

'Where are we?' I said. I thought of eBay and Gagarin's flight socks and wondered if what I was doing was altogether wise. In my mind's eye, just for a second, I saw my wife standing dumb in the hall of our home, the *Daily Mail* with its headline – 'Writer Found Murdered in Red Rocket City' – in her hand and the sound of Kiss FM on the radio in the kitchen.

Inside, the place was not what I'd expected. I'd expected some kind of student hovel; what I found was a comfortable and fairly smart bar: tables and chairs, the latter red-upholstered, a long dark bar with beer taps and glasses overhead. In the corner, from a jukebox, came the voice of Bruce Springsteen.

With Feliks standing beside me, I ordered two beers. The barman glanced at me, then at Feliks. He said something

I, of course, didn't understand. Feliks responded with a shrug. 'Come on,' he said, picking up the beers. I smiled at the barman as we turned away. He didn't smile back.

'What's the matter with him?' I said.

We were seated at a table in the corner, the man behind the bar still glaring in our direction. Feliks downed a clear half of his beer and set the glass down on the table. The man at the bar, he said, was his father.

'Your father?'

The bar, he said, was his father's bar. His and his brother's – Feliks's uncle. They'd bought it cheap from a man who'd been arrested for smuggling children across the border from Iran. It was the only place in the city, he said, where fucking Muslims weren't allowed. In fact, he said, if one came in now and ordered a beer he wouldn't stand a chance. His old man, he said, would fucking kill him – cut him up with the carving knife he kept under the bar and then feed him to the dogs out the back.

I glanced around. Certainly, if you had a darker face, you'd have felt out of place.

'Hey,' said Feliks. 'Do you want to know something funny?'

Cut him up with a carving knife.

He leaned forward across the table. 'See him?' he said, nodding towards a table in the far corner. I half-turned. An old man with a white beard was sitting hunched over the table, playing dominoes.

Feliks leaned closer, dropped his voice. The old man, he whispered, had been in charge of a camp up the road.

I glanced over at the old man, then back. 'How do you know?' I said.

Feliks frowned, as if surprised by such a foolish question. 'Everybody knows.'

'Would he speak to me?'

Feliks shrugged.

'Can we try?'

Feliks drank the rest of his beer. 'Come on, then,' he said. He stood and crossed the room. I took a gulp of mine and followed.

Standing perhaps two feet away from the old man's shoulder, Feliks said something. The old man with the dominoes just went on playing.

'Excuse me,' I said.

The old man sniffed.

'He doesn't speak English.'

The fingers of a chubby, liver-spotted hand lifted a domino, turned it around, then set it back down.

'What about Russian?'

'Only if he wants to,' said Feliks. 'And he doesn't want to.'

'Can you just ask him which camp?'

Feliks hesitated. Then, as he said the words, I studied the old man's face. Not a flicker, not a twitch, not a single sign that he was even aware of our presence.

'Come on,' said Feliks. A hand found my elbow. 'We should go.'

I looked at Feliks. Something was different – a change in the tone of his voice. I asked him if there was something the matter. He shrugged, looked away. I looked back at the old man playing dominoes. The old man turned a domino over, then another, the faintest trace of a smile (I was certain) creeping over his clean-shaven face.

From the top-floor windows of the Shalyapin Palace Hotel, much of the city of Kazan is laid bare. The lake in which – people will tell you – the Tartars fleeing Ivan the Terrible hid their gold; the old town, once made of wood but demolished by the Soviets in the name of progress; the first few miles of the continent's wild east: all this and the Kremlin with its slowly crumbling tower is visible for three hundred dollars a night at the Shalyapin Palace Hotel.

I stood on the balcony, looking out into the night. The highway heading north was a red, twinkling necklace of slow-moving tail lights; to the west of the city was the airport. Every now and then a plane would lift off, rising slowly, then climbing into the thick, freezing air. It would turn, arching away, heading for Moscow or St Petersburg or Vladimir or Kursk, while below it lay the road, unheeded in the darkness, snaking here and there, silent and knowing, its secrets kept as close as a convict's rusting chains.

The fact that Bugulma Air Enterprises had once been the least reliable division of the famously unreliable pan-Soviet airline Aeroflot should have prepared me for what greeted me the next morning at Kazan International Airport – that, and the knowledge that the millennium that the rest of the world celebrated in the year 2000 was celebrated in Tartarstan five years later. Combined, they should have warned me to expect at least delays and quite possibly the airport's sudden and completely unexplained disappearance. Though the latter, of course, was a fantasy, the former was not, my ten a.m. flight east across the Urals to the city of Yekaterinburg, site of the murder by the Bolsheviks of the last Russian tsar and his family, scheduled now to take off a little later than planned.

'Later?' I said.

'Yes,' said the woman at the BAE counter.

'How much later?'

She shrugged.

'But it will be today?'

Her attention drifting to a young man across the concourse emptying rubbish from a bin into a small yellow cart, she nodded. Which, of course, at best meant somewhere between a possible maybe and a definite no.

I picked up my backpack and found a seat in the waiting room. I was too tired to read, but too restless to doze. I pulled out my map. The stretch of road over which I'd be flying was apparently in the process of repair – a situation, according to Kazan's tourist office, that meant it would be (for a period no one seemed willing to even guess at) impassable. All of which, in itself, would have been no great problem had it not been for the thought that had woken me in the night and had been bothering me ever since – pestering me and tugging at my coat-tail like a beggar. What, I wanted to know, would happen to the bones? Would there be someone there whose work it was to see that – though disturbed by workmen with pickaxes and bulldozers and loud, grinding mixers – the bones of all those who'd given up the struggle for life on that part of the road would be preserved and treated with some kind of care? That I'd come to think this most unlikely (who, after all, really cares for old bones?) had kept me awake and was responsible now for my sitting in the waiting room, glassy-eyed and hungover from the heavy Russian wine I'd employed to help me sleep but which had merely served to broaden and strengthen my doubts.

I settled back, squinting at the posters on the wall. They were old and curling, pale and blue-tinged, each opening a window on a world that hadn't for several decades – if ever – existed. The centre of London fashion was still Carnaby Street, and Rome still the city of Antonioni, of *Bicycle Thieves* and the long-ago fantasy of Anita Ekberg's *La Dolce Vita*.

'Sir?'

I jumped.

'Your flight is boarding. Last call.'

I picked up my bag and hurried to the gate. Last in the queue, I stepped on to the aeroplane.

'Welcome,' said a young man with pink, scrubbed-up skin. 'English?'

I nodded. Behind him, the crew were just taking their seats. The captain looked about fifteen years old and in need of a good meal.

I moved down the aisle, took my seat by the window. The flight was an hour and a half. I looked in the seat pocket. A sick bag and a half-eaten Snickers bar. A *ping* overhead; I fastened my seat belt, closed my eyes and tried not to hear all the rattles and bangs and terrible creaking that seemed to accompany the crew's every movement. For distraction, I took out my guidebook.

Nikolay Alexandrovitch Romanov, Grand Duke of Finland, King of Poland and Emperor and Autocrat of All the Russias, gave his name to a sheep, a vodka and – among, no doubt, many others – the Cafe Romanov on the island of Waiheke off the east coast of New Zealand where, long ago it seems now, Max chose to tell me he was dying. It was, he'd said – a bottle of Stoneyridge Merlot in his hand – a tumour, something to do with his lymph nodes. Later that day, when he'd lain down to rest, I'd sat with his mother, her thin, gentle hand in mind, watching her face seem to age right in front of me as she told me again how he'd always been a joker as a child. But not this time. This time was no joke. Her face, I remember, was a face already in mourning – mourning for the death yet to come, of course, but also for the final, irrevocable passing of her role as mother and protector.

'Something to drink, sir?'

I ordered a beer and thought again of the lounge of her neat house in Howick. There'd been pictures of Max everywhere – Max the actor, Max the Buddhist, Max the little boy. In a while the plane started moving and was soon gaining speed. A few seconds more and – groaning and reluctant, the overhead lockers twisting and shaking – its wheels left the ground, leaving Tartarstan behind us and rising high into the clearest of clear blue skies.

Half an hour out, the plane banked sharply, turning east, then flattened out. The seat belt sign blinked off. I looked out of the window. Despite the lateness of the season, only the peaks of the mountains were white; below them, the slopes were a dingy, scrubby brown.

According to my guidebook, the Ural Mountains – also known as the Great Stone Belt – form the natural geographical boundary between Europe and Asia. Skimming the details of geology and mining and how high the mountains are and how long, I settled again on the section I'd read several times before – the section having to do with the Dyatlov Pass Incident. As I had the night before (foolishly thinking it would help me to sleep), I settled down to read the strange and gruesome details.

In February 1959 it seems a group of ski-hikers set out for a trek in the Ural Mountains. They took with them all that was necessary for a trip lasting two to three weeks – not least a pair of guides whose knowledge of the terrain was second to none. After a week, as arranged, contact was attempted with them by radio, but unsuccessfully. The next day it was attempted again, then the next day, then the next. Still nothing. On the eleventh day, a helicopter was dispatched in an attempt to locate them, but poor weather forced the search to be abandoned. Another day passed, then another. After another two weeks, with the weather lifting, the search by helicopter was resumed. This again brought nothing.

It wasn't for another month that the bodies were discovered, semi-naked and scattered over a large area. An official investigation concluded that the cause of the deaths would for ever remain a mystery, so fuelling speculation that something more than the weather had been the cause of the disaster. One school of thought had it that the group had been attacked by some kind of mountain creature (newspapers employed artists to offer their increasingly ghoulish interpretations of what might have occurred), another – this soon gaining ground until today it's generally considered to be the unproven, indeed hidden truth – that the death of the climbers had been caused by a radiation leak from some underground military facility, an accident the authorities refused either to confirm or deny.

'May I ask you to secure your seat belt, please?'

'Are we there?' I said.

The flight attendant smiled. We would, she said, be landing in ten minutes.

'So we're in Asia now?'

She nodded. 'Asia, yes.'

I asked her if she knew about the Dyatlov Pass and what had happened there – if she thought it was radiation that had killed the hikers or some kind of bear.

She glanced down the aisle, then back. 'It's a mystery,' she said. 'Only God knows the truth.' She moved away; I looked out of the window. Down below, the city of Yekaterinburg was glittering in the light, distant but growing closer with every passing minute, first of the East, last of the fast-fading West.

*　　*　　*

At two o'clock in the morning on 17 July 1918, Emperor Nicholas II along with his wife Alexandra, their son, the Tsarevich Alexei, their four daughters, Olga, Tatiana, Maria and Anastasia, their physician, Dr Eugene Botkin, Alexandra's principal lady-in-waiting, Anna Demidova, their cook, Kharitonov, and a footman named Trupp were woken, told to dress quickly and then led with some urgency down into the basement of the Ipatiev House, the former home of a prominent merchant and banker which had, for seventy-eight days, been their prison. Captive since the February Revolution of the previous year, the Ipatiev House was to be their last prison, their having been moved regularly to avoid any attempts at rescue, from the Imperial Palace in St Petersburg to the Governor's Mansion in Tobolsk, a former capital of Siberia, and thence to Yekaterinburg and the Ipatiev House.

Believing that they were at last to be rescued, the tsar and tsarina did their best to reassure their children, the tsarina even playing a game of hide-and-seek with her son Alexei. Rescue, however, was not forthcoming, for, when the cellar doors opened, their jailer, the Communist officer Yakov Vurovsky had with him ten militiamen. The executions were swift and brutal. When the shooting stopped, those of the family who were still alive were dispatched with bayonets, Anastasia having to be prised from her dead mother's arms in order that her life too should be ended. Later, the bodies of the dead were stripped, then thrown without ceremony down a mine.

In this way did the 300-year-old imperial Romanov dynasty come to a bitter, bloody end.

I asked my guide why the house had been knocked down and a church erected in its place. It was, he said, President

Brezhnev who had ordered the destruction. I asked him why – what possibly could have been gained by such an act?

Pavel, full-time student at the Ural State Academy of Medicine and part-time church guide, was a young man, clearly, for whom the past was important as a means of preparing oneself for the future – and one quite as serious as his sombre suit was dark. 'I think,' he said, frowning as if my question were not one he'd ever previously considered and deserved his best attention, 'the President thought it was a place of too much sadness. That it is better to have a happy place. Shall we enter now?'

Rising spare and magnificent, the walls of the church were quite unreasonably white in the hard winter sun, the five golden domes, on the top of the largest of which stands a three-barred Russian Orthodox cross, glorious and gold in the sun.

'Excuse me? Yes?'

I wondered if Brezhnev had had it knocked down for fear that it might become a place of pilgrimage – a meeting place for disparate anti-Communist groups.

Pavel shook his head. 'I think,' he said, 'it was good for accidents. People stopping to look. There were people being killed. But now not so many. I think it's good that people are alive – mothers and fathers, little children.'

'And the Romanovs?' I said. 'Weren't they a mother and father? Weren't their children little ones too? Don't they deserve to be mourned?'

'Of course,' said Pavel. 'But why must there always be a *place* – somewhere where the dead are gone?'

'A place of pilgrimage, you mean?'

'Pilgrimage, yes.' He patted his chest with the palm of his right hand. 'Here is thinking,' he said. 'Here is remembering. Will you come now?'

We climbed the steps and entered the church. It was cool inside, sombre and dark, a place of tiny chapels, of shadows and gold.

'You like?' Pavel whispered.

I nodded. For an hour nothing more was said, as the arms of the church seemed to wrap themselves around us, so preventing us from speaking and forbidding us anything but unquestioning devotion.

Outside and glad to breathe the air again, I asked Pavel about Compound 19, and if the radiation that it seemed likely had killed the Dyatlov skiers had originated there.

'You know about that?' he said.

I opened my guidebook and showed him:

On 2 April 1979, at Military Compound 19 on the outskirts of Sverdlovsk (previously and subsequently known as Yekaterinburg, after Catherine, wife of Peter the Great) the secret production of anthrax was disturbed and revealed by a simple act of negligence.

Due to the direction of the prevailing wind, only a hundred people died from the resulting dust-leak. Had the wind changed direction, hundreds of thousands would almost certainly have perished.

'You knew about this and you still came?'

'Shouldn't I?'

He shrugged. Many people, he said, had stayed away.

'But it was twenty years ago. Are you saying there's still danger here?'

'I don't know. Nobody knows.'

'But you're still here.'

'I live here. This is my home.'

'Is that what the people of Chernobyl said?'

'The people of Chernobyl had no choice. The government told them to leave.'

'But they could have refused.'

Pavel shook his head. 'If a soldier with a gun tells you to leave, then you leave.'

'Even if it means taking nothing with you?'

'You must understand that every Russian wakes in the morning expecting disaster. Every Russian knows he'll be made to leave his home one day and all he has will be burned. And when he goes he will burn the land behind him too. Every Russian knows this – knows it will happen one day.'

'And what if it doesn't?'

Pavel glanced up at the great golden domes of the Church on the Blood. 'Do you think,' he said, 'if a tsar can lose everything, the rest of us are safe?'

I followed his gaze. I thought of the children, cold and scared, holding hands in a dank cellar room, and then I thought of my own child and the children of my sisters and wasn't so sorry in that moment that Boris Nikolayevich Yeltsin had, on his first day as President (and years after Brezhnev had first ordered it), finally signed off on the much-delayed destruction of the Ipatiev House and so set in motion the removal from the landscape of such a brutal house of horrors.

He was born on a train on its way to Siberia and didn't stop moving until he wasted away and died at the age of fifty-four. The son of a Red Army major, the youngest of four children, there was, from the start, only drudgery ahead of him – nothing more, it seemed, than the usual endless, inglorious fight for survival. He would live and die and soon be forgotten, just another Tartar boy from the ramshackle city of Ufa, capital of the Soviet Socialist Republic of Bashkortostan.

The young Rudolf Nureyev had no shoes for school, and little to eat save potatoes. He was small and skinny and undernourished, and – as if that weren't bad enough – he showed no interest in the people's revolution. A shameful disappointment to his father, the major, he was – all but his mother agreed – worse than useless to a family so poor. He was hopeless and pathetic; he was sullen, a halfwit, a waste of precious bread.

Yes, others said, perhaps so – but have you not seen him *dance*? When he danced, they said, all earthly bonds were severed. It was as if the young boy could truly fly.

Svetlana Rutskoi, Assistant Commercial Director of the State Opera House of Bashkortostan, said, as a young girl, she'd seen the young Nureyev from a seat in the stalls. She'd watched him dance the part of a knight in Glazunov's *Raymonda* with the Kirov in Leningrad. She'd been wearing, she remembered, a hand-me-down coat for the occasion – one that pinched beneath the arms and made her shoulders itch.

'So, despite the coat,' I said, 'did you know then that you were watching a genius?'

'A genius?' She laughed. All, she said, she could think about was that coat – not the little skinny boy with a nose like a beak.

'Then you didn't fall in love with him and dream of one day dancing as his partner . . .'

She shook her head. She was by then, she said, already in love with Tony Curtis, the American film star. 'Did you know he was here,' she said, 'Tony Curtis? In Ufa. For an exhibition of his paintings at the Opera House?'

I said no, I didn't know.

'Of course, he's in a wheelchair now.'

'Was he in his wheelchair when he was here?'

Svetlana Rutskoi nodded. She pointed to the stone ramp at one end of the shallow, graceful steps that lead to the building's main entrance. 'We call them "the Mr Curtis Steps",' she said. 'When I told him we'd had them made just for him, he cried. Right here. He stood up and took me in his arms and kissed me and cried – Tony Curtis! It made me think of my life as a girl, and that horrible coat, and sitting with my mother and my best friend Tatiana at the Opera House in Leningrad, having my special warm secret inside me, and while everyone else was wanting to be dancers, all I could do was wonder if I'd ever kiss Tony Curtis!'

'And you did. You and Marilyn Monroe.'

Svetlana smiled. She was in her sixties now, and though she was a mother (and seven times a grandmother) and rather forbidding, the girl she'd once been – the girl who'd been in love with Tony Curtis – was obviously still inside her, the possibility of life's chances still before her, still alive.

'You were in good company,' I said.

She nodded. We stood for a moment in silence. I asked her if she'd ever thought of becoming a dancer.

'Me?' She shook her head. Clearly, the idea was preposterous. 'Why not?'

Her father, she said, wouldn't have approved. And anyway, her feet had always been too big.

I looked at her feet. They were tiny.

And *anyway*, she said, she was glad. If she'd been a dancer, then the chances were she'd have been in London or New York or at the Teatro dell'Opera in Rome and not in Ufa on the day Tony Curtis came to visit.

'Maybe in the next life,' I said.

'Maybe.' She straightened up. 'So, now,' she said. 'Are you ready?'

Her arm through mine, together we climbed the Opera House steps. Did I know, she said, what Tony Curtis had called him?

'Who?'

'Nureyev. He sat in his wheelchair in one of the boxes and said: "How about this Hoofer from Ufa?" And do you know, he knew everything about him – about Leningrad and the Kirov and all his bad times as a boy. He said he even met him once – in Hollywood. He *said* they'd been lovers.'

'Did you believe him?'

Svetlana Rutskoi said maybe, though she didn't like to think about it. 'Come on,' she said. She slipped her arm back into mine.

As we paused at the doors of the Opera House, I thought of Max and how he would have loved such a story. I glanced up at the sky, half expecting in that moment to see him up there looking down, a big smile on his face as warm as the sun.

'Is something wrong?' said Svetlana.

I said I was thinking of a friend.

'He's gone, this friend?' She gripped my arm tighter as I nodded. 'Then he's with God.'

I said Max was a Buddhist and that he didn't believe in God.

Svetlana smiled. 'He gave us minds, God, so why should we not use them to challenge Him?'

I said he believed in peace. In acceptance. In kindness. Not God.

'And *you*? What do *you* believe in?'

'I believe in what I see.' If there was a God, I said, then He should show me a sign – make it clear that I was wrong.

'How could He if He doesn't exist?'

'So are you saying,' I said, 'that you know He exists *because* there's no proof of it?'

'Yes.'

'But that's ridiculous!'

Svetlana shook her head. That was faith, she said.

I sighed. I felt tired, suddenly. She squeezed my arm. 'Do you really want to go in?' she said. 'We could come back tomorrow.'

I had a ticket, I said, on a train that left early in the morning. I was heading for Omsk, to see where Dostoevsky had lived and worked – how he'd lived when he was sent down the Vladimirka Road into exile. Svetlana nodded. Her friend, she said, had often talked about that road – how it was like a river, how it rose from nothing – not in the mountains but in Moscow – and ended in oblivion. It was swallowed up, her friend had said, not by the sea but by the endless snow-bound land where men drown and are buried where they lie – a place where the cries of the dying are lost in the vast frozen wilderness of Siberia.

My train, I said, was at seven in the morning.

'Oh, so early!' she said.

I felt a heaviness settling slowly on my shoulders – why, I didn't know. I took out my wallet, showed Svetlana my tiny school picture of my son Joel.

She smiled. 'Do you think he'll be a writer like you?' she said.

I said no, I hoped not.

'Maybe a dancer,' she said.

I thought of my little boy and the strange twirling movements he made to the theme song from *Neighbours*. I shook my head.

'You don't think so?'

Then I thought of the children – the little girls and little boys – left to die on the hard, frozen roadside, crying out for their mothers, of the story of the massacre near Bazilevka (itself just a few miles from the centre of Ufa) in which – so the story has it – a trainload of children, each one the child of an Enemy of the People (and therefore certain future enemies themselves), bound for the Gulags was removed from the train at the first light of dawn by personal order of Comrade Stalin himself. I remembered then how the children were marched several miles through the bitter winter frost to a field wherein, one by one, they were shot in the back of the head, and how their bodies were left for the scavenging wolves – a much less troublesome means of disposal of the bodies than the tiresome business of gravedigging. As was the custom of the time, one child – a witness to the slaughter – was allowed to live and encouraged, once the transit camp at Omsk had been reached, to tell what he'd seen, and so deter others (for the news of these things will always find a way out and back to the rooms of traitors and unbelievers) from defying in future the word of the Party.

Built between the slopes of the Ural Mountains and the banks of the Belaya (White) River, Ufa is a city – like so many others in the region – whose sole purpose was and is the taking from the richly endowed land all that can be economically taken. Consequently, oil, gas and all kinds of minerals are harvested with scant care for the land's future life. People came to dig, to drill and, in time, to refine, and, in time, the scattered dwellings became a town and the town became a city whose humble origins no one cares now to remember. Mosques and grand churches were built for the faithful and opera houses and vast civic areas levelled and paved, making promenades where newly married couples wander on their wedding day, posing for pictures by the Yulayev[1] statue, and where children play on summer afternoons before they too, of course, must either leave or take their turn with the diggers and the drills, so selling their future health – as did those who went before them – for the iPhones and Reeboks and HD Blu-ray LCD televisions that make the problems of the present so temporarily avoidable.

1 Salavat Yulayev was an eighteenth-century soldier and poet – and Bashkir national hero – who fought Moscow in the doomed cause of Bashkortostan independence.

But mines collapse and gas explodes – like the gas that exploded close to the city on the Trans-Siberian Railway in the summer of 1989.

Although its conclusions were suppressed for some years (to have published them would have been to reveal to the world the parlous state of Soviet infrastructure already well known to the native population), an investigation by the Ministry of the Interior was later shown to have determined that sparks from a pair of passing trains had ignited the gas from a leaking pipeline and so caused the resulting explosion that killed nearly 800 people, many of whom were children returning from their holidays. The explosion has since been calculated by the US Department of Defense to have had approximately the same destructive power as the Hiroshima atomic bomb.

We were standing now, Svetlana and I, in the sumptuous lobby of the Opera House. I asked her about the explosion – what they'd been told at the time.

'To start with,' she said, 'we were told nothing. All we knew was that there'd been a terrorist bomb that had killed a great many people. In the end they said it was Tartar extremists, although, of course, no one believed it.'

'Why not?' I said.

'Because that's what they told us, and we knew that what they told us would never be the truth. And they *knew* that we knew but they didn't care.'

'So what did you do?'

'Do?'

She shrugged. 'What could we do? We buried the dead and went on with our lives.'

She held open a door that led to the auditorium. I passed through; she followed. Although I wanted to, I felt sure that to speak more about the explosion would have been hurtful and in some way an act of desecration. Instead, I returned to the safety of Tony Curtis. I suggested that she should have asked him to paint her.

She stopped, frowning hard. 'A portrait? I don't think so! What would my husband say?'

'Surely he'd be flattered,' I said, 'that Tony Curtis, the famous American film star, had wanted to paint his wife. Wouldn't he?'

She shook her head. Her husband, she said, wouldn't have understood – or, rather, he'd have understood one minute but not the next. For fifteen years he'd been suffering, she said, from dementia; to start with it had just been little things – an inability to manipulate his grandson's plastic toys, constant fumbling with the car keys – then, gradually, pretty much everything else had slipped away, until, more and more often these days, she'd find him wearing three pairs of underpants or standing by the front door, unable to remember her name. 'Who are you?' he'd say to her, or he'd wonder why his car was no longer in the street and want to call the police to report the thing stolen. He'd try doors that she'd had no choice but to lock; he'd rage against all those – including her, *especially* her – who were so obviously out to murder him, then weep inconsolably two minutes later when a terrible, cruel lucidity crept over him. He would sob, she said, like a child, and only sleep, in the end, could quieten him. And then he'd sleep so peacefully and she'd watch him sleeping, and how he'd become again for a while at least the wonderful man she'd married – before the gas and fumes from the refinery had taken him from her and she'd lost him to a faraway place from which he'd never really return.

The Road of Bones

We stepped into one of the Opera House's twelve boxes. It was the box in which she'd sat all those years ago with Tony Curtis – where he'd taken her hand and kissed it. She smiled at the memory. 'Do you know what Nureyev said about dancing?' she said. I said no, I didn't. 'He said that every step must be stained with the dancer's blood.'

'And were they, do you think?'

'Of course. He was amazing. He would work so hard that his feet would really bleed. He would leave footprints across the stage – thousands every night. People used to say he would never escape to the West as he'd be too easy to follow.'

'And when he did were you sorry or glad?'

'I was glad. But sorry too. Sorry for what people in the West would think of us.'

'But it wasn't your fault. You were only a child.'

'I was a young woman. I could have spoken out.'

'But you knew what would happen if you did.'

'What we knew was that the ship was sinking. Why else would the best of the crew keep trying to jump overboard? We were frightened, and we told ourselves that waiting would be enough.'

'And it was. In the end.'

'In the end, yes. But if we'd known how long we'd have to wait, maybe things would have been different.'

'You and your friends would really have taken to the streets?'

Svetlana shrugged. 'I don't know,' she said. 'Maybe.'

Back out on the steps, I shook Svetlana's hand. I watched her make her way back indoors. She turned at the last minute and waved – said she'd see me tomorrow.

'Tomorrow?' I said – but she had gone.

I made my way down the steps and along the path that ran between neatly trimmed lawns. I thought about the explosion and the death of so many children, and I thought of the massacre near the hamlet of Bazilevka. I wondered if the boy who'd been spared in order that his voice should tell the tale had survived the camps, and whether by some chance he was still alive today. I couldn't help hoping that he wasn't, for what could he see when he closed his eyes at night but the death of those children in a distant, misty field – and how could such visions of hell ever give him up to sleep?

That afternoon I walked alone through the streets of the city, gazing into the windows of shops and the narrow cool darkness of the alleys that form a gloomy maze in the city's north-western quadrant. From a shop close by the station I bought a bottle of wine, some biscuits and a postcard of Rudolf Nureyev. In the picture he's lean and determined, his legs and torso muscular and taut. In the hotel that evening I propped it up on the night-stand, and later, when I closed my eyes, I dreamed I was him and that, though my feet were bleeding and my heart thumping so hard I thought it might burst, all I could feel was my body's perfect grace. So perfect, indeed, was I – so strong and supple – that in that one single moment I couldn't believe even God Himself, had He had another go at it, could have improved on what He'd already done.

Yearly host of Ufa's *Celebrate!* song contest, the President Hotel is so vast that it could put on a dozen such events without fear of any two overlapping. The place is big enough, after all, to offer not only a solarium and a dental surgery but a Cosmetological Room[1] and a casino. All of this, locals say, is a good thing, as among those competing for the *Celebrate!* first prize (a year's worth of groceries in a local supermarket and a contract of some kind with Ufa's PopPop radio station) are representatives of nations and ethnic groups who would normally rather slit each other's throats than stand together in the same room, breathing the same air. There are Kazakhs, Armenians, Cossacks, Tartars, Azeris, Jews, Orthodox believers, Ukrainians, Belorussians, Georgians and a barbershop quartet from Chuvashia. They sing everything from ancient steppe folksongs to 'The First Time Ever I Saw Your Face', accompanied by everything from a single, mournful zither, to a man with an old Atari keyboard and the blondest and most improbable toupee, to downloaded karaoke backing tracks.

1 The Cosmetological Room is not, as I'd hoped, a room dedicated to the cosmos, containing telescopes and maps of the stars, but merely a beauty-treatment room run by a woman whose son is an actor and had once appeared in the Russian equivalent of *The Bill*.

What the judges are looking for is impossible to say, and the result is notoriously difficult to predict. Whether or not money changes hands, no one – in public at least – will say.

On my last night in the city I was sitting in the Sports Bar on the edge of the casino, watching Dynamo Moscow on the plasma TV (they were beating Zenit St Petersburg 1–0, thanks to a deflected free kick from the Ukrainian midfielder Denys Skepskyi) when the barman, whose advice I'd sought previously about the Opera House, and who'd given me Svetlana Rutskoi's name (his sister had often babysat *her* sister's chocolate Labrador Rudolf), asked me if I knew what was going on downstairs.

I said no, what?

He said I should go and see for myself.

And so, making my way downstairs, I did.

It was hard to talk in such a racket and barely possible to think.

'What do you think?'

'Who are they?' I shouted to the man in the blue and white tracksuit who seemed to have some kind of role in the whole thing. He leaned in close. 'Jews from Armenia,' he said. He nodded towards the couple on the stage. 'You like?'

The duo, who called themselves 'Brother and Sister' (who, I later discovered, were – despite looking uncannily alike – not related at all and had, in fact, only known each other a week), were making their way energetically through 'Every Breath You Take', the young man (who'd quite clearly taken the title at face value) pausing every now and then to pant like a dog, much – at first at least – to the surprise not only of the audience of perhaps 200 but also his partner, who seemed constrained neither by the burden of such literalness nor any discernible musical ability.

'I think they're very committed,' I shouted.

'Committed? Yes!' The man in the blue and white track-suit beamed. He leaned in close again; his breath smelled of whisky and stale cigarette smoke. They were, he said, his.

'Yours?' I said.

He nodded, red-faced from (I assumed) drink, and, raising his right hand, rubbed his thumb and first two fingers together. They would, he said, make him rich. After all, he said, had I not seen *American Idol*?

On stage, their song concluded, the couple took a bow. This was greeted by a smattering of half-hearted applause and looks sharp enough to have cut them severely coming from a bunch of bearded Armenians in the corner.

I watched the man in the tracksuit weave his way towards the stage, his arms aloft like a boxer on his way to the ring. Just visible in the wings, a plump woman in a long, close-fitting gown and glasses was nervously shuffling her feet and glancing back over her shoulder. Clearly a favourite (she was, I found out later, a Ufa native, the granddaughter of a man famous for his exploits during the siege of Leningrad), while the tracksuit man was congratulating his charges, she stepped out to enthusiastic applause (even, this time, from the Armenians) and, with a high piercing voice, launched into a song about long roads and exile:

> Long is the road upon which I stumble,
> Cold is the ground that will be my grave,
> Home is the shoes that encircle my feet,
> My head is free thanks to onrushing death.

There were more verses and a rousing chorus of foot-stamping and handclapping and, when she'd finished, scarcely a dry eye in the room. With the room thus in tumult, I eased my way out; I felt urgently in need of some air.

Outside, the night sky was rich, deep and dark, the air so cold it could freeze a man's blood.

I let my eyes close. I sucked in the icy air, felt it fill up my lungs. *Yes, there's winter and real winter*, a native of North Carolina's Outer Banks had once told me, and this, surely, was what he'd meant. This, surely, was the kind of winter that no harbinger of spring would recommend; the kind of winter that nothing – not even the hardiest steppe grass – could ever survive. I blew on my hands in an effort to delay the flight of feeling. The world, that night – the one that existed beyond the lights and warmth of the city – seemed as vast and still as a battlefield at dusk, a land strewn with corpses of which neither sight nor memory has endured. In a while I went back inside, drawn as much by the reassurance to be had from the sound of other voices as for the need for the hotel lobby's warmth.

Railways everywhere attract and accumulate statistics. Ask the wrong person how long, how far, how often or how much, and you're likely to be bombarded with the kind of information in the kind of detail that could make the sanest of men take a razor to his wrists and slash away until he can no longer stand unaided and all talk of branch lines and tenders and the Great Age of Steam is but a thing of the far-distant past.

It was early. The station was empty – even the ticket office was deserted. There seemed, as a consequence, little likelihood of a train.

I wrapped my coat around me and sat on a bench. *First railway track*, I thought, *St Petersburg to Pushkin, home of the Romanov dynasty. First train? 1832. Or was it 1837?* I thrust my hands deep into my pockets. How easy it is to clutter one's mind with things that don't in the least matter, and so push out the things that really do.

Like birthdays.

My father used to say – quoting who, I don't know – that first you forget names, then faces; then you forget to zip up your fly, then you forget to unzip it.

I withdrew my hand from the warmth of my coat pocket and fed it under my coat.

Zipped.

I looked at my watch. The seven o'clock train to Omsk was already late. Probably not coming at all. I stood up and marched around, the breath pouring out of me like steam.

Svetlana Rutskoi saw me at once. I was the only one there, so why would she not? She raised her arm in a wave. For a sixty-something woman, she walked with the ease of someone much younger – with absolutely no hint of arthritic joints. I stood up.

'You're still here,' she said.

I said indeed I was – that the train was either late or not coming at all.

She held out a slim package.

'What's this?'

'For you,' she said. 'A souvenir.'

The gift was an exhibition catalogue: *American Eye: The Paintings of Tony Curtis*.

'Do you like the name?' she said. She said it had been her idea – one much praised by the man himself.

I nodded. It was good, I said. But not as good as the gift itself.

It was nothing, she said. Just something to read on the train.

I turned it over. On the back was a picture – a little gaudy for my taste – of a long, sweeping beach and palm trees and an obviously elegant hotel.

'Thank you,' I said. I gave her a kiss on the cheek and, in the brief passing awkwardness that followed, asked her what she knew about Omsk.

'What everyone knows,' she said, a blush crossing her face. 'That Omsk is a White city.'

'You mean anti-Communist? Even now?'

She nodded. Despite, she said, being chosen during the war as the new capital should Moscow fall, later, when Communism *itself* fell, it returned to its former character. 'When people in Russia used to say, "Wait for the Revolution", people in Omsk would say, "Wait for the *end* of the Revolution". And they did, and now they say, "Didn't you listen to me?"!'

I asked Svetlana if it was something you could see – this independent spirit – whether it was visible in the ordinary people.

'I think so, yes,' she said. 'Like in American movies. You leave Omsk, you leave civilization.'

'So it's a sort of border town.'

She nodded.

'And the other side of the border?'

'The other side?' She shrugged. 'The other side of the border,' she said, 'it's just *out there*.'

'You mean Siberia?'

The two-tone horn of a train in the distance announced its imminent arrival.

She pointed out across the tracks – to a place somewhere beyond the station buildings and the streets of the town and the cars and their drivers all heading out early on their way to work. 'Out there,' she said, 'is where we all belong. And where we will all return one day.'

'We?'

'Russians. One day we will all return to the fertile plains. One day – when all the oil is gone and cities like Moscow and Petersburg and even Omsk have turned back into dust.'

'When will this happen?' I said.

'Perhaps in the lifetimes of our children,' she said. She shrugged. 'Who knows?' She stepped back.

The train pulled in: the stink of diesel, the squeal of metal on freezing tracks.

I kissed Svetlana again, then climbed up into the carriage. I closed the door, pushed down the window. I thanked her for her present and, as the train pulled away and Svetlana and the station grew ever smaller, was struck by a sadness that was quite unfamiliar. Leaving – getting out – for me usually carries that thrill of escape, but not this time. This time, with the city falling back until it was out of sight and I was once again alone, I felt a great sadness at the thought that I would never see Svetlana again.

I pulled up the window and found my seat. The carriage was empty. I opened the catalogue. *Tony Curtis*, I read, *is an American actor and an artist*. In his photograph, he was smiling, the beauty of his youth still evident in his old man's mask of age. I closed the catalogue and set it down beside me. I suddenly felt terribly tired.

I looked out of the window – at the endless, frozen land where, only an hour ago, a great city had stood before me but where now – as if it had never been – there was nothing.

The further east you go, the thicker the fur; the thicker the fur, the more desirable; the more desirable, the higher the price; the higher the price, the more willing will a man be to set out across Siberia's bleak beauty and into the wild, wild east.

'Why Omsk?'

Always the same question, but no *one* answer will ever tell the whole truth, so, in the end, all you can do is settle for the half-truth and hope it's enough to buy perhaps another ten minutes of solitude.

'Because,' I said, 'I was cold and there was no other train.'

The young man nodded earnestly, as if such an explanation was both reasonable and common.

'And you?' I said.

He was, he said, a student at the Dostoevsky University in Omsk, returning home after three days with his girlfriend in Ufa. His girlfriend, he said, was having a baby.

'Congratulations,' I said.

He shook his head. The baby, he said, wasn't his – though he'd promised to look after it as if it was.

'So whose is it?' I said.

He shrugged. The father, he said, was dead – killed when a mine collapsed in Santa Clara, Cuba.

I asked him if he'd known the father.

'Of course,' he said cheerily. 'He was my brother.'

The city of Omsk is both the centre of things and on their very furthest edge. A dozen railway lines cross here – including the Trans-Siberian – and the port, situated on the confluence of the Om and Irtysh Rivers, is the third busiest in all Russia. Seen from the sky, the city too is the meeting place of highways. Stand in its centre and all in the city is movement, movement. Perhaps more than any other, the city of Omsk is equipped for escape, its citizens for ever looking west and to the south, while all the time bracing themselves against the east's bitter harvest.

The boy's name was Yuri. He was twenty and in his first year of modern languages. Spanish was his favourite, though Chinese the most useful. He planned to go there – China – at the end of his studies; he could find work there, he said, as a translator and send money home every month for the baby.

The train slowed, as if reluctant to advance any further into such down-at-heel suburbs.

'Are we there?' I said.

Yuri jabbed at the grimy window. 'Do you see those houses?' he said.

The 'houses' were a collection of dirty high-rise blocks – the kind that seem to surround all Russian cities like a ragged, stained army keeping those cities for ever in a perpetual state of siege.

I asked him if that was where he lived.

'Number two,' he said. 'Do you see the little flag?'

I looked hard, scanning the second block. At last I saw what could have been a flag. 'What is it?' I said.

'It was Sergei's,' said Yuri.

'Your brother?'

He shook his head. The flag, he said, had belonged to their cousin Sergei. It was Sergei who'd persuaded Anton (that was his brother) to go to Cuba, and Sergei who'd got him the job in the mine. 'He said it was good money – that he could make enough in one year to get everything they would need when the baby comes. Maybe even a car to drive around in.' He shrugged. 'But now he's dead.' It was a gesture not of blame but of resignation – a recognition of man's impotence in the face of fate's unbending determination to never lose control.

'Is there no one else to help?' I said. 'What about your parents? Or *her* parents?'

His parents, he said, were dead. Hers he'd never met. She didn't talk about them. He thought they lived in the Ukraine somewhere and that they were possibly teachers. He didn't think, anyway, they'd be interested.

'So there's no one? What about if you go to China? Who will look after mother and baby then?'

He had a sister, he said, in Moscow. He'd written her a letter – though, as yet, had received no reply. She was a nurse in the army in the old days and had served in Afghanistan in the war.

'And today? What does she do now?'

He shrugged, then brightened as a thought suddenly struck him. 'After Omsk,' he said. 'What will you do?'

A good question. In actual fact, I hadn't a clue. *Just onward* was as far as I'd ever got. Just keep going. I told Yuri this; again, such a plan seemed, to him, quite acceptable. I told him about Levitan and *The Vladimirka Road*, and the book I would write on my return.

He wanted to know if he'd be in it.

'Of course,' I said.

He turned his face to the window. The station at Omsk had crept up with great stealth – a dark and grimy cocoon filled with bustle and noise.

'Aren't you happy to be home?' I said.

Yuri shrugged. He turned. '*You're* lucky,' he said. 'You can go anywhere you want to.'

'Can't you?'

He shook his head.

'Why not? When you've finished your studies you could travel – and not just to China.'

He said no, there was the baby to think about.

'But money can be sent from anywhere.'

The station at Omsk was the end of that particular line. From here you either took a connection or headed back the way you'd come.

I stood up.

'Can I ask you something?' said Yuri, and straight away I knew what was coming.

'I travel alone,' I said. 'I have to. It's the only way to meet people. People like you. And to get lost.'

Yuri looked puzzled.

'Getting lost is the only way to find places and people that other people haven't found. So . . .'

'Do you know about Tomsk?' he said.

I thought of Max – of his great-grandfather and the piece of orange cloth in my bag. 'What about it?' I said.

Tomsk, he said, was famous – a distant transit area, a place where exiles were sent to learn their final destination.

With the fall of Communism, it too had fallen. Now, he said, it was little more than a place for ghosts – and for children who had neither mothers nor fathers.

'You mean it's an orphanage?' I said. It seemed quite bizarre enough to be true.

'Orphanage, yes.'

I asked him if he'd been there. He nodded. Of course, he said. Hadn't he just explained *he* was an orphan?

'You mean you lived there – in this orphanage?'

He nodded. 'Would you like to go?' he said.

I said what about his studies – weren't they important? He shrugged. His studies, he said, could wait. And, anyway, wasn't studying the past a useful thing?

'Sometimes,' I said.

We parted in the station's grand hall, having arranged to meet again in three hours. He had his tutor to speak to and transport to arrange. When I asked him what he meant by 'transport' he just smiled. We embraced and I watched him walk away. He turned and waved, and I wondered if any word of what he'd said had been true and if, as a consequence, I'd ever see him again.

Having long since abandoned any notions of God and, consequently, having not once in forty years sought His help and advice in prayer, it seemed to me that if I was ever going to believe again, then there would surely be no more persuasive a place than Krestovozdvizhensky Cathedral in the centre of Omsk.

Not that it was exactly the pursuit of faith that had me letting myself in by the iron latticework gate and then wandering through the cathedral's tiny, intimate rooms, each one smaller than the last, each one more golden and brightly coloured like the contents of a matryoshka doll. It was the knowledge that somewhere in that grand and peaceful place there was a wall unlike (or so I'd read) any other – a memorial, a list of names not carved by a stonemason but written in cement still wet by the men and women who, fifty years ago, had sought refuge in this place from the harshness of the cold and unbending brutality of those to whom they were nothing but cattle to be herded up the road and into the Gulag pens.

To call it a siege would be to lend the scene a dignity it didn't earn. It was a huddling together amid the tools and materials of renovation work, a clinging to the skirts of a clergy too cowed to any longer feel a duty of sacrifice. It was a bunch of ragged men and women whose only hope (although truly, in their hearts, they knew there was none) was God and His merciful protection. But His mercy and protection were compromised by the weak, craven cowardice of His servants – and a bargain was done by those servants: their own survival (and that of their church) in exchange for the lives of those whom by any standard of brotherhood and piety it was their God-granted duty to protect. Go, they said, and prayers were stopped, invocations to God abandoned, and, at the point of a bayonet, those whose names had been written on the wall were returned to the world of bitter winds and death.

It is said that one man looked back, and that none among the clergy would meet his gaze. They looked away, ashamed, as the soldiers with their bayonets and no fear of God smashed the golden altar and, one by one, relieved themselves against the dark and heavy doors.

But it wasn't just them, for there were others. Whole nations, people say, would seem to pass by on their way to the camps, but not a face, any longer, would turn to the face of the church. The church, they knew, had abandoned them – perhaps God too.

People say also that, from the church's high tower, the great shifting masses heading north to their doom would move as slowly as a great black slick – and always in silence, save for the occasional, merciful crack of a rifle, the sound of which – so sharp in the still air – would echo across the cold and desolate land, disturbing the birds in the wind-bent trees and leaving in their path corpses in the snow like black dots on the landscape.

'I wasn't sure you would be here.'

We were standing outside the station in the hard and bitter cold. Yuri was studying a map, one gloved hand, finger extended, clearly following a particular route. Satisfied, he looked up. His breath was thick, like smoke.

'But why would I not?' I said.

'People say things all the time they don't mean.'

'So what now?' I said. 'Is there a train?'

Yuri said yes – but not for us. For us, he said, there was something different. 'Come and see,' he said. He turned and headed for the station exit. I followed him. Once we were outside, he stopped, looking this way and that. 'It's that way, I think,' he said. He nodded to the right.

'*What* is?'

The road was jammed with cars, angry commuters late for the office and sullen-faced children on their reluctant way to school.

'So?' I said. 'What now?'

He slipped off his large backpack and set it on the ground. Dropping to his haunches, he withdrew first one pair of walking boots, then a second.

'You're kidding,' I said.

He looked up. 'What's kidding?'

'We're walking?'

He shrugged. 'You want to know what it was like – to walk? You want to know how it feels to walk and to have nothing?'

I opened my mouth to say *no*, but something stopped me. He was right. I watched him pull on his boots. Then, feeling a strange mixture of dread and exhilaration, I sat down beside him and, mostly unable to believe what I was doing, reached down and started pulling on my own.

How different would a life be if a birth certificate – like a driving licence or a library ticket – also carried a date indicating expiry? Would such a thing make us act more recklessly or would good husbandry of the time that remained prevail? And if a man were to know where and when the end would come, would he give up the struggle or fight on – even uselessly? – or would he simply endure as so many on the road endured, neither welcoming that end nor attempting to retard its arrival?

For more than two hours we'd been walking through the city of Omsk's bleak northern suburbs, passing shabby, run-down shops, whose shelves often seemed to be empty, and deserted chain-fenced lots. The place had a feeling of distemper – as if it were suffering some kind of disabling infection of the spirit that had drained the streets of colour and made the most simple joy in living as irretrievable as any faith in the future. A sullen desolation seemed to rise like something noxious through the cracks in the pavements; at the cross-streets at which we waited, traffic lights blinked red to amber to green, entirely independent of the reckless, grinding movement of the traffic.

'What are you doing?'

I was sitting on a low wall, tired already and utterly dispirited. 'I'm sitting down,' I said.

'Why?'

Because, I said, I was old – old enough, in fact, to be his father.

His father, he said, was dead.

I glanced over. The sparseness of the phrase – its strength and simplicity – matched perfectly the strength, simplicity and sparseness of Yuri's face. Both face and phrase were angular and to the point – each stripped of all adornment and affectation. It was a face unmarked by age or excess – a face smooth as if sandblasted or sculpted over centuries by the harsh Ural winds.

As we stood and walked on, I began to wonder if I'd not been too hasty to identify so few tales of rebellion on the road. Perhaps, I thought, as a colour-blind man takes blue for green, I had taken stoic bitter silence for meekness. It made me think that maybe endurance – *strada* – is its own rebellion. It made me think that, like the Jews queuing in such orderly fashion on the selection ramps at Auschwitz, the millions who had passed in silent agony down the road knew that for a man to embrace his opponent is in the end to defeat him – that, by offering himself as a sacrifice, God might – if He's there – raise Himself from His slumbers and lift His swift and righteous sword in defence of all those children – those men and those women – who have yet to take the walk to the ovens under ground or the camps cast adrift in the wilderness of white.

Isaak Levitan's father, Elyashiv, was born in Kybartai in south-western Lithuania, a shtetl[1] located in the Pale of

1 A shtetl was an exclusively Jewish town most frequently found in pre-Holocaust Eastern Europe. With the arrival of the Nazis, such concentrations of Jews was, of course, useful to their plans of extermination and, as a consequence, the Jews living in such communities were the first to be deported and slaughtered.

Settlement, then part of the Russian Empire. Elyashiv was a Jew who had suffered – as all Jews had suffered and would continue to suffer, in Russia and elsewhere, for the practice of his faith, and all he wanted for his sons was an end to the wandering that for a thousand years had been the fate of God's Chosen People. So in early January 1870 he had the family pack their bags, and they set off. One last move – to Moscow – and that, he thought – *hoped* – would be that.

He couldn't, of course, have known that the move to the city would be in fact the start of Isaak's wandering – that, with sketchbook, paints and easel in hand, his son would travel the lanes and crude highways of the country, seeking to capture the very essence of his new, adopted land.

He tramped lanes like this one – *that* one – that is now a six-lane highway heading north-east to Siberia through the barren Russian hinterland whose shabby, poorly made, tumbledown tower blocks (once referred to without irony as 'palaces for the people') are home now to the new and ever-burgeoning urban poor.

I asked Yuri what he thought the people who lived there did all day – how they passed their time.

He shrugged. 'I don't know,' he said. 'Maybe they steal cars. Maybe they drink vodka.'

We were sitting at the side of the road on an upturned plastic bath. All around us was the now-familiar legacy of the slovenly post-Soviet world: broken-down fences, old abandoned washing machines, walls of rain-streaked concrete, behind us an old car-breaker's yard, all mud and old tyres and heaped-up rusting Ladas. Across the main road, heading east, stretched scrubland littered with old crates and broken bottles and thick-growing sinewy weeds. Among the weeds, three young men, feral-eyed, were half-heartedly playing football in the oily standing water with a sodden, rolled-up piece of material – an old shirt, perhaps, or a coat.

Suddenly, Yuri called out. The young men stopped their game. They stood eyeing us with both malice and disdain.

'What are you *doing*?' I said.

The tallest of the young men walked over with a swagger to the bowed and buckled chain-link fence.

Before I could stop him, Yuri was halfway across the road, dodging the traffic; the cars blew their horns, and voices and fists were raised in anger. Seeing a gap and seizing his chance, he dashed the last twenty yards. He turned, grinning. 'Come on!' he called out. 'It's easy!'

I pushed myself up and made my way to the edge of the road. The cars were passing by so close I could feel the cold air brushing my cheek. Yuri was talking to the young man by the fence; he, the meanest-looking one, was gripping the wire, his face blank but for the faintest twist of a sneer.

I looked left, then right; I waited.

'Go!' Yuri called.

'Now! Now!'

I ran without daring to look, the soles of my boots slipping and sliding on the road.

Yuri was smiling when I reached him. 'What took you so long?' he said. 'Come and say hello.' My heart was racing from the sharp and sudden exercise. I looked over his shoulder at the mean-looking young man standing sullenly behind the fence. I smiled, despite my terrible wheezing; he did not. He just stood staring at me, his pale face a hard blunt instrument, in his eyes a dumb and distant challenge. He'd been told, apparently, I was writing a book and he wanted to know what I'd say.

'About what?' I said.

Without shifting his gaze, the young man muttered something low and harsh-sounding.

'He says, mmm, he knows you think he is – how to say? – not clever. But he says he has read many books.'

Another phrase, barked low, eyes still challenging.

'Dostoevsky, he says.'

I looked at the young man. 'Does he know,' I said, 'that Dostoevsky passed down this very road on his way to exile and prison?'

Yuri translated.

The young man nodded. A further exchange took place. He said, apparently, that a truck the old people called the Black Raven went by the same time every week – that it was a truck from the Interior Ministry.[1]

I asked Yuri to ask him how he knew that it wasn't just some ordinary truck carrying fruit or biscuits or something else quite mundane.

More talk, back and forth. The young man huffed.

'He says he knows what everyone knows. He says every week the truck goes by and old people make the sign of the cross. He says everyone knows but only the old people care.'

'*What* do they know?'

Yuri translated. The young man shrugged.

'He thinks,' said Yuri, 'that you already know. He says he thinks you are going where the truck is going. He says it is a long way.'

I said did he mean to the camps.

The young man said maybe.

1   The Interior Ministry police were (and some say still are) responsible for the transporting of prisoners to the Gulags.

'But I thought,' I said, 'they were closed.'

Hearing my words, he shrugged. I looked at his pale, undernourished-looking face; not for a single moment did the angular harshness of his features soften. It was as if life and experience had fixed his face like that, and – thanks, but only in part, to the wire fence between us – as if one of us was an unwilling boarder in some down-at-heel zoo and the other a visitor looking on.

Then, unbidden this time, he said something more.

I looked at Yuri.

'He tells me to tell you that he thinks what you are doing is a good thing.'

'It is? Why?'

Yuri turned; the young man listened hard. He flicked his eyes to mine. As before, his words came fast and brutal like bullets from a machine gun.

'Well?' I said.

'He says to write in your book what you see is a good thing. He says people in the West should know about Putin.'

'Know *what* about him?'

'About the truck. About the people in the truck. That not all the camps are closed.'

I asked him if the people in the trucks were criminals.

Another exchange.

'He says there are no criminals. Only people who speak out.'

'You mean against the government?'

Yuri shook his head. 'He says there is no government. Only money. Business. He says the people in the truck are guilty of speaking out against those with money.'

I asked him if he thought things were better in the old days.

Another consultation.

'He says he doesn't know about the old days. He says he is too young, but . . .'

Yuri paused.

'But?'

He glanced at the young man; the young man nodded.

'He says soon things will change. He says soon the people will rise up. He says they will slit a great many throats. He says the blood of the rich will soak the land, and the people in the trucks and in the prisons will be set free. This is what he says.'

I said it sounded like a revolution.

The young man nodded and smiled. 'Revolution,' he said, the word awkward and unwieldy on his tongue. He lifted his right hand, one finger extended. He drew it with a smile across his throat. Then he turned away and wandered back to his friends across the uneven, rain-spattered concrete.

'Come on,' said Yuri.

I asked him if *he* thought that that's what would happen.

'A revolution?' He shook his head. There were, he said, too many iPods, too many Nokias. And, anyway, nobody really cares.

I nodded towards the young man and his friends. 'He seems to care,' I said.

'He's nothing,' said Yuri. 'He will live and die and nobody will notice that he was ever here.'

I took another look. The young man with the pale face was arguing with his friends, their game of football – for the moment at least – forgotten.

I turned away. Yuri was already halfway across the road. I looked back. The young man and his friends were gone, the wasteland suddenly deserted. It was as if he and they had never been there at all.

We stopped at a roadside vendor and bought coffee and sweet Russian cake. Sitting on a low bank, we looked out at the road and the traffic and the empty land beckoning beyond. I asked Yuri if he felt a presence – anything left of the millions of souls who had once passed this way. He lowered his cake and narrowed his eyes, scanning the grass verge and the highway beyond like a man seeking figures in a fog. In the end he shook his head. The dead, he said, were gone, and souls, he said, wither like flowers in a frost.

I asked him if he thought it was important to remember. He shrugged. Sometimes, he said, forgetting was best. Sometimes forgetting was necessary for a person to survive.

Later, as we were picking our way along the verge, our boots sinking deep in the mud of a broken sewer pipe, I thought of Nikolai Ilyanovitch and the page I'd removed from his copy of the *Moscow Times*. I thought of Anna's story, and wondered if Yuri was right about the withering of souls.

'What are you thinking?' he said. He was looking at me hard and frowning.

I said I was thinking about the road and the people who'd been forced to walk it at the point of a gun – about one in particular.

'Who?' he said.

We walked on and, as the ground beneath our feet began slowly to dry and harden, I told him about Anna and how her story and that of her husband seemed to me to stand for so many, so profound had been her loss, and how wicked were the actions of the butcher in the Kremlin for whom the death of one was a sentimental tragedy, but the death of millions was nothing more than a casual and supremely unimportant statistic.

She told everyone he just disappeared, as if at the will of some sequinned illusionist. One minute he was there and the next he was gone. All he did, she would say, was step out to greet a friend who called up to him as he did some mornings from the street, leaving unfinished a breakfast that would never be finished and business unfinished – the promises of a husband, the duties of a father – that would hang suspended for evermore like washing on a line, growing paler and more ragged as the months and years went by.

But that then was all still to come. Then, there was just that morning – those first minutes, those first hours.

At first there was nothing strange (for heaven's sake, after all, how many times had Anna told him to finish one thing before embarking on another?), but then the usualness of things receded with the passing minutes.

Curious, a slow dread creeping over her, she edged back the curtain.

Nothing. No one.

She'd kill him, she thought, when next she saw him for doing this to her.

She cursed, moved on, the worm of the truth barely moving inside her.

In time, the breakfast dishes were cleared away, and, in time – after calls on neighbours and hours spent waiting – the darkness fell, familiar and unchanged, and when morning rose again it rose not for those whose loved ones were missing – those whose husbands like Anna's had been taken – but for those stretching and yawning at the new day's dawning and for those mothers and wives preparing a breakfast that would be eaten and not so thoughtlessly abandoned.

Days for Anna passed in numbness. Things that had to be done were done. A baby cries and has to be comforted or winded or fed from the breast regardless of a father's sudden absence. All this was done but no joy attended a mother's loving tasks. The days were hollow, the months dragging by like a coalman with his bag.

In time, she noticed that the season was changing, that the ground – once frozen solid – was softer now, more pliant. New life, she started thinking, and she started thinking now and then of the old one. His eyes, she remembered, were they the darkest brown or the purest black? Step by step she began shedding his memory like a winter coat in spring.

Life goes on; even hearts quite broken keep beating. Without tears, she put his shoes in the back of the cupboard. She burned his clothes – those she was too ashamed to give away.

He just disappeared, she would tell people if they asked, as if by the will of some sequinned illusionist. All certainty, she realized, she said, is false – itself an illusion. At night she closes her eyes and wonders whether he was taken because of his work at the printmakers or for some other reason, and she wonders abstractedly where he lay in the moment of dying – but not with sorrow and barely with regret. For Anna the past was over, the future too.

All there was now was *now*.

And even that, in time, she knew would pass.

He returned in the spring of 1958, his freedom a gift from Stalin's successor. For six weeks he walked – now and then hitching rides – until he found himself standing outside the house that over twenty years ago had been his home. He fed his hand into the hole between the bricks where he'd always kept a key for the nights when the drink and the cold had caused him to mislay his own. Like a miracle, it was there still. He withdrew it and, with a shaking hand, slipped it into the lock and turned it. But the door would not open. He tried it again. Still it resisted. He removed the key and stared at it, turning it in the harsh early light, as if demanding of it some kind of explanation. But none came – not until, still standing there like a fool, an old woman approached him and asked him if he was looking for Anna. 'Yes!' he said, his heart suddenly racing. The old woman shook her head. Anna, she said, was dead. 'Dead?' he said. The old woman nodded. She had taken her life three years exactly after her husband had been arrested for his crimes – on the day when news of his death had reached her. The old man opened his mouth to speak, but no words were forthcoming. He watched the old woman walk away, realizing only then that the old woman was his sister. A part of him wanted to go after her, but the greater part knew that to do so would be pointless. He looked at his hands, raising them and turning them over slowly. Once they had caressed his wife's face, but now they were the hands of a dead man. Once they had held his baby, a tiny hand light in his palm. For a while he sat quite still on a bench in the square. *So this is what it's like to be dead*, he thought. In a while he stood up. He had nowhere to go now, so he just started walking.

According to the article accompanying his picture in Nikolai Ilyanovitch's copy of the *Moscow Times*, Andrei Liubimov somehow made his way to the city of Archangel in the far north on Russia's Baltic coast. Here he resumed his former work as a printmaker's assistant. He never married again, nor did he attempt to make contact with his only son. People said he kept himself to himself and seldom spoke if silence was an option. That he had decided to speak out now – to tell his story – had surprised all his former co-workers at the printmakers – as had the news that the blood disorder that was responsible for his increasing inability to fight off infection could not be reversed.

'So when will he die?' said Yuri.

I said I didn't know – that no one knew for sure.

'He had children?'

'A son,' I said. 'But no one knows where he is.'

Yuri said maybe he'd read the article and that maybe they'd be reunited.

'Maybe,' I said, though it seemed then so unlikely. For two people so distanced by a lifetime's history to find each other again seemed to me in that moment nothing less than the stuff of the most hopeful fairy tales.

A vast and distant place once the preserve only of outlaws and exiles, Siberia today – though no less vast and scarcely less distant (it constitutes, in fact, nearly eighty per cent of the land mass of the Russian Federation, but is home to barely a quarter of the nation's population) – is a land of extremes: in the north, above the Arctic Circle, the winter is long and bitter – a freeze relieved only by a brief, fleeting summer, itself a period of perhaps a few weeks, during which temperatures scarcely reach above thirty below. In the south, however, along the route of the Trans-Siberian Railway that runs from Moscow in the west to Vladivostok on the coast of the Sea of Japan, the climate is much milder, the extremes so much less severe that they scarcely warrant the description. From minus twenty in the winter, temperatures climb to the positive mid-teens, so making possible – when combined with the region's rich soil – the production of barley and wheat, potatoes, cabbage and so on which had meant the difference, to those sent there in exile but not in chains, between survival and a slow, hungry death.

'What's that?'

Yuri and I had slowed our pace, as if evening's arrival was weighing us down bit by bit. He'd been rummaging around in his backpack, producing in the end a pale plastic box.

'For us. Red cabbage. And onions.'

With the city at last behind us, the air seemed to have turned colder, the land become harder underfoot.

'So do you know where we are exactly?' I said.

'Would you like to try it?'

He held out the box.

'Well, *do* you?' I said. The cold and the walking and what seemed to me then the whole wretched senselessness of the enterprise had a grip on me that I couldn't seem to shake.

'Exactly?' said Yuri. He looked around.

I said approximately would be good enough.

All around us – on either side of the road – there was nothing but flat, empty land.

He shrugged.

'So you don't know, then.'

'Cabbage?' he said, shaking the lunch box.

I shook my head. Thank you, I said, but no. I didn't want cabbage. I looked around. *I don't want this – any of it* is what I wanted to say. I was cold and miserable and whatever foolishness had possessed me to come to such a desolate place – whatever absurd and quite uncharacteristic sense of duty had made me leave behind all that was comfortable and familiar – had drained away, leaving me longing for home.

'Do you know,' Yuri said, 'that tea from China is what to drink if your head is bad from vodka?'

I said no, I didn't know. Right then, right there, I really didn't care.

'It's true,' he said. 'Here.'

I turned at the sound of a top being unscrewed from a bottle.

'After this we'll need some,' said Yuri, a broad smile stretching like a banner across his face.

An hour later we were walking in open country. Thanks to the vodka, the air seemed a lot less cold now than you'd expect from such a weak winter sun, the fields down beside the highway softer to the eye and more forgiving. What we talked about – Yuri and me – I can no longer remember. My notebook the rest of the day was pretty much a blank. I do remember, however, a kind of inventory being taken in my head as I walked – a crude sort of list of all the reasons (or all that I could remember) for the journey I was taking, particularly those that had to do with Max.

Of which, of course, there was really only one.

Reunite the generations, my wife had said. I thought of the square of orange fabric in my bag and wondered if such a thing – such coming together after such a long absence – is ever possible, or whether such a notion is nothing but a fantasy made to make the pain of loss less acute.

Stand where he stood and look close enough and maybe you'll see a white building – a chapel, perhaps – far away in the distance. Give yourself up to the painter's invitation and you'll find yourself drawn towards it along the loose, rutted track as if by a team of invisible horses. Pass the milepost on your right and head for the small copse of trees. Though the sky hangs low and grows ever greyer, don't despair; you can pause beneath the trees and take shelter. You can stand where he stood and listen to the voices of the ghosts that pass before you.

Truly, what you hear is a chain of voices.

Pavel, *exiled*, denounced by his lover for the harsh words rashly spoken about the family of the tsar.

Svetlana, *exiled*, sentenced for the theft of a dozen sweet potatoes.

Nikolai, *exiled*, for speaking out against the Bolshevik land reforms that would leave his family starving and without shelter against the thick winter freeze.

Ilya, *exiled*, for failing to cheer the ICBMs' arrival one May Day in Red Square.

Exiled – a dozen, a thousand, millions – all lost, all but a few, all but the unlucky lucky ones who came back down the road, old men at thirty, women barren and for evermore childless, those left standing but for evermore cursed with survival's bitter legacy.

I squinted hard. It seemed too unlikely to be true. But, surely, there it was: the chapel – *his* chapel – away in the distance, way out across the fields, small and white against the vast grey sky. One minute there'd been nothing, then, as if by a divine sleight of hand, there it was.

I fumbled through my pockets for the picture. I pulled the crumpled thing out, flattening it on my thigh as best I could. *The Vladimirka Road by Isaak Levitan*. I held it up.

Yuri took the picture. He flicked his eyes up and down from the chapel in the painting to the chapel on the distant horizon.

'Well?' I said.

He looked a little more, then lowered the picture. Yes, he said. He was certain.

I took another look. It was similar, yes – but could it really be the same? What were the chances – after so long? 'It's been over a hundred years,' I said.

'So?' said Yuri. 'Those trees,' he said, pointing towards the copse, 'you think they grew yesterday?'

'Of course not.'

'Then let's go.'

'Go?'

Then, without a word, he started walking – away from where the highway now ran, towards the chapel and, a little to its right, the small copse of trees.

The idea was to rest for a while beneath the shelter of the trees, drink some soup and then carry on up to the chapel. We shared the only cup, all the time looking out across the darkening fields, as if expecting something. I couldn't believe we were really there.

Yuri shrugged when I told him.

I'd studied the painting for so long – pored over it obsessively, tracing every brushstroke and twist in the paint – until it had become largely invisible to me: so familiar that I could no longer see it as once I had.

Yuri poured the last of the soup from his Thermos. He passed it over. I took a sip.

'This Max,' he said.

I looked over. 'What about him?'

'Do you think he is here?'

I passed the cup back. 'What do you mean?' I said.

Yuri blew on what was left of the soup and then drank it down. 'Did he come with you? To visit his grandfather?'

'It was his great-grandfather,' I said. 'And I don't know. Why?'

Yuri shrugged.

For some reason I thought of the small lacquered box in my pocket that Professor Rodianova had given me in

Moscow. I thought also again of the piece of orange cloth in my backpack.

'Maybe his great-grandfather was right here. Maybe he walked past these trees. Maybe he looked at the chapel like us.'

'You believe that?' I said.

'Of course.'

'But he could have been anywhere. Nobody knows. Isn't that what "disappearing" means?'

'Then here or another place – what does it matter?'

For that I had no answer, and as we walked on, stumbling across the stubbly field towards the white chapel, all I could think was what, some many years ago now, Isaak Levitan had disclosed to his diary. About the bones of those abandoned on the road, he wrote, in his elegant, sloping hand, *they are always there – sometimes so close to the soles of your boots that to walk where they fell is like walking on the very bodies of the dead.*

I told Yuri this; again he shrugged. I said didn't the thought of such sacrilege bother him? He shook his head. The bones of the dead, he said, were a useful source of calcium – enriching the land and making grow there crops and spring flowers that otherwise would not. To prove this, he stopped and reached down, scraped the snow back with the side of his boot and pulled from the earth a tiny white flower. He held it out; I took it, unable not to wonder in that moment just exactly whose bones had made it grow, and whether they'd have been gladdened or saddened by what to me seemed such an unequal trade.

But then Yuri turned away and commenced walking again, and I followed him, the tiny white flower pressed for safety in my notebook, the fall of my boots a little lighter on the rich, dark earth.

Following a stop for another shot of vodka (the stuff being, according to Yuri, as vital to survival in such a place as warm clothing and a strong selfish will), we walked hard for an hour, not a single word passing between us. Though the air had grown colder and the light was really beginning to fade now, I didn't seem to feel it as much as, only an hour ago, I had. As I walked I tried to imagine (it felt like trying to *remember*) how it must have felt to walk this land in chains, growing further with every step from all that had for so long been familiar, and closer to the dread of the unknown.

'The taken' is what they were called – those who were there one minute and gone the next, men like Max's great-grandfather, Aleksandr Kazazhkov, who died somewhere out there – out *here* – and whose corpse was left to rot by the side of the track somewhere or frozen solid on a bunk in the Gulag at Tomsk, and then heaved into a pit and left to the scant and fickle mercy of the wolves. They were legion – these men, these women and these children – a phantom army of the dead and missing that if mobilized by some avenging deity would scatter their executioners and those who attended them like leaves before the first winds of March.

'Can you hear that?' said Yuri.

The chapel was deserted – a roofless wreck now whose only congregation were the weeds and wild flowers that, even in the big freeze of autumn, fought their way through the rich soil in search of another season's sun.

But I could hear nothing – and maybe that was the point. Maybe the point was that the body really is everything and the spirit – the soul, perhaps – just make-believe, and when you're gone you're gone completely and all that remains of you is a shadow-life lived in the memory of others: a picture in an album, a voice deciphered from the whisper of the wind, a link in a chain of long-departed voices.

And yet . . .

Which one of us has not spun around at the touch of ghostly fingers, only to find there a presence unrecorded by the eye that cannot with good sense be explained? And which of us has not found relief in the thought that those loved ones who were taken from this life prematurely are awaiting us somewhere, their arms outstretched and ready to receive us, their words once again a gentle whisper in our ears? We all fear aloneness – an empty, cold eternity. We all fear – do we not? – the exile of death. We ache for the warmth of our mothers' perfumed skin and the gentle, guiding strength of our fathers. We long to know that they're waiting for us – and so we listen, our ears straining for the sound of their beckoning voices, while our hearts all the while are yearning to return to the safety of the womb.

During the time of the tsars, a man – a serf, the property of others – was not a man entirely without hope of escape. He could join the tsar's army and gain liberty for his children through a glorious death – or he could, if so inclined, release himself from his chains of service by the act of his own hand and become, in time, a kind of free man.

Assuming a deal of spirit and determination to succeed with his own self-destruction, there was, first, an unlikely truce to be negotiated with God (who frowned on such wilful waste of life) and, second, the shame that the shadow of self-murder would cast on those left behind to be considered. All of which is just to say that the only aspect of life, in other words, held in the gift of such a lowly person was the manner and time of its ending. He was a prisoner as much as was the criminal in the prison cell, or the man – the son, husband, the father – forced from his bed in the middle of the night and sent east on the road far away to Siberia and the brutal, ice-bound Gulags.

Yuri asked me what it was that he did – Max's great-grandfather – to deserve such terrible treatment.

We were sitting bundled up in blankets in the furthest corner of the ruined chapel. We had waterproof sleeping bags, a dozen blankets each and even a small tent in case of rain or snow.

I said he was a musician – that, like his father before him, and like those who followed him, including Max himself, he played the violin.

'So what did he do wrong, this musician?'

'Nothing,' I said. 'He just played the violin. In fact, he was so good he played under Rachmaninov at the Bolshoi.'

Yuri whistled.

'And then one day the Cheka knocked on his dressing-room door and told him his services were no longer required – that he had precisely thirty minutes to gather up what was his and leave. He begged to know where they were taking him and why, but all they'd tell him was that criminals had no right of explanation. But what about my family? he said, but the men from the Ministry told him he no longer had a family – and that already half his time for preparation had gone. After that, there's not much more to tell. He was never seen again. He just disappeared.'

After a while Yuri said, 'Maybe it was the violin. Maybe he was too good. Maybe he made people feel things that were against the Revolution.'

'Like what?'

'Like happiness. Maybe he made people think that they didn't need the Party to be happy. Maybe he set them free.'

'And for that they killed him?'

'He was a problem, and death solves all problems. No man, no problem. Did you know Stalin said that?'

I nodded.

We sat for a moment in silence, as if Max's great-grand-father's disappearance and death demanded, even at this distance in years, a duty of silent respect. A further minute passed; the silence was stifling. To break it, I asked Yuri how often he came to the chapel.

He shrugged beneath his blankets. Just sometimes, he said. Whenever he had the time.

'Does anybody know?' I said. 'Your brother's wife, for example.'

He shook his head.

'Doesn't she wonder where you are?'

'She's busy.'

'But still she must wonder. Are these her blankets?'

He nodded.

'She doesn't mind you taking them?'

'They're blankets.'

He looked pale. He pushed himself down into his sleeping bag, leaving one hand out to pull up the blankets. That done, he slipped the hand back in. Soon, buried beneath his blankets, he was fast asleep and snoring.

I closed my eyes. The pattern of stars for a moment remained. How strange, I thought, that they should do so – that they should stay for a moment on the lid of the eye, lingering like the soft touch of a lover's fingers when the hand is finally withdrawn.

Thinking of the star a friend had had named for my son, I opened my eyes and studied the darkening sky, searching abstractedly for one among the millions. But, of course, such a search was useless, for there were so many. Indeed, the odds of finding a single, particular star are no better than those of finding the particular skeleton of a son or a daughter, of a brother or a sister, or of a father or a mother in a world where names had long ago been abandoned and identities subsumed into one great mass of bones. A man, they used to say, sent east to the Gulags may as well have been boiled on arrival and his flesh eaten for supper – for nothing more of him than they – his bones – would, in the end, remain.

In a while a single star caught my eye. (Maybe it was a satellite; at any rate, it was brighter than the others.) It was white and cold, its gaze hard and unforgiving – the same star (if star it was) that my boy could see if he stood in the garden; the same star that Max's great-grandfather would have seen had he glanced up towards the heavens, seeking reason or God or some hope that the pain and dislocation would in the end one day bring some kind of peace – and that forgiveness would come one day to the hearts of those left behind.

I settled back, the search abandoned. I wrapped myself up tight in the blankets and closed my eyes. There was so much to think about – so many stories, so many lives – that I was certain sleep would never come. I was certain that the ghosts in the chapel would not let me rest and that the cool watchful eye of that single, brightest star would suddenly fade to nothing – all hope of direction for those lost on the ocean of memory gone – should I give myself up to the shadow world of dreams.

Born in the spring of 1873, Sergei Vasilevich Rachmaninov arrived in the world with the ear and the hands of a pianist. The only son of aspirant middle-class amateur musicians,[1] by the age of four, his fingers had a spread wider than a boy twice or three times his age, and everyone knew what

1 As well as possessing some musical ability, Rachmaninov's father was also a drunk and managed with some ease to spend well beyond the value of his wife's estate, so, as a consequence, eventually forcing the sale of that estate, including Sergei's precious piano.

he would most likely one day become. Indeed, the young Sergei's was a star with a quite definite trajectory: he would study, he would write, he would perform and he would conduct. Thus, all in the life of the young boy was set – and the journey of that life would surely have continued with scarcely a bump in the road (his first piano teacher having given up after only a month, there being, he said, no more he could teach such a pupil) had debt and revolution not risen unexpectedly to stand – albeit temporarily – in his way.

A branch breaking; I opened my eyes. Yuri was still sleeping (and still snoring) beside me. I sat up. The night was freezing – literally so, the moisture of early dawn frozen into crystals on the surface of my hair, all evidence of life quite absent from my feet. I pushed myself up and hobbled around; slowly, the feeling returned to my legs. I passed through what had once been the chapel's main doorway and stood where there had clearly once been a shallow flight of steps.

Behind me in the chapel, Yuri stirred. He half sat up, bleary-eyed. 'What is it?' he said.

I told him *nothing*, and that he should go back to sleep. He laid his head back down and in a moment was gone.

I turned again to see the vast land foreshortened now by the dense screen of night. As I stood there, my ears and nose freezing and the air so clean and sharp that breathing it hurt my lungs, all I could hear, in the ear of my mind, was Rachmaninov's *Chorus of Ghosts* and all I could feel were the passing spirits of a line of shackled prisoners, among whom – I felt certain – was Max's great-grandfather.

I never saw him, of course, except in the pictures my father smuggled out.

I stuck out my gloved hands, spreading the fingers.

I'd never thought before about height being an advantage to a pianist – or even broad hands and long fingers. Even looking at the man in Max's smuggled pictures, the length of his hands (held straight down by his sides as if he were a soldier) had – like Rachmaninov's himself – seemed to me no more useful (and scarcely less an embarrassment) than the composer's oversized nose or Max's great-grandfather's heavy, dark suit. In my memory, Max's great-grandfather is looking out from the picture with that stillness and hauteur peculiar to the subjects of early photographs. One hand on his hip and the other on the back of an empty chair, he stands, chest out, proud and self-possessed, pathetically unaware, of course, of the holocaust to come.

But then a flash of nitrate powder and the picture is done. And what then? Back to work? Another hour at the piano with Rachmaninov and his exquisite Prelude in C Sharp Minor? Or would he stand in the garden and smoke a cigar and listen for some sign of the gathering storm that so many fools said was coming?

I gathered my blankets and went back to the corner of the chapel. I sat on a wall and tried to remember the tune of the Prelude. Once so familiar (Max would often play it on his violin), it was, then, just out of my grasp, and in a while I gave it up. Instead, I just sat, huddled up, aware of little beyond my own heart's beating. I looked up at the stars, but they were as distant, cold and lifeless as the eyes of fishes. I closed my eyes. There was nothing to do now but wait for morning.

A little of the worshipper dies with the idol: so it was for Sergei Rachmaninov when the musical colossus that was

Pyotr Ilyich Tchaikovsky succumbed to cholera in 1893.[1] Three years of depression followed, during which the composer could neither write nor perform. His friends diagnosed a broken heart, his enemies madness – and all manner of 'cures' were proposed. Medicines of all kinds were prescribed and exercise regimes, some of which were quite bizarre. Even a visit to Leo Tolstoy was recommended, though this hardly went well, the meeting ending in argument and rancour and the composer pulling hard on the great author's beard. Finally, the composer fell into the hands of the famous psychologist (and amateur violinist) Nikolai Dahl, under whose direction a course of autosuggestion therapy succeeded where everything else had failed. Soon he began writing again, and in 1904 was offered the role of conductor at the Bolshoi Theatre. His fame spread throughout the world; offers of overseas tours were made and accepted. Chaos, for Rachmaninov, had finally coalesced into a life of music, domestic bliss (he at last, after a long engagement, married Natalia, his childhood sweetheart who would remain his wife until his death) – a well-earned life of well-ordered success.

But then along came the Bolsheviks and took it all away.

They fled north one night along the Vladimirka Road, Sergei and Natalia and their two young daughters, huddled up on a dog sled in the harsh winter's freeze. Stripped of all he owned by the new kings of Russia, he had little left but his family – that and a pair of leather-bound notebooks in which were written ideas for future projects and the score of

1 Though cholera caught from drinking unboiled water is the most likely (and popular) explanation for the composer's death, many still believe it was murder (a jealous rival, a sentence imposed clandestinely by the tsar as punishment for his homosexuality, and many others), and some have convinced themselves that he died by his own hand.

a work in progress. This, the opera *Monna Vanna*, was, at the moment of his death in the spring of 1943, still unfinished – and it would, of course, remain so, a monument to a life so abruptly interrupted, a voice for ever silenced by the red despotic tide.

He would lead me to the highway and show me where best to stand that I might flag down a bus; more than that, he said, he could not do. He had, he said, changed his mind about Tomsk and the orphanage. He asked me if I still wanted to go.

'Yes,' I said, 'of course. But why don't *you*?'

He shrugged.

'You *have* been back before – haven't you?'

He was rolling up his sleeping bag and stuffing it into its heavy plastic cover. 'Of course,' he said. 'Many times.'

'So why not now?'

Another shrug.

'Would you go if I weren't with you? Would you go if you were alone?'

He shook his head.

'Then why not?'

It was, he said, his birthday.

'Today?'

'Tomorrow.' He zipped up the cover and started folding up his blankets. 'Tomorrow,' he said, 'I will spend with Natasha and the baby. So today I will show you the road and tell you the way. If you stand where I tell you, a bus will come. The bus will take you to Tomsk. From there you must ask.'

I nodded. As we piled up the blankets and sleeping bags and covered them with the tarpaulin, I tried to catch his eye but could not. It seemed he wouldn't look at me.

I bent down to tie my boots. I looked up, meaning to ask him how far it was to the road, but he had already gone, already striding out across the hard, frozen field, his breath swirling all around him like the pale, acrid smoke from a *Baltic* cigarette.

The black earth of Siberia, said Isaak Levitan, the *dark sacred land of my fathers.*

'Why are you doing this?'

'A souvenir,' I said.

Yuri was up ahead, looking with what seemed like disapproval at my chipping away at the soil with my penknife. When he asked me why I was doing it, I said I'd keep it as Levitan had done, and I told him how, on the painter's long journey up the road he'd often stop and pick up a handful of the earth like a scientist taking samples. It was blood and bone, he said, and a million years of history – the most fertile land anywhere between the oceans. It was the spirit, he said, of Mother Russia. By the end of his wanderings his pockets and knapsack were full and he carried it all the way back to Moscow. Here, having removed his boots and socks, he'd scatter it across the floor of his studio every morning, in order, he said, to commune with the restless souls of generations past – to hear their voices and feel their despair.

'And that is what you will do?'

Later, he said, he would gather it, ready for his burial.

I said maybe – although, on the other hand, maybe Customs would think it was theft of a precious Russian asset. *In the black earth is contained the spirit of Russia.* 'Do you think,' I said, 'I'd have to get a permit?'

Yuri shrugged. 'Come on,' he said. 'We're wasting time.'

An hour later, it was Yuri down on his haunches and digging around in the dirt at the edge of a field. His hands were red with the cold, the flaps of his fur hat pulled down low over his ears.

He raised his head and called out. 'Bones,' he said.

I crossed to him and dropped down beside him. Before him in the dirt were four sticks lined up, each one no longer than a pencil (though perhaps two or three times as broad), brown in colour, one rounded at one end. To me they could have been anything.

'How do you know?' I said.

He picked up the round-ended one. 'You can see,' he said.

'Are you sure?'

He said of course he was sure.

'Who was it, do you think?' I said.

He half-turned his head. 'Who?'

'Do you think he was a prisoner? Somebody on his way to the Gulag?'

He shook his head, a slight smile on his face. 'No,' he said. 'I think he was a rabbit.'

Later, as Yuri walked ahead and I followed (the pounding of my feet on the hard ground keeping any numbness in my toes temporarily at bay), I tried again to picture the faces of the lost and condemned, as – every one of them weary and some close to death – they trudged the hard road into exile. How was it, I wondered, for a man to be as certain as any man can be who's had the last of his hope extinguished that, once they're gone and behind him, he'll not see those fields again, fields that in spring will sway like a yellow sea with shoulder-high rye, nor the milepost on which some previous pilgrim has placed a sun-whitened skull? And how must it have felt to know that he'll never again see that chapel on the low hill, or feel again his child's hand – its bones tiny like a little bird's – nor the warmth of his bed and the smell like barley of his wife's flaxen hair? How *was* it to know that all will pass behind him and be gone, gone, gone? How was it that when all hope was gone so many hearts kept pumping and so many muscles bunching and stretching? A man would stumble and catch himself before he fell – for to do so would be to invite a savage beating. Something beyond hope pushes him on and on. But what? Is there something in these people that lasts beyond last hope's extinguishing? Whatever it is, you see it in the faces of Repin's *Barge-Haulers* and in the eyes of his *Cautious One*, and you hear it in the words of Frederick the Great, who said of such people that, though you can kill them, you can never really defeat them. For confirmation of this, ask Fieldmarshal Paulus at Stalingrad or Napoleon on the bloody fields of Borodino. They are as stoic as cattle in winter and as numerous as the land is vast, and their will to endure the greatest of all suffering inexhaustible. In their millions they have stumbled, they have frozen and they have died – but something of them in the land and on the road remains.

Two months before his death in 1900, while Isaak Levitan was staying at the Black Sea home of Anton Chekhov, he was visited, so the story goes, by an old man whose work, the old man claimed, had been the upkeep of a faraway chapel. The chapel, he told the sick and dying painter, had been a mile or so from the road they called the Vladimirka, but had by the time of the old man's visit long been abandoned, the roof having caved in one winter following a particularly severe snowfall. All that was left of it now, he'd said, was a shell – a home to the wolves that hungrily stalked the surrounding steppe, endlessly searching for food. According to the report of the visit recorded by Chekhov's sister Maria, when Levitan – by then drifting in and out of lucidity – had asked the old man about the chapel's congregation, the old man had raised his hands as if to say, 'What congregation?' All that was left there now, he'd repeated, were the wolves – the wolves and the ghosts. At this, Isaak Levitan had, according to Maria, turned his head on his pillow, his rheumy eyes suddenly open wide. 'You have spoken to them – these ghosts?' he'd said, his voice low now, his breath coming hard. The old man had nodded. The ghosts, he'd said, would sit in the fields, lying back in the summer, enjoying the heat of the day. At night, however, they would walk the mile or so to the road and there they'd stand in silent remembrance of the lives of so many so brutally lost. On hearing this, the painter, it is said, had turned his head away and closed his eyes, his tears running down his pale face and on to the fine linen pillow.

Two months later, when Isaak Levitan died, Maria Chekhovna is said to have written to a friend, describing the painter's last weeks. They were, she said, weeks of bitter torment, the great Levitan suffering a pain far beyond that of his illness. To her it was clearly the weight of the pain combined of all those who'd sought shelter in that chapel on the road, but for whom, in the end, even God's protection had not been enough to prevent their suffering at the wicked hands of man.

We said goodbye at the highway, then I stayed this side, while he crossed to the other. Six lanes away, he looked tiny – as I suppose I did also. Vast lands will do that to a man – make him see himself and others on a scale more modest than he's used to.

Yuri was the first to get a ride – after maybe ten minutes, a beaten-up slate-grey estate with the rear bumper hanging half off. He raised his hand in a wave as he got in; I raised mine, but by then he'd disappeared inside. I watched as the old car pulled away in a cloud of fumes, its exhaust hanging down and raising sparks as it was dragged along the highway.

I looked at my watch. According to Yuri, the local buses came about every two hours and were a great deal safer (especially for a foreigner and especially *here*) than hitch-hiking.

Why here in particular? I'd said.

Because, he'd said, of the murders.

Murders?

There'd been three in the last month alone, apparently – and another two before – all the work of the man the newspapers were calling the Killer of the Highways.

According to the newspapers, his modus operandi is every time the same. Every time, the crime occurs on a stretch of empty road – empty, that is, but for a single (preferably female) hitch-hiker. He slows down as if he's going to give the hitcher a lift; the hitcher relaxes, delighted at the prospect of at last escaping the cold. Then, at the last minute, the driver swings the passenger door open, slamming it into the hitch-hiker. Then, while his victim is either unconscious or hurt so badly that he or she can neither run nor defend him- or herself, he lifts them up and puts them into the boot of his car on a bed of blankets he has previously prepared. This task completed, and the boot properly secured, he drives off, almost certainly taking each new victim to the same abandoned house. Though no closer as a consequence to finding the killer, the police are aware of these details thanks to the remarkable testimony of the man who escaped. This man – a twenty-one-year-old student from Holbæk in northern Denmark – managed to flee the scene within an hour of his arrival at the house (an outside door had been left unlocked in an uncharacteristic moment, it seemed, of inattention) and alert the local police, who, in turn, raided the house only to find that the man – of course – had gone. Where he is now no one knows, nor, indeed, does anyone know the fate of the five missing hitch-hikers. As for the young man from Denmark, he is currently – according to a blog purporting to be his – writing a book about his experiences, for which project he has already (or so he claims) been advanced a significant sum.

Perhaps a little over an hour after Yuri had gone, a dirty brown bus appeared. It ground to a stop in a great hiss of brakes.

The door opened.

'Tomsk?' I said.

The driver nodded. I stepped up and pulled out a pocket's worth of change. This he scooped into the tray.

'How much?' I said.

He gave me a look that said I'd be receiving neither change nor an answer to my question.

I took a seat by the window. It was an unfamiliar feeling to be warm, and it made me feel sleepy. I leaned my head against the grimy glass and fixed my eyes on the vast, endless, slow-moving land.

A while later a jolt made me sit up. I looked around. The bus was maybe a third full now – old women mostly with shopping bags and heavy tights and hands thick and rough from a lifetime of work. Some were toothless; one had hair the colour of an aubergine. One of the only three men that I could see was carrying the head of a pig, its eyes staring out in understandable surprise.

I turned back to the window. Again I drifted off. In a sudden, sharp dream I was walking in the company of a single ragged child, our feet raising thick summer's dust on the road. Up ahead, beyond a small copse of trees, stood a chapel shining white in the sun. We walked on, but with every step the chapel grew no nearer. I asked the boy what was going on – why, however hard we walked, we made no progress. He shrugged, then said, 'Look behind you,' and I turned at the sudden sound of hooves, just in time for the blackness of horses to overwhelm me as they blocked out the sky, throwing everything into darkness and the chaos and crashing of a fearful, fevered nightmare.

But then another jolt – this time a poking at my shoulder – woke me a second time.

'Where are we?' I said, the darkness, the nightmare receding before the light.

The old woman with the aubergine hair was standing in the aisle beside me, jabbering something I couldn't, of course, understand. She pointed to the window. I looked but could see nothing. She reached over me in a cloud of old sweat and potatoes and knocked on the window as if testing it for strength, then withdrew once again to the aisle.

'She says to look at the sky.'

I twisted around. The man with the pig's head was leaning forward from his seat a few rows back; his eyes were bloodshot and staring – the pig's too.

'What about it?' I said.

Thanks to a tinge of early morning pink, the sky carried with it, apparently, a warning of bloodshed.

I looked again. Sure enough, the sky – when not obscured by low cloud – had a pink look about it. I turned back to the pig man. I told him that maybe the sky was wrong. He shook his head. He looked down at the pig in his lap. But the pig, mute and, of course, unblinking, was saying nothing.

An hour later the driver turned his head and touched the horn. Those around me stood up and started gathering their things.

'What's happening?' I said. 'Where are we?'

The man with the pig's head leaned forward. We were, he said, in Tomsk. We were, he said, at the end of the line.

We were commanded to gather for breakfast by eight-thirty, having first ticked our names on Marina's clipboard as we entered the dining room. An hour, then, for breakfast (there was a buffet of hot food as well as cereals, toast and a waiter primed to take any individual requests), following which a short talk was scheduled in the ballroom – an opportunity, according to the itinerary, for those as yet unacquainted with each other and/or the Terror to, with regard to the former, have a chat and perhaps compare highlights of the trip so far, and, as far as the latter goes, learn a thing or two about the ways and means of the NKVD. Those with little or no knowledge of torture (the special box in the brochure warns) might find this talk distressing. Small children, it advises, would be best to spend the time in the hotel's Pushkin Conference Room, where suitable entertainment had been provided. Finally, all members of the tour were reminded to wrap up warm, for, though the weather was, as always, likely to be bracing, its effects could still be quite unexpectedly severe if proper precautions were ignored.

'Your name, sir?'

I told her. She ran her pen down the list of names on her clipboard.

'It's not there,' I said.

She looked up.

'It won't be.'

Clearly new to the job, she seemed suddenly lost. She would look again, she said.

I said there was no point, and that, though I wasn't part of the tour group, I would, if possible, like to join the day's excursion.

She looked up again.

'To the prison?'

She had the pale face and high cheekbones of a Slav; her nails were bitten back, and, though her blue suit was clean and sharply pressed (and its Union Jack badge declaring her fluency in English gleaming on her lapel), the scuffed toes of her court shoes made her seem like a little girl dressed up in what she'd found that morning on the rail in her mother's wardrobe.

'Is it possible?' I said.

She looked down at the clipboard as if for an answer.

'I'll pay, of course,' I said.

She looked up. She would, she said, have to ask Mr Hagen. Mr Hagen, she said, was in charge of everything.

'Everything?' I said. 'He must be busy!'

'Busy?' said Marina.

I smiled. She did not.

It is without apparent irony that the highest point in the far-distant city of Tomsk is known as Resurrection Hill. I couldn't help thinking how bitter must that name have seemed to all those for whom the city was, though not quite the end of their journey, at least the point from which that end would very soon be reached. Stand on the hill's summit and you seem to be standing on the earth's furthest point – as far from warmth and comfort and a family's embrace as it is possible to be. Indeed, that afternoon – my first in the city – had been the bleakest, coldest, most desolate afternoon of my life, and I'd longed to go home.

Home.

If such a place seemed then so far away to *me*, how impossibly distant must it have seemed to those men, those women and those children who were gathered here – those poor hopeless wretches standing in that very place and on a day such as this, shivering with cold and with fear, as bereft of hope for the future as they were tortured by memories of a fast-fading past? How was it for them – such misery? How did so many survive for so long? And, above all, I couldn't help wondering what they would have said if they'd known the purpose of my journey. What would they have thought of the man standing there in the shadows cast darkly on that road, taking notes while all the time wrapped up in a thick borrowed coat, a ticket for home in his pocket and plans for the coming Christmas season?

I was finishing my coffee in the lobby when Marina returned. Mr Hagen had apparently said yes. She mentioned a price and I passed the money over, feeling guilty like a man buying a ticket for a hanging. A thousand roubles for a trip to the Museum of the Terror. The world, in that moment, seemed perfectly insane.

Ten minutes later a coach pulled up outside the hotel. We stood in the foyer in a line. Marina attached a little gold sticker to our names as we passed by, and out we filed into the bitter morning air.

I sat by the window, hoping that what lay beyond it – the busy streets, the gingerbread houses, the department stores selling Lancôme and Prada and Whitney Houston CDs that could have been anywhere – would at least for a while be my only company.

But tour groups are groups first, their destinations a distant second. Step on to that bus and, whether you like it or not, you've stepped into a world where talk is the currency and silence the enemy of fun.

'Say, where did *you* spring from?'

I turned reluctantly away from the window. The man was maybe in his sixties, large-bellied, crisply dressed in a check shirt and slacks. Around his neck was a string tie with a silver clasp in the shape of a steer's skull. His name, he said, was Dean, and he was a doctor, retired, whose home was in San Diego. I shook his hand. He frowned hard. Not really caring about the answer, I asked him what the matter was.

'No, sir,' he said, shaking his head. 'It's OK.'

'What's OK?'

He held up his palms. He'd promised Loulou, he said, and was bound to keep his promise.

'Loulou?' I said.

He lowered his hands. Loulou, he said, had been his wife of forty-six years, and it was Loulou whose death six months ago had nearly ended his. 'People ask me,' he said, 'what's the secret? And I tell them, if you got a nurse and she's pretty, then marry her. That way you get care as well as looks.'

I asked him for the sake of politeness how long he'd been a doctor.

'Nearly fifty years,' he said. 'And let me tell you that's a lot of busted fingers. Still, I guess I did more good than harm in the end. And you, sir?' Again, abruptly, he held up his hands. 'Nope. Don't tell me. Let me guess.' He narrowed his eyes, as if a man's occupation was hidden in his face and needed only a little concentration to be successfully divined.

'You, sir,' he said, 'are an artist.'

My heart sank. I'd been planning to say I was an acrobat, or a man who sells vegetables from the back of a van.

He nodded. 'So am I right?'

Grudgingly, I said *sort of*, annoyed that the deception had crumpled before it had even begun. He smiled and tapped the side of his nose. At once the smile dipped.

'What now?' I said.

He leaned in close, dropped his voice to a whisper. 'Were you aware,' he said, 'that you are suffering most probably from a hiatus hernia?'[1]

'What?'

'Ssssh,' he hissed. He glanced left, then right. 'Remember Loulou,' he said. 'She may be gone, but you can bet she's looking down.' As if to confirm this, he cast his gaze upwards, then down again, a broad smile on his face – just as the coach swung into the courtyard of a grand-looking building and a voice from the front (not Marina's this time) announced our arrival at the Museum of the History of Political Repressions.

'So what do you think?' said Dean.

He pointed to the building. 'Bugged or not?' he said. 'What do you reckon?'

Opened in 1994 by Alexander Solzhenitsyn,[2] the Museum of the Terror occupies the basement area of what is today the

---

1 Amazingly, on my return I discovered he was right.
2 A famous resident of the Gulags, Solzhenitsyn spent several days at the Tomsk detention centre, during which time he carved his initials on one of the cell doors.

Tomsk Regional Museum and is dedicated to the memory of all those who suffered from repression 'in the great land of Tomsk'. Victims of many different Soviet ethnic groups are represented as well as several dozen different nationalities (chief among whom are the Poles, who suffered greatly), and though there is much for the visitor to read – individual stories, descriptions of camp life (though very little in English) – it is, of course, as with the mound of children's spectacles at Auschwitz or the pile of discarded shoes at Dachau, the physical remains and extraordinary reconstructions that take the most attention. The four rooms – themselves former torture cells – have been restored to their 'working' appearance – the benches and buckets and crude detritus of misery gathered again as if in preparation for the next vicious purge.

I looked over at Dean. We were standing before a dark-stained execution block. There were tears in his eyes.

'Do you see that?' he said.

I looked down. The block had been well used, worn smooth by the pressure of the many victims' necks. I shook my head. 'It's terrible,' I said.

'Yes, but do you see?' he said.

I looked again.

And then it struck me what he meant – the size of the dip in the block. It was no bigger than the size of my hand, fingers outstretched. Too small to comfortably accommodate the head of an adult, it had clearly been used in the execution of children – the instrument before which they'd be forced to kneel, and on which they'd been made to rest their pale, downy necks, thence to await the terrifying moment of death.

Dean raised his hand to his face. I touched his shoulder and eased him gently away – away from the chairs bolted tight against the far wall, where, with exquisite venality, the parents would be forced to sit and watch as the child on whom they'd lavished such love and whose future they'd so tenaciously guarded for so long was struck from this life with the kind of brutal cruelty exclusive, in a world of harsh and bloody nature, to the creative and superior mind of man.

A while later we were sitting in the cafe, two bottles of Sprite before us on the plastic table. I told him about the plans I had for my book – and the title *A Distant Road*.

'Not so distant now, eh?' he said. He tried to raise a smile. It withered and slipped away. I sat and watched the woman behind the counter arranging Mars bars and the Russian equivalent of Hula Hoops on a shelf.

'I was thinking I might skip the rest of the tour,' I said.

He looked up. 'What about your book? Won't that make it incomplete?'

'Who'll know?'

'You'll know, for one.'

'Yes,' I said, 'but I'm not telling.'

'What about me? You think I won't be writing in, saying what a fake you are? How you chickened out?'

'Maybe I don't want to see any more. Maybe I don't see the point.'

Dean shook his head. 'So you came all this way just to shut your eyes? Don't we owe 'em something, these people – these children?'

'But they're all dead,' I said. 'Gone. They won't know if we open our eyes or keep them closed. They won't even know if we were ever here or not.'

In a gesture quite as tender as he was large, Dean from San Diego laid his hand on my shoulder. 'Doesn't a dead man,' he said, 'cast a shadow just the same as a man that's alive?'

At that moment Marina appeared in the doorway with her clipboard.

'Perhaps,' I said.

Dean patted my shoulder. 'You know so,' he said.

I said I thought he was a doctor, and that being a doctor – a scientist – he wouldn't believe in anything you couldn't prove.

'I believe what I feel. So do you,' he said. 'Or you wouldn't be here. You wouldn't be travelling this road of yours. I mean, what would be the point of such a journey? It would be like buying a ticket to the circus way after the circus left town – and where the heck's the point in *that*?'

'You must come now,' said Marina. 'The man is showing the tortures right away.'

Dean stood up. 'You coming?' he said. 'Or will the poor man in the hood just be wasting his time?'

I said OK, I was coming. I pushed myself up. In the face of such certainty it seemed useless to resist.

On the way back in the coach, I asked Dean where his interest in Russia had come from. He asked me in return if I'd heard of Louis L'Amour.

I said yes – sort of. He was a writer, Westerns mostly, wasn't he?

He nodded. 'And who,' he said, 'do you think has the largest collection of Louis's books in the entire United States of America?'

'You?'

'Yes, sir. Me. In fact, it may be the biggest collection in the entire world.' He leaned towards me then, as if he were about to share a secret. Did I know, he said, that Louis L'Amour was Russia's third-highest-selling author, behind Tom Clancy and J. K. Rowling?

I said no, I didn't know.

'Well, it's true. Which is why I'm here. I'm here for the conference – the Worldwide Friends of Louis L'Amour. It seems while my expertise as a doctor is no longer required, my knowledge of the works of Louis L'Amour most certainly is.'

'Will he be attending?' I said. 'The man himself?'

Dean shook his head. 'No, sir,' he said. 'The man himself died in June of 1988. Histoplasmosis.'

'That sounds awful.'

'Fungal pneumonia to you.'

We sat for a while then in silence, just watching the flat, endless land passing by. The fields had a dull grey cast to them, as if their years of fertility were far behind them now. Now and then an old piece of rusting farm equipment lay abandoned in the corner of a field, a reminder of the expensive disaster of centralized state planning.

It was dark by the time the coach pulled up outside the hotel. I said goodnight and made my way up to my room, leaving Dean in the bar going over his speech to Louis L'Amour's Worldwide Friends.

Later, I took a shower and was just writing up my notes when a package on the floor just inside the door caught my eye. It was a pale brown envelope with what felt like a book inside.

I picked it up and turned it over. The envelope wasn't sealed. I reached in and pulled out a slim volume of poetry: *Smoke from This Altar, Poems by Louis L'Amour.* Taking a vodka from the minibar, I sat on the bed and slowly turned the pages. A bookmark had been inserted at page twenty-three. I flicked on the lamp, the better to read the words.

> *For I'm a stranger here, of other clay;*
> *A guest within this house, a passer-by –*
> *A roving life whose theme has been 'Goodbye',*
> *A shadow on the road, a thing astray.*

I set down the book. *A shadow on the road, a thing astray.* I thought of my boy and how long it was since I'd seen him. I lay back, but couldn't sleep. I thought then of the block in the prison and its surface worn smooth by so many tiny necks. Again I crossed to the minibar. I drank another vodka, then another, then a fourth.

As the dawn rose slowly above the distant Russian steppe, I found myself standing pale-faced at the window. Far away and below on the Vladimirka Road, the early morning traffic was already building, the drivers wrapped up at the wheels of their cars, their thoughts no doubt of the day ahead and not the years gone by, their eyes and ears tuned neither to the gaze of the ghosts by the roadside nor the rattling of their rusted, freezing chains.

Often, when we talked about our trip to Russia, Max would recite a poem he knew by heart, written by Irina Vladimirovna Odoyevtseva. The lines, he said, made him think of his great-grandfather, who, as a young man long before Tomsk, would take a walk every afternoon in Moscow's Gorky Park, in the hope of seeing again a girl he'd seen there once before – a girl with whom he had fallen in love.

The lines were these:

> He had said, 'Goodbye, my darling. Maybe
> I won't come back, ever. Time will tell.'
> And I walked off down the lane, not knowing
> If this was Summer Park
> Or hell.

That they did meet again and in time were married was where I always used to hope the story would end. But it never did end there, for, as well as being the birthplace of their love, the park, in the end, was also the place from which, one spring afternoon, Max's great-grandfather had made his way with his violin to the Opera House, from where he'd later that day disappeared – taken, it was later discovered, by the Cheka, and sent there – *here*, where I stood, in the city of Tomsk.

Standing next morning in the hotel lobby (my head was banging from the vodka, my fingers numb at the tips), I turned over the postcard I'd just bought and tried to think what to write. But my mind refused to be corralled; instead, it started wandering, considering all it could remember of what, early that morning, I'd copied into my notebook.

My eyes fell back on the postcard. *The Statue of Lenin at Lenin Square.* There was Lenin, arm raised, standing on his plinth in the centre of the square that still – even after the collapse of his experiment – bears his name. Behind him stood the grand Epiphany Cathedral, stark white against skies quite improbably blue. I turned the card back. *Dear Joel*, I wrote, *Am having a lovely time, although it's very cold. Will be home soon. All my love, Daddy.*

'Marina says you're not coming with us today.'

I picked it up and slipped it into the postbox by the lifts and heard it drop.

'That's too bad. So what will you do?'

Dean from San Diego was standing, dressed head to foot in pale blue, fully armed with his camera and annotated guidebook. I said I wasn't feeling so good – that perhaps it was something I'd eaten.

'Should I call someone?' he said.

I shook my head.

'Would you like me to take a look?'

No, I said, I'd be fine. Unfortunately, I'd have to give the Epiphany Cathedral a miss. I was planning, I said, to spend the day in my room, relaxing. Maybe I'd write up my notes. I asked him to bring me something back.

'Will do.'

He crossed the foyer to join the group, turning at the swing doors. He raised his hand in a wave, then was gone. From the window of the bar I watched the coach depart, then went up to my room. I lay down on my bed and opened my notebook. A picture of Isaak Levitan fluttered out. I stooped to pick it up. I stared at his solemn face.

In a while I returned the picture, closed the book and lay back. It all suddenly seemed too ridiculous. *I will follow the road*, I had said. *I will listen to the voices and tell you what they say.*

But there are no voices.

The dead are dead.

The dead are silent.

The dead are saying nothing.

The bus to the Gulag was scheduled to leave at two. I had an hour to wait. I sat in the corner of the waiting room at the bus station on the other side of the city and watched the people buying their tickets or saying hello or goodbye to friends and family. Outside, amid the newly thick-falling snow, filthy diesel-spewing buses came and went, each one growling, gears wrenching as if they were working entirely against their will.

'Hey!' A rapping of knuckles on glass.

The man in the ticket office was stabbing the air with his finger, pointing to a rattling, wheezing bus that had somehow pulled up outside without me noticing. I closed my notebook and made my way out to the bus, passing through an airlock of bitter wind and swirling snow that could rob you of your breath as surely as an unexpected punch to the gut.

Once aboard, I nodded to the driver; he scowled. I chose a seat by the window. The window was thick with grime; I touched the glass with the tip of my finger, but the grime was on the outside and so beyond removing. The bus started up, backfiring badly. I settled down, making myself as comfortable as the dipping plastic seats would allow. Though in the end the bus was nearly full, the seat beside me remained resolutely empty.

The journey from the centre of the city to the outskirts was like travelling through the rings of a fallen tree. Once we'd departed the grand, historic, 400-year-old heart of the place (a fort built by Tartars on the banks of the fast-flowing River Tom), the suburbs didn't so much spread as rise in the usual ring of several dozen tower blocks – buildings that cast their blind and broken eyes over a narrow, bleak hinterland of broken cars, disfiguring power lines and a feeling of hopelessness and boredom that, in every Russian city I visited, seemed to come directly from the stares of the aimless, sullen youths, who every hour of the day and night seemed to prowl such left-behind places with their concrete yards and boarded-up stores like shabby, ragged wolves. For them, the winter days – though shortening – are clearly still a burden, still far too long for all that there isn't to do. They watch as you pass by, raise a casual middle finger, then are gone, lost behind, many of them more than half the way towards the army meat grinder, with its murderous hazing to look forward to and its unheated barracks and pay every other month if you're lucky. That or – for some of them – a half-life spent begging at the traffic lights – standing, staring dead-faced at the window of a bus, the boys, pale-faced, arms punctured with needles, the girls most often with a baby held aloft – a child so emaciated and close to death, with cheeks so shrunken that you can clearly see the shape of the skull beneath the translucent skin.

'She wants to sell her child to you.'

The girl was staring hard through the thick, grimy window, the baby in her arms just a lump in a rough, tangled bundle of rags.

The voice came from behind me – a woman's, young, educated, clipped precise English.

'She can see you are not from here. And she knows that Americans all the time want babies.'

'I'm not American.'

'She thinks anyone who is not from Tomsk is from America. May I sit here, please?'

The voice belonged to a tall, thin girl in her twenties. She was wearing a heavy army surplus jacket, thick wool trousers and a pair of working boots. She was a journalist, she said, who'd spent two years studying in Blackfriars in London and was currently on an assignment for the Internet magazine *Yabloko* ('the magazine for women and not only for them'), her brief at this time being to travel around the city in search of romantic stories for their new 'Living on the Go' section. She pulled off her right glove and offered her hand. Her hand, despite the glove, was freezing. Her name, she said, was Katherine.[1] I told her mine, and something of what I was doing.

---

1 Her mother, she later told me in a letter received a month after my return, had been an actress of some note. Following the birth of her daughter, having decided to name the girl Audrey (after Audrey Hepburn), she discovered that the name was on the list of names proscribed by the local soviet. Her second-choice name – Katherine (after *Katharine* Hepburn) – however, was not.

'So what will you do when you arrive?' she said.

The bus pulled away from the lights, leaving the woman and the baby to disappear, abandoned.

'Do you have a plan?'

'No,' I said. 'No plan.'

She frowned.

I told her about Max and the piece of his robe I had stashed in my backpack.

'And this you will do what with?' she said.

I told her I would bury it. Hearing the words made the whole thing suddenly sound crazy – to go all that way just for *that*, the act of a madman or a fool. I wanted to do something for Max, I said – to reconnect him somehow with those of his family that were long gone.

'And what about you?' she said. 'What about your family?' She was scrabbling about in her bag for something. 'You have a family? A wife?'

My wife, I said, was at home.

'And do you love her,' she said, 'your wife?' She had a notebook on her lap now, a pen poised above the page.

'Is this for your readers?'

'Do you mind?'

In my mind, suddenly, I had a picture of some great red-faced babushka sitting somewhere in poor light at a rickety table, a bowl of potato peelings and an open copy of (the now printed) *Yabloko* before her, her toothless mouth set firm and contented in a sentimental smile.

'Why should I mind?' I said.

She noted down my answer. She paused, then looked up.

'Does she know?' she said. 'That, even though you're so far away, you still love her?'

'Of course.'

'And you have children?'

She smiled when I told her I had a son. Her readers would apparently be happy to hear that. They would, she said, be happy to hear of a family reunited after so long apart. Russian people like nothing more, she said, than happy family stories.

I said maybe that was because so many Russian families had been so brutally split up – so many brothers and sisters, mothers and fathers separated. This she considered for a while, her head to one side. Finally, she nodded. She would tell me, she said, the story about Grigory the Cossack.

Grigory the Cossack was a paper merchant who for many years had delivered paper to the offices of the newspaper that had become *Yabloko*. He was, apparently, famous for his reticence, scarcely uttering a word to a soul unless it was necessary for him to do so in the execution of his work. One day, however, this all changed. One day, apparently, when Katherine had been sent to do an inventory of the storeroom, she'd found Grigory the Cossack sitting in the darkness, his head in his hands (in one of which also he'd been holding what looked like a medal) and weeping. At first quite intimidated by such an unexpected sight, she'd left the room, closing the door behind her. Something, however, had stopped her and had made her go back. In the storeroom once more, she'd sat beside the weeping man and had asked him what was wrong.

Which was when, quite unexpectedly, he'd told her his story.

Like so many people over so many years, Grigory's father had been arrested one day and exiled the next, not for what he'd *done* (for he'd done nothing but try to survive in the dying trade of thatching) but for who he *was* – a Cossack, that is, and a man consequently whom the great leader and teacher Joseph Stalin, sitting out on the porch in his dacha on the Black Sea, believed to be plotting his downfall. And so, with a simple stroke of his pen, the fate of Grigory's father was sealed – along with that of a million others. A whole people, in fact, in a single moment, ceased to be citizens and were, *in* that moment, cast out into the bitter endless wilderness from which few would return and those who did – like Grigory's father – would for ever walk crippled, unable to shake the snow from their boots, unable to forget what they'd seen.

Grigory the Cossack had not asked his father how it was he'd survived when so many others had not – and would never have known had, a week following the old man's death, a letter not arrived from the Re-Education Committee of the local soviet. The letter had contained notification that, as a result of his father's exemplary work as camp executioner, his father (and therefore he, Grigory, also) had had the revoking of his citizenship itself revoked, and was therefore, from that day on, entitled to all the benefits that such an honour will bestow. Among these, Grigory only discovered many years later, was the right to wear the medal that had been awarded to his father for his work – a medal that, according to the notification, had still been awaiting collection. This was the medal Grigory had been holding when Katherine had found him that day in the storeroom. It was, he'd said, all that was left of the man who'd been his father – all that was left of a man who'd chosen to kill his own people in order to survive, but whose survival had, in the end, killed the very thing inside him that had made him a man.

'Is that a true story?' I said.

Yes, she said, it was a true story.

I asked her where he was now – this Grigory the Cossack.

He was, she said, dead. He'd killed himself – hanged himself from a tree, his father's medal pinned to his chest, his shoeless feet as white when they'd found him as the pure Siberian snow.

The bus ground to a stop – all hissing brakes and diesel smoke – at what looked like the outskirts of the greyest of all Russian towns.

She stood up. She zipped up her heavy coat. 'This is my stop,' she said.

I looked out of the window. There wasn't much to see – just a line of low concrete buildings, a petrol station, a rain-stained CrapDog fast-food stand.

'What's here?' I said. It all seemed hopeless – the kind of place from which nothing good could ever come – except for a distant, pointed spire gleaming golden in the light.

'My grandmother lives here,' she said. She pointed to a bag full of groceries on the floor before her feet. 'I bring her groceries and any news.'

'What kind of news?'

'News about my grandfather. But every week I have to tell her no news.'

I asked what had happened to him – certain I knew that she'd say he'd just one day gone missing – that one day the boys from the Ministry had picked him up off the street and had taken him away in their truck. Some days such a thing seemed to have happened to everybody.

She reached down to pick up the grocery bag and heaved it on to her shoulder. Her grandfather, she said, was in the hospital, his lungs so congested with fluid it was hard for him to breathe; even the morphine they gave him couldn't cancel out the pain. All he wanted to do, she said, was die, but the doctors wouldn't let him.

'Does your grandmother go to visit him?' I said.

She shook her head. Her grandmother, she said, was too old and too frail to make the journey. So she just sat by the window, waiting for news.

'And when it comes?' I said. 'What then?'

Katherine sighed. 'Then she will follow him and at last they will be together.'

The doors at the front hissed open.

'I have to go now,' she said, and for the second time that day she held out her hand. Her hand was still cold, as if it were too far away from any source of warmth to really benefit. She turned and made her way to the front of the bus and down the steps. The doors closed behind her. She waved and I returned it. Then the bus pulled away, and I thought of Grigory the Cossack hanging from a tree, his medal pinned like a prisoner's ragged number to his chest, and of an old lady in a broken-down tower block somewhere, waiting for her granddaughter to bring her the news of her husband's final passing. As the bus rumbled on, wheels bunching and stretching on the uneven road, it seemed to me extraordinary how closely and openly some people will associate with the stark fact of death, while others will deny its very existence in an effort to avoid it – but how neither, of course – acceptance nor denial – will lessen the burden for those left behind, those for whom the end, like the whistle of a distant train, is still but a warning, a promise, a threat.

The number of passengers on the bus thinned the closer we got to the last stop, those leaving offering those of us remaining the sort of acknowledgement – a nod halfway between pity and good wishes – that the lifer might offer the condemned man as he makes his final, one-way journey, all hope at last spent.

In the end – at the end – only four of us remained.

The driver drew the bus to a stop at what seemed a quite arbitrary point at the side of the road, then opened the doors, turned off the engine and made his slow, wheezing way down the steps and across the icy road towards a low hut butted up against the fence. It seemed an act of quite outrageous abandonment – a casually stark reminder of what, for so many years, had gone on here.[1]

I glanced at my fellow passengers. Of the three, two were old women, swaddled up against the cold like ancient bloated babies, their heads swathed in thick scarves until only their eyes and the tips of their noses were visible. I

---

1 Although such a reminder was, of course, accidental, elsewhere, in similar places, the visitor will find himself a part of a sly but telling reconstruction. On arriving at Auschwitz, for example, the visitor is forced to wear a badge of a different colour, each denoting a different nationality. Thus are those present segregated and any bond of communion broken.

smiled at them, and – though, for all I know, they might have been smiling back – their scarves made them inscrutable. I looked away.

The third passenger was a woman also, but younger and neater in appearance – a schoolteacher, perhaps, or a secretary in an office on some kind of day out. She was pale-faced but still youthful-looking. *I'm off to the Gulag tomorrow*, I imagined her saying one Friday afternoon. *Is there anything I can get you?* She turned her head, as if drawn by my attention. Then she looked blankly away and began busying herself with her bag.

I pushed myself up, stepped into the aisle and made my way down to the front of the bus. On the dashboard behind the steering wheel, a small icon – a triptych of blues and gold – sat casually propped up on an old cloth.

When people describe a place as existing in 'the middle of nowhere', of course they think they know what they mean. But – the chances are – they've not been to Siberia. The chances are that such people haven't taken the four-hour bus journey north-west from the city of Tomsk. What's more, they probably haven't been to the Gulag that to those incarcerated within it was simply *out there* – the place that for so many years now has lain almost entirely abandoned in the snow.

At first, when you cross the road the camp is hard to see. There's a long fence, heading to the left and to the right as far, it seems, as the horizon, behind which, a dirty grey against the whiteness of the snow, lies a series of low buildings. Only from the air, perhaps, could the eye get a grasp of the vastness of the place – the sheer size which, when combined with the cold and the distance from the world, produced in so many a kind of paralysis of the will – for, from the ground – from where I stood – it seemed a modest endeavour and all a little ramshackle – certainly not a factory of misery and death.

The main gate was padlocked. Beyond it, the compound that had once been filled with activity – the arrival and assessment of new prisoners, the roll-call of the guards morning and night, the daily caravan removing the day's dead to the pits beyond the wire – was eerily quiet, like a school playground in the winter holidays, the new fall of snow undisturbed.

I fed my fingers through the wire. The wire was thin – a marker, clearly, rather than a means of containment, as working to keep people in was in such a place a redundant activity, for what better guard could there possibly have been than the hundreds of miles of emptiness that lay beyond? In such a place as this, gates would often remain unlocked, while the fence posts were only shallowly buried. All men knew that no man could survive for long beyond the wire, and that no man – however strong, however bound to the land and its ways through centuries of tenancy – could long elude tracking. Consequently, no panic – no shouting, no running around, no ear-splitting blast of sirens – attended the actions of the man who, glancing over his shoulder, ducked down and under the poorly made enclosure and, suddenly free, took his first steps towards the home left so long ago that he would never, in this life at least, see again. No – on the contrary – instead of such a fuss, the samovar would be filled in a stifling-hot guardroom and the first light of morning awaited. And when the body was discovered, perhaps a quarter-mile distant, no prayers would be said and no preparations for burial be made. The body, frozen hard, would be left for the yellow-eyed, lean Arctic wolves to devour, their sharp teeth stripping the bones of their weak and meagre offering as surely as had the heart been stripped by loneliness and despair of all but one single hopeless dream. Indeed, really the only hope of escape is summed up in the words – neatly written in a childish hand (in Russian, of course) – written on the wall beside the door inside the main latrine block: *The only escape is the escape within.* The only certain way out was a numbing of the mind to match the numbing of the senses handed out by the cold. For many, the only way out was through the tunnel of madness whose darkness protected all from the light of despair.

I followed the fence for an hour, seeing no one and hearing nothing but the shifting of the distant trees and the crunch of my own footsteps in the snow. Then, as if from out of nowhere, a truck I'd not heard coming – a black Hyundai with thick tyres and a polished-chrome roll bar – pulled up on the road behind me, wheels crunching on ice. The back of the truck was stacked up with boxes, each of which had the Stars and Stripes printed on the side. A man was leaning out of the driver's side, lean with copper-coloured hair. 'You speak English?' he said.

'Yes,' I said.

'You lost?'

I looked around me. Aside from the fence and the low buildings beyond, there was nothing to say where I was or how far I'd come. 'Maybe,' I said.

'You want a ride?'

'Is it warm in there?'

'You betcha!'

John C. Delaney, pillar of the United Methodist Church of Shiloh, Tennessee, is a man of great faith who wears that faith lightly and with a great and often wicked humour. He had, before our meeting on that distant, icy road, made twelve other trips to Siberia, each one at a cost only to himself and his church. Every winter, accompanied by a half-dozen colleagues from the simple, high-spired red-brick church on Shiloh's South Main Street, he flies to Moscow Domodedovo, where, in association with the local office of the Russian Red Cross, he leads the expedition of relief to the orphanage – Orphanage Number 10 – that now occupies a tiny corner of what had once been one of the region's largest and most brutal Gulags.

We stopped at the gate.

John Delaney turned to consider me with his kind blue eyes. Would I, he said, care to hear a joke? It was something a colleague had told him on the plane coming over.

'OK,' I said.

A serious look settled on his face. 'OK. So how many Methodists,' he said, 'does it take to change a light bulb?'

'I don't know,' I said. 'How many Methodists *does* it take to change a light bulb?'

The serious look lifted. 'Three,' he said, smiling, triumphant. 'One to replace the bulb, and two to cast out the spirit of darkness!'

I smiled.

I felt him turn to consider me. 'Tell me,' he said. 'Do you have faith?'

'You mean in God?' I said, my heart sinking. I thought of Max. Why couldn't I have just said I was a Buddhist and be done with it?

John Delaney nodded.

I said no – that I could see no reason to. 'No offence,' I said.

'None taken. No, sir.' Smiling, he looked away. 'Do you see that?' he said.

I followed his gaze through the gate and across the compound. There was nothing to see but low buildings and snow. 'Third block on the left. Do you see it?'

I counted blocks. 'Sure. What about it?'

'The execution block. Do you know what they said to their victims, the executioners – the last thing? They said that God had abandoned them. *He has forsaken you,* they said, *otherwise why would you be here?*

'Was it true?' I said.

John Delaney shook his head – not in answer to my question but, perhaps, in answer to one of his own. 'Time was,' he said, 'when I would have said yes.' He paused. 'Does that shock you?'

'I hardly know you, so no,' I said.

'Well, if you *had* known me, then I can tell you you *would* have been shocked. Back then John Delaney was a poster boy for God. Back then I suppose you could say I was a little crazy. God was all I talked about, all I thought about. God was everything.'

'So what happened?'

'I had a son and he died. In a car wreck. On Elvis Presley Boulevard in Memphis.'

I said I was sorry to hear that.

'They said he was driving intoxicated, which I guess would have been true. They said he was lucky he didn't kill nobody but himself. Anyway, we took him home, his mother and me, and buried him at the cemetery in Shiloh. Which means *Place of Peace*.' He paused, as if things were coming back to him – memories and dreams. 'Well,' he said, 'that's when I thought, Hey, God, where were you on that road? Where were you when my boy was dying in that wreck? And that's when I thought, God is dead, and I quit the church and everything.'

'So what happened,' I said, 'to bring you back – to get you here?'

'You don't want to know.'

'Try me.'

'Well . . .' he said, hesitating.

'What is it?'

'OK. This is it. I had a vision. And in my vision I was driving my truck down a long icy road in Russia, and I was lost and kind of starting to panic, when I came to a place – this place – with its fence and low buildings, and I knew I was meant to be there. Here.'

'In a prison?'

'In an orphanage. You see, I knew in my heart that I was lost – that in giving up on God I was giving up on the good things that come from Him. I was lost. Adrift. An orphan myself.'

'And now you're here,' I said. 'That's a good news story.'

John Delaney turned towards me. His breath was like smoke. 'Hey, you want to come see the kids? You might find them kind of noisy . . .'

I said of course, and we climbed in his pickup and drove around the perimeter, this time in an anticlockwise direction. We stopped at a second gate. This one was open. We drove through and parked between a pair of long huts. He turned off the engine. 'One thing,' he said. He paused. I turned to meet his gaze.

'What is it?' I said.

He asked me if I was planning to write about what I saw.

'Would you mind if I did?' I said.

He shook his head and said of course not – but there was clearly something more. He sighed. 'You see . . .' Again he hesitated.

'If it's a problem, I won't.'

'No, really,' he said, 'there's no problem. It's just, well, do you think you could maybe relocate us?'

'Relocate?' I said. 'Why?'

And then he told me how there were still people out there who believed that places such as the orphanage – places that had witnessed the murder of so many people – were bound to be riven with ghosts, and that those ghosts were bound to want revenge. And he told me also how several former camps had been razed to the ground, the fires burning through the night, until all evidence of their having been there had been erased. That some people said it was the government acting in the name of these deranged people was, he said – even if it was true – of little consequence when the lives of children were at stake. That, he said, was why.

I looked around me. *Bound to be riven with ghosts.*

'Well?' he said.

'Of course,' I said. 'Consider the orphanage and any ghosts it contains relocated.'

He nodded. 'Hey,' he said, following a moment's silence, 'you know anything about soccer?'

'You mean football?'

'Sorry. I forgot. Football.'

Smiling as if all talk of ghosts and burning had never occurred, John C. Delaney opened the door and stepped out. 'They're just crazy for it,' he said, his breath spilling out like smoke. I slung my backpack over my shoulder and followed him across the hard ground to the door of one of the huts. *Ghosts.* I thought of Max and the duty I had yet to perform, and how, as a young man, he'd always been the one to hear voices in the bush. *Can't you hear them?* he'd say, and I'd stand, quite dumb, listening but hearing nothing but the tuis and pukekos. I looked up, just as a tiny distant V of black birds crossed the sky.

'Are you coming?'

I pulled my gaze down from the sky and asked him if he believed in ghosts – if whether, when a person has gone, they leave something of themselves behind.

He nodded. 'Can't you hear them?' he said.

I listened – and, yes, sure enough, there they were. Voices.

We walked on then, and the closer we came to the hut, the louder and more distinct the voices became. They were the voices of children, laughing, playing. In such a place as this, such a sound seemed suddenly peculiar – as if God Himself, regretting His carelessness, had decided to make amends in the strangest and most unforgettable of ways.

At first I'd thought the camp entirely isolated – an island of brutality set in a vast, white sea – when, in fact, it was not. There's a village – I'll call it Bogrovka – perhaps eight kilometres away, a ramshackle collection of huts and primitive houses boasting neither running water nor electricity. The former is available through the once-weekly visit of a water-truck[1] (which also attends to the needs of the orphanage), the latter an entirely unknown resource. In the old days at least, just about the only thing, it seemed, present there in any quantity was fear – fear not of the camp itself and the terrible howling like wolves to be heard there at night, but fear of the arrival in their midst of a camp escapee. That such an event had only ever once occurred had not, it seemed, in all those dark years lessened this fear – nor even, for some, the knowledge that the camp had itself been abandoned to all but the elements and a hundred once-homeless orphans whose home it now was and would, in all likelihood, in perpetuity remain.

1 When I suggested they might melt the snow of which there is an unnatural abundance and then drink it, the only villager who seemed willing to talk to me looked at me as if I were mad. So bad, apparently, had been the poisoning of the earth by the aluminium plant over a hundred miles away that even the snow was toxic.

John Delaney touched me on the arm as a father might. 'They'll be wary at first – but don't let that worry you, OK?'

I nodded, although – not knowing what to expect – I was anything *but* ready.

He twisted the handle and opened the door. I took a deep breath and followed him in.

My son will tell you that there's no such thing as an unsinkable ship – the *Titanic* and many since are witness to that – just as (although I doubt he'd tell you this) there's no such thing as an inescapable prison. Alcatraz, Robben Island, the Tower of London: all in time, like Colditz castle and many others, saw their reputations compromised by the daring, foolish or simply deranged. Tunnels were dug and disguises prepared, and thoughts of home entertained for the first time in years. And a few even made it – walked into the parlour, the kitchen or the garden one fine spring morning and began, by so doing, the relearning of so much that had been lost.

Not so Gulag 20.

Not so the ghosts of men, of women and of children lost in the wilderness beyond the rising Russian steppe. Here, aside from those who'd struck out in the dark Arctic night whom gentle morning and the lean, sharp-toothed wolves had discovered frozen and face down in the snow – aside from *them*, not a soul made it out of this particular place, before the whole rotten system itself imploded and everyone left within it was cast adrift to fend for himself in the new and quite terrifying world of freedom.

From Tomsk, barely a single soul.

Just one – and he was just a boy.

His name was Abram.

He was fourteen years old.

His father was a Jew and an educated man, a hotelier from St Petersburg and a veteran of the civil war (during which he had distinguished himself at Vladivostok, the war's last engagement, and was later awarded a medal for his bravery in destroying a White-held machine gun), who had nevertheless been imprisoned by Stalin along with his wife – Abram's mother – and later executed as part of the generalissimo's cull of the nation's intellectuals. Cast adrift, the boy Abram drifted, sinking step by step into a world of thieving and prostitution.

In the end – an end that wasn't, as it turned out, quite the end – he curled up one winter in a stand of birch trees on the outskirts of Moscow.

And there – for the first time – he died.

His heart stopped in the freeze for so long that the doctor who found him felt no special need for urgency. He wrapped the boy in his coat and carried him home. The boy, he said, was so light, there being so little flesh on his bones. The doctor laid him on the floor of his parlour and, though convinced of the boy's death, decided, for the sake of completeness, that he should listen a final time to the silence now settled within the boy's chest.

But the boy's chest, of course, was silent no longer, for a heartbeat had returned and, with it, further signs of life. The boy opened his eyes. Stumbling back as if he'd been struck, the doctor called for his wife, thinking himself deluded or suddenly mad; his wife appeared and was able to confirm, then, that neither was her husband deluded nor mad, nor that the appearance of life in the boy was anything but genuine.

'It's a miracle,' said the doctor.

'A miracle indeed,' said his wife – and, later that day, she made the rounds of her friends on the outskirts of the city, telling all of the miracle of the boy's flight from death, emphasizing, each time the tale was told, her husband's vital role in events.

The following morning, early enough to find the doctor and his wife still asleep in their beds (and, indeed, the boy, whose recovery was continuing apace, the colour returning to his cheeks like the arrival of spring after winter), their sleep was interrupted by the sounds of talk coming from outside, and the shuffling of feet in the snow. 'Doctor!' a voice called, which soon was joined by another, then a third. Soon, forced from his bed, the doctor went to the window. A hundred of his neighbours were there, every one of them eager to catch a glimpse of the boy who had cheated death. The doctor shook his head but knew that such a gathering would not be satisfied with anything less than the boy's appearance.

When they saw the boy, the crowd grew silent, as if in the presence of a deity. Some asked for his blessing, others that he might cure them of some illness. All sought his attention and all were glad of his presence among them.

All but one.

The man from the Party looked on, they say, from behind the trunk of a tree. His eyes, they say, were cold like a wolf's, and his dedication to godlessness unwavering. The boy, he knew, had a power greater than any army, and posed a threat, as a consequence, to the great leader Joseph Stalin himself. Action, he knew, would have to be taken, and such a spring of shallow hope quickly buried. And so, three nights later, when the immediate protection of celebrity had dwindled (though not the hundreds of requests every day for his help), the boy was bundled up in the yard by three masked men and delivered like a criminal to an ad hoc local court.

The verdict, of course, was guilty.

The sentence, of course, was exile. He would take the Vladimirka Road to Tomsk and beyond, and never, in this life or the next, return.

And so he disappeared – this Abram – down the road along which so many had disappeared before him – and there, one more among the hundreds, the thousands, the millions, he slaved and suffered and dreamed of another place – any place that wasn't here.

How he made it to the village is a journey unrecorded; not so the reception he received when he got there.

For the villagers, those distant souls for whom the glory of St Petersburg, of the Golden Horde and the Battle of Blue Waters, of the tsar and Rasputin, of Stalin, of Khrushchev, of Brezhnev and the growing evidence of utter, utter failure – for those innocents, indeed, for whom the swirling, bloody tides of Russian history meant nothing, the camp (the existence of which many still disbelieved) stood for everything unknown and fearful, and, as a consequence, talk of it was restricted to those hours after nightfall when the spirits of the land were sleeping and words found their way only to the listener's ear. For those who believed in it and those who didn't, the camp was a bad thing, from which only bad things could come. Some had heard the howling and the cries in the dusk light and knew that the devil was at work in such a place, and many were convinced that, sooner or later, he would send out an emissary to satisfy their greed in exchange for their souls.

And then one day there he was – a skinny apparition, little more meat on his bones than the meat on a skeleton.

He came, as expected, crawling on his belly, his eyes big and wild with the things that he'd seen. He rolled over in the snow in the centre of the village, clearly, as once before, close to death.

But everyone knew that the devil's dogs don't die from hunger or neglect. Everyone knew that they must be slain, the poison drawn from them with the slowness of the seasons.

And so it was.

They tied him to a stake in the depth of winter – crucified him as once Christ had been crucified – a young boy dressed only in a soiled shirt and a pair of thin canvas trousers that scarcely reached his ankles – and then they watched and waited until he was dead. His name was Abram and this, for the second and last time, was how he died. He was – and would for ever remain – fourteen years old.

The room was long and narrow, a row of tables arranged down the centre like a spine, along each side of which sat a line of pale-faced children, some perhaps only four or five years old, others maybe sixteen or seventeen. Perched on a table to one side, a CD player in the shape of an American football was playing 'We Are Family', while several women – two of them alike enough to surely be sisters, perhaps even twins – were making their way from one child to the next, their smiles as broad as their teeth were straight and white, doling out portions of some kind of steaming-hot stew.

I glanced at John Delaney. He was smiling with the satisfaction of a modest man certain of God's reward. 'I can't believe it's so warm in here,' I said.

He nodded. 'Do you hear that?' he said.

'You mean Sister Sledge?'

'Who?'

'The music.'

'Oh, no,' he said. 'I mean that thumping noise. Isn't it wonderful?'

I listened. Sure enough. *Thump, thump, thump.*

'The new generator,' he said. It was big enough, he said, to run pretty much whatever they wanted to run. Big enough, if the need ever arose, to power up air conditioning in the summer.

I caught the eye of a pale-faced, dark-haired boy; he held my gaze with an unblinking stillness that was quite unnerving. I looked away, then glanced back. He was still staring. I lifted one arm, clenching and unclenching my fist high above my head. His eyes didn't move.

'That's David,' said John Delaney. 'Blind from birth. Father an alcoholic. Abused by his mother. Found wandering the streets. You should hear him play the piano, though.'

'He can play?'

'Sure. He's blind, not deaf. Would you like to hear him play?'

I looked again at the boy. Everything about him was utterly still, as if he feared that to move would be to give himself away and so draw down on him some terrible violence.

John Delaney called to one of the women. She clapped her hands with joy, then whispered something in the blind boy's ear. He shrugged, then stood.

'Where's the piano?' I said.

The woman led him to a table by the window. He sat, straight-backed.

'Come on,' said John Delaney.

I followed him to the table. We stood around – five, six of us – clearly waiting for something. The boy sighed and raised his hands, fingers extended. Then, slowly, he lowered them, until the tips of his fingers were touching the very edge of the table.

He paused.

A hand – John Delaney's – found my shoulder.

And then the young man began, his fingers rising and falling above imaginary keys, his feet beneath the table pressing with great care imaginary pedals.

I looked at John Delaney. He was smiling. He drew in close. 'Shostakovich,' he whispered. 'The Piano Concerto.'

I nodded as if I knew it, which I did not. But it didn't matter, for it was something I shall never forget – a moment both wonderful and absurd. I closed my eyes, and in the ear of my mind I thought – for a moment at least – I could hear what the young man at the table could hear, maybe feel in my heart what he, in his blindness and through the pain of his long-ago abandonment, could maybe feel in his.

His recital over, David laid his hands on his thighs. He was breathing steady and hard, as if he'd run for a bus and only just caught it. Then he stood, pushing back his chair as he did so. I stepped back, out of his way, and watched as the woman who'd led him to the table led him away.

'Have you ever heard him play?' I said. 'I mean, *really* – on a *real* piano?'

John Delaney looked to another of the women, who was standing close by, and shook his head. The woman glanced over at David, who was sitting back at the main table, his nimble fingers peeling the wrapper off a cupcake. 'They said he's good, though,' she said. 'The folks who brought him here. They said they heard him and he was really good.'

I said it was a shame they didn't have a piano.

John Delaney nodded. I thought I saw something like a smile way back somewhere. I looked at the woman. Though she tried, she couldn't stop a grin.

'Should we tell him?' she said.

'Tell me what?' I looked from one to the other. 'What is it?' I said.

Apparently, should things go to plan, the piano will arrive in the week before Christmas – in time for the camp's 'reconsecration'. What form this secular service of thanks will take no one as yet really knows – there never having been such a thing before. Never before (as far as anyone knows) has a prison camp in Siberia – a Gulag – given up its life as a harbinger of death in favour of providing a new life for those for whom abandonment and even death had for so long been so close.

'It seems like a miracle,' I said.

John Delaney shook his head. 'It's a gift,' he said, 'from the folks back in Shiloh.'

'A gift from the Place of Peace,' I said.

'Amen,' said John Delaney, and then, looking out across the room to the children for whom the title orphan was really, thanks to him, no longer quite accurate, he smiled a smile so full of love and kindness that for the rest of my life it is something I shall never forget.

It was three o'clock and already growing dark when I slipped out of the building unobserved. I closed the door behind me, sealing the warmth of the electric heaters and the laughter of the children inside. I looked around. The snow had been trampled between the dormitory and the recreation blocks by the feet of close to a hundred children; beyond this, however, the thick whiteness of the ground remained untouched.

I searched around in my bag. At last my fingers found the soft cloth of Max's orange robe.

He'd always said that the orange of his robes was a beacon for those seeking answers to all sorts of questions. People, he said, would approach him on the street, or sidle over to his table in a restaurant (the 'Amber Samba', he'd call it) and ask him everything from how they might find the swiftest path to enlightenment, to how much they might expect to get for their second-hand Subaru. It was, he said, no more than, long ago, he'd been warned to expect. Long ago, he said, when he'd first put on the robe, he'd been told to expect a great deal of mistrust and aggression, for, according to his teacher, an unenlightened man sees a challenge in another man's enlightenment, and will seek to rob him of it if he possibly can.

I took out the cloth and set my backpack in the snow. The orange of the cloth was as bright still as it had been on the day all those years ago I'd first seen it – as rich still and as full of promise as the most garish and audacious of sunrises. With the cloth in my hand – held as tightly as a child will hold a father's hand – I walked on, my boots squeaking in the snow as I set out to explore what remained of the camp.

Aside from the half-dozen low buildings occupied by the orphanage, there were perhaps another two dozen still standing, while – of several dozen more – all that was visible now were the lower halves of their brick chimneys. Of still others, not even *this* remained; having once been buildings housing between one and two hundred souls, all that was left of *them* now was the slightly raised oblong of their poorly made foundations.[1] As to the question of why some of the buildings had remained while others had perished, it's a mystery that seems destined to remain so. The elements, it seems, choose their victims with care and to a plan quite impenetrable to others. However, standing or not, and despite this tenacious grip on existence, it's difficult to think of the camp's long-term future as anything but bleak. Indeed, considering how much of the camp has already disappeared since its abandonment by all but a few homeless children, it's hard not to think that soon it might all be gone – orphanage and all – and the land returned to the silence and emptiness of life before man.

I thought of Abram as I moved across the hard, snow-covered ground, the collar of Aleksandra Rodianova's brother's coat pulled up high, all the time wondering if I

---

1 The crude foundations of the camps are said to contain the bones of the inmates who built them, so many having died during construction, their bodies having simply then been rolled into the pit.

was walking where *he'd* walked, whether the building I was passing had been *his*, and if there was anything left of him here after so many years of absence.

I pushed on a wooden, slatted door; it swung inward, reluctant, grinding on rotten, rusted hinges. The darkness inside the low building was dense, the cold air thicker, darker, almost tangible. Two rows of crude wooden bunks, a double row in the centre; two passageways between the outer rows of bunks and those in the middle. The slatted walls, always thin, were buckled now, the swollen planks splitting apart, allowing the bitter winds easy passage through. Thick tufts of hardy grass had risen through the dirt floor, and the roof was heavy with snow. A farmer would surely not have kept cows in such a place, for fear that the milk yield would dwindle to nothing; no bird would surely roost here, so malevolent is the air. Breathe in and breathe out and human despair passes through you like a virus; lie down on a slatted bunk and when you rise it is to a morning as dark and as bitter as nights spent adrift in a nightmare. Listen to the whispers that assail you in half-sleep and know that they're only the whispers of madmen, and of women made barren by the harshness of their treatment, and children whose lives, like their spirits, are shrinking, dwindling down to nothing.

Children like Abram.

Men like Max's great-grandfather.

I turned at the sound of something moving in the darkness.

Abram, I thought.

I turned to find David standing in the passageway. He had followed me with the stealth that comes only to the sightless. For no reason that I would ever divine, in his arms he was carrying a box of knives. I smiled; he did not. He was

339

frowning, something clearly on his mind. I asked him if he was all right – but, of course, my language wasn't his and my words fell between us like shot birds.

He turned and walked away, pausing as if encouraging me to follow. This I did. He led me from the building and out into the snow. His boots sank up to his ankles as he walked; mine matched his stride for stride, my soles fitting neatly into his.

Soon we left the buildings that still remained half-standing behind us and passed between what was left of those that are gone. We kept walking, trudging on, bundled up against a new fall of snow that seemed to assail us now from a low and sneaky angle, as if it were seeking out the flesh of our faces. On and on we walked, with the snow soon up to our knees, until after perhaps ten minutes' walking the boundary fence rose up before us, its wire all spidery lines drawn in ink on a pure white sheet of paper.

David slowed and stopped ten yards or so from the wire. I stood beside him. Together we looked out at the land beyond. He said something I didn't catch.

'I'm sorry,' I said. 'I don't understand.'

He half-turned his head, repeating the word. It sounded to me as if it had no vowels, just consonants.

I shook my head and shrugged.

'Svo-bo-da,' he said slowly, and he pointed to the wire – to the heavy wooden post where, the nails that had held it having rusted, it hung down, drooping as if beneath some great invisible weight.

'Svoboda,' I repeated, no idea what it meant, when suddenly it came to me that maybe this was the place from where Abram had made his escape.

David nodded.

Or maybe here – *right here* – was where Max's great-grandfather had stood, eyes turned instinctively towards home, in those moments of panic and longing before death.

David rattled the box of cutlery; I looked up. Then, in one swift movement, he lowered the thing nearly down to the ground, then, springing up hard, he hurled it high into the air, sending the knives spinning and turning and glinting silver like daggers in the light, before returning to earth and their burial in the snow.

He turned to me again. 'Svoboda,' he said. 'Svo-bo-da.'

And then it came to me – what it meant. The word had been painted on the side of a T-34 tank outside the Armed Forces Museum in Moscow.

Svoboda.

David smiled; I thought of Abram and of Max, and something inside made me smile too. I looked at the ground. Here it is, I thought. The place.

'Svoboda,' I said.

Freedom.

The ground was hard, but not so hard that it couldn't be dug with a handful of knives. Slowly, a mound of earth appeared – and a mound-shaped hole beside it in the ground. I knelt before it, felt the sharpness of the stones and frozen earth beneath my knees; with hands shaking and numb now with the cold, I folded the orange cloth corner to corner like a flag is folded for a fallen soldier and laid it in the ground. I scraped the dirt in after it and pushed myself up. The following lines from Pasternak had been Max's chosen words. With no one to hear them but a slowly gathering host of spirits, I recited:

I am no more but you live on,
And the wind, whining and complaining,
Is shaking house and forest, straining
Not single fir trees one by one
But the whole wood, all trees together,
With all the distance far and wide,
Like sail-less yachts in stormy weather
When moored within a bay they lie.
And this not out of wanton pride
Or fury bent on aimless wronging,
But to provide a lullaby
For you with words of grief and longing.

A moment's silence, then I buttoned up my coat and made my way slowly to the road. The snow was falling hard now, but it didn't seem to matter. All that mattered were the faces and voices in my heart. I set my feet by the roadside and peered through the white haze, my ears hearing nothing now but the distant coughing of a slow-moving bus.

The same road that takes us away leads us home. The same road returns us to all that we love. But beware, for the same road – *that* road, the Vladimirka, a turning, twisting ribbon of misery stamped out across the land by the tramping of so many feet – won't be there for ever, for all in the end will surely return to the land from which it sprung, and all that will remain then will be the cooling heat of memory – memory and voices that, unless we choose to hear them, will dim too in time, leaving nothing behind them but the earth and the wind and the snowfall in winter.